To Charlie

On your 80th Birthday a
a happy holiday in Southern Ireland.

Love

Kay x

AN ARCHAEOLOGY OF SOUTHWEST IRELAND, 1570–1670

For Claire

An Archaeology of Southwest Ireland, 1570–1670

COLIN BREEN

FOUR COURTS PRESS

Typeset in 10.5pt on 13.5pt AGaramond by
Carrigboy Typesetting Services for
FOUR COURTS PRESS LTD
7 Malpas Street, Dublin 8, Ireland
e-mail: info@fourcourtspress.ie
and in North America for
FOUR COURTS PRESS
c/o ISBS, 920 N.E. 58th Avenue, Suite 300, Portland, OR 97213

A catalogue record for this title is available
from the British Library.

ISBN 978-1-84682-040-3

SPECIAL ACKNOWLEDGMENT

This publication was grant-aided by the Heritage Council
under the 2007 Publications Grant Scheme.

AN
CHOMHAIRLE
OIDHREACHTA

THE
HERITAGE
COUNCIL

Printed in England
by MPG Books, Bodmin, Cornwall.

Contents

Illustrations

Preface

This study consists of an overview of the historical archaeology of southwest Ireland over the hundred-year-period 1570 to 1670. It does not pertain to be an exhaustive study of the region nor is it necessarily highly innovative; instead it is largely an empiricist attempt to establish an archaeological context for this formative period which gave rise to such fundamental changes in landscape character and landownership across the province of Munster. This work was prompted initially by research undertaken along the coast of the southwest concentrating on the later medieval lordship of the O'Sullivan Beare. During the course of that work it became increasingly obvious that the demise of the Gaelic lordship across the region was intrinsically linked with the advent of plantation. This process played a significant role in landscape change yet it has been under researched from an archaeological perspective. The same is not necessarily true of researchers within history and historical geography who have long recognized the importance of the period and its role in shaping contemporary society and landscape. Writing a book of this nature is as a consequence fraught with difficulty. Much of the relevant data is buried within excavation and survey reports primarily concerned with earlier periods. There is also a pronounced shortage of directly relevant data. Nevertheless a significant debt is due to the archaeologists and researchers who have carried out many of the projects upon which this volume is dependant. It is with a certain trepidation then that I attempt to use and incorporate these data here. Such a synthesis project will hopefully bring together existing information in a meaningful and accessible manner. The study does not overly engage in theoretical readings of the data as the archaeological community in Ireland is currently under served by published material dealing with the recent past.

This volume will take the following thematic approach. The opening chapter outlines the research context of the study and places it firmly within the emergent study area of historical archaeology. Chapter two provides a historical context and overview of this region from the Desmond revolt through the immediate post-Restoration period in the 1660s. Chapter three examines the morphology and socio-economic aspects of the larger urban centres in the region – this includes the major settlements of Cork and Waterford and the associated port towns of Dungarvan, Youghal, Kinsale and Tralee. A number of important inland towns like Bandon are also addressed here. Chapter four addresses various aspects of the port economies and physical waterfront structures associated with the urban centres. It also looks briefly at the limited archaeological evidence available for boats and shipping during this period. Chapter five examines the nature of rural settlement in the landscape looking at the smaller towns and villages as well as settlement clusters and isolated sites. Chapter six discusses monuments associated with the defence and protection of the region and the role of the military in society. Chapter seven presents the available evidence for the varying forms of industry in the landscape including agriculture, fishing and other emerging forms of production. Finally, chapter eight attempts to bring all of these varying threads of evidence together and construct some form of interpretative framework around them.

Invariably for a work of this nature thanks and acknowledgement are due to a variety of landowners, colleagues and friends. First and foremost, again I would like to thank Dr Kieran O'Conor of National University of Ireland, Galway for the direction and advice. His expertise was the guiding hand in this volume although of course all of the mistakes, misinterpretations and misunderstandings are mine. The debt remains unpaid. Further thanks go to the staff of the archaeology department at National University of Ireland, Galway including Prof. John Waddell, who has been hugely supportive, Prof. Billy O'Brien (now at UCC) and Dr Liz FitzPatrick. Colleagues at the University of Ulster have been supportive as usual including Dr Rory Quinn, Dr Wes Forsythe, Dr Ciara Herron, Tom McErlean and Dan Rhodes. Killian McDaid and Lisa Rodgers once again hugely helped with the illustrations while Nigel McDowell greatly facilitated the photographic process. Thanks to the library staff at Trinity College Dublin and at the National Library of Ireland; John Sheehan and Dr Colin Rynne, UCC; Maurice Hurley and Prof. Eric Klingelhofer for permission to use their work; Stella Cherry, Cork Public Museum. The staff of Four Courts Press have again been highly professional and capable. Thanks to Egerton Shelswell-White, Bantry House and Alec O'Donovan at Newtown

The continuing and ever present support of my wife Claire and children Dáire and Caoimhe is once again acknowledged.

CHAPTER I

Introduction

The end of the sixteenth and beginning of the seventeenth centuries was a complex period of change and disruption in Ireland. A period of significant political and religious upheavals, it was also a formative time in terms of landscape and settlement development throughout the island. Unfortunately, though, there has been little systematic archaeological survey undertaken on its monuments and landscape forms. This book attempts to develop a short synthesis and overview of a number of key emergent themes in the southwest from an historical archaeology perspective during the period 1570–1670, in particular the study will set the archaeological context of these developments against the historical background of plantation, Cromwellian intervention and economic expansion. Specific themes include the process of landscape transformation and change brought about through a variety of changes in management of the land, extensive transfers of ownership and developments in agricultural practice following the Desmond revolt of the 1570s. Subsequent undertakings involved the introduction of more intensive and innovative industrial processes and the reconfiguration and expansion of existing industries like fishing. Significant developments in both urban and rural settlement were a key feature of this period and an overview of the known archaeological evidence for settlement elements including architecture, housing, waterfront infrastructure, defence and town morphology will be provided. Important developments in rural settlement also occurred with a network of agricultural and trade settlement clusters being established or re-developed, related to the new emergent capitalist networks of trade and centralized control. These settlements were often established at pre-existing Gaelic house clusters and the consequent changes in settlement morphology provide important insights into community negotiation and response to change. Physically, landscape was substantially altered through new patterns of ownership, enclosure and intensification of rural practice.

HISTORICAL ARCHAEOLOGY

The last ten years have seen a major upsurge of interest in the archaeology of Ireland's recent past. Investigations of this period have long been a feature of the archaeological profession of North America and Australia where the subject became known as historical archaeology. In the US archaeological study is focussed on the post-contact period and the era of European expansion (Orser 1996). Dominant themes have included the settlement and landscape practices of these new arrivals and their role in emergent modernity and the consequent expansion of early capitalism. The value of these studies has been their ability to often give voice to the subaltern and to reengage past silent voices of the non-elite minority. Negotiation between the settlers and indigenous peoples, as expressed through material culture interchange and landscape negotiation has been an additional multivocal aspect of these studies, leading us away from the often one-sided textual-based evidence of the past. In later centuries increased multi-culturalism, exploitation and demographic movement, whether voluntary or forced, have emerged as foci for archaeological-based explanation. Britain has also had a long association of archaeological involvement with the last four centuries of human endeavour. However, there the subject area has been known as post-medieval archaeology, often dually referred to as industrial archaeology through-out the 1970s and 1980s (Donnelly and Brannon 1998, 22). Indeed the majority of investigations and projects that have taken place have carried out a highly empirical look at industrial process and monument interpretation. Both regional areas have been dominated by studies grounded in artefactual analysis with many specialists emerging in small focussed artefactual categorization groupings – the clay pipe study group or English brick society immediately spring to mind.

Archaeology of the recent past received little attention in Ireland until the late 1990s. There are a myriad number of reasons why this has taken place, probably most notably as a consequence of the island's recent colonial past. There was a reticence amongst the archaeological community in the newly formed Irish Free State, and later Republic of Ireland, to engage with the essentially colonial elements of the landscape. Instead, researchers were actively encouraged to look further back at the so-called 'Golden Ages' of the prehistoric and early Christian periods. It should, however, also be stated that there was a perceived framework to the division of research in the state where any cultural relic post dating 1600 was regarded as the domain of folklife researchers. The research that did take place subsequently was either focussed on developing extensive artefact chronologies or very site specific analyses of certain site types. This work was not without validity. Ireland has now strong tightly published chronologies of a range of artefact types such as the work of Joe Norton and Sheila Lane on clay pipes (Lane 1997a; 1997b; 2005). These are extremely useful data sources for comparative and dating work although gaps are evident (see the work of Clare McCutcheon, Roseanne Meehan, Nick Brannon and Audrey Gahan). For example, there are comprehensive under-standings of imported pottery but we as of yet know little about local pottery production across the late medieval and immediate post medieval periods (Gahan 1997; McCuthcheon 1995; 1997; 2003; 2005). Similarly, through the work of the industrial archaeologists certain industry types are also well understood. The near exhaustive work undertaken by Rynne on the iron industry is pre-eminent here (Rynne 2001). Archaeological work more rooted in landscape or theoretical approaches was less well served until the emergence of the Irish Post Medieval Archaeology Group (IPMAG). Donnelly and Horning (2002, 560) have suggested that there are four primary challenges which need to be addressed in order to redress the limited volume of research undertaken to date. Firstly, historical or post-medieval archaeology does not have a sufficient profile with both profes-sional and public arenas. Secondly, the archaeological resource dating to this period has been under-investigated as part of the recent explosion in commercial development. Thirdly, historical or post-medieval archaeology must also include nineteenth-and twentieth-century remains including, for example, the military heritage of the island during the world wars and the 'troubles'. Finally, researchers in this study area must become more integrative and contextualize their work in an international framework. A number of projects which have adopted a broader world view have taken place in Ulster but the southern half of the island has only begun to see systematic programmes of investigation in the last two decades. The American archaeologist Eric Klingelhofer has for a number of years been involved in a number of innovative programmes in Munster, all of which have been pub-lished (Klingelhofer 1992; 1999; 2000; 2005). Charles Orser, the internationally renowned historical archaeologist, has also undertaken a number of projects in the west and northwest of the country and has been very supportive of work in this country through the pages of the *International Journal of Historical Archaeology*. IPMAG has developed an annual conference and is now actively promoting new and exciting avenues of research on the island. Closely linked with similar organi-zations in Britain and the US, it has succeeded through its outreach work in centring historical archaeology in Ireland within a North Atlantic research frame-work. More specifically an awareness of the importance of material culture from our recent past has been strongly generated and this material is now being approached both in a far more applied and engaged manner. Historical archaeology is now taught at both at both third and fourth level in the island's universities and the material is treated as an integral part of the commercial process.

Historical archaeology has moved in a number of different directions over the last number of years. What started as an overtly empiricist and structuralist study area has become increasingly theorized. Specifically this latter approach has seen projects questioning and mapping the emergence of modernity and the advent of early capitalism. Increasingly, projects are moving away from elitist monuments and landscapes to engaging with the subaltern. Somewhat subconsciously there has been a distinctly left-wing allegiance to a significant portion of this work with Latin American scholars, perhaps unsurprisingly, taking a firmly Marxist approach to their engagements. Similarly there has been a notable attempt in a North American context to deal with archaeologies of slavery and the African Diaspora. Archaeology, to paraphrase Spike Lee, has almost developed to be seen to be doing the right thing. This increased politicization of the subject must surely be a product of its time. Rapid economic globalization is leading to increased disparities across the globe and the increased homogeneity of culture is an anathema to many archaeologists. Historical archaeology is firmly placed to question many of these processes and the often bland statements of past development emerging from these neo-liberal quarters. It has the potential to create and become an advocacy based on its integrative understandings of past process and development. Specifically it must have a strong input into debates about trans-boundary demographic movement and subsequent societal negotiations. It can demonstrate the historic character of globalization and case study its past excesses and problems. It can also highlight and contextualize past injustice and suggest ways in which society can better cope with change in a more egalitarian and equitable manner.

Dating framework

With what period should historical archaeology concern itself with on the island of Ireland? We have noted that in a North American context historical archaeologists deal with the period from European arrival. In Britain post-medieval archaeology is commonly held to begin from the 1540s post dissolution (Newman 2001). Both dates are associated with the advent or beginnings of modernity and researchers in Ireland have adopted a similar approach. Historical archaeology is not then necessarily about making association with the written record. Such historical documentation has been available from the fifth and sixth centuries AD yet it is only the recent past that concerns this field of study. Supporting documentation and evidence is an integral part of historical archaeological study but it is not its primary feature. Instead, the subject area is driven by the concerns listed above and by a desire to develop understandings of contemporary society through study of its formative phases.

Some comment is required here as to the chronological definition of this study. Both the start and end date – 1570 and 1670 – were especially important in the political context of the era. 1570 marks the beginnings of increased English interest in Munster and an emergent period of revolt by a number of Gaelic lords. The following one hundred years witness a number of highly significant events including plantation, famine, large-scale war in the 1590s, the gradual erosion of Gaelic power and an intensification of trade and communications within a North Atlantic sphere. The defined period ends with Cromwellian government and finally the Restoration of royal power. It was a time of profound landscape and architectural change which in effect herald the advent of modernity across the region. Such an intense period of macro-political activity requires integrated study. Traditionally archaeology has not overly concerned itself with event-based research but is instead largely content to examine more long-term process of change and societal development. Much of this approach is due to the nature of the evidence where isolating or identifying events in site stratigraphy is complex and often not possible due to the nature of relative dating and uncertainties associated with absolute dating methods. Complex site formation processes can also make precise association difficult. This long-term view is most evident in approaches to prehistoric investigation. Increasingly, however, we are recognizing that archaeology has a valuable role to play in developing understandings of the recent past and creating more integrative frameworks for its study. This field of study, as we have noted, has been labelled by the academy as historical archaeology or post-medieval archaeology. The former is preferred here. Of course this from of categorization is artificial. It is not a terminology that people in the past would have been familiar with but is instead a convenient mechanism with which archaeologists can deal with and order the past. Also, while the term historical is enjoying increasing usage it does not imply a separate or sub-discipline but rather a term of convenience employed by the profession to clearly define particular periods of study and research interests.

STUDY AIMS

This study will then attempt to produce a synthesis of existing archaeological information drawn largely from excavation evidence produced over the last forty years. Specifically this book will try to meet the following objectives and examine a number of emergent themes including:

- the contextualization of the development of society and landscape using available historical and archaeological sources for the period 1570–1670,

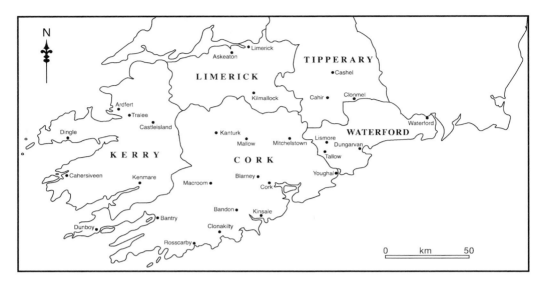

1 Map of the study area

- analyse the varying forms of settlement present in the landscape,

- question the processes and agents of landscape change in southwest Ireland following the undertakings and plantations of the later sixteenth and seventeenth century,

- attempt to extrapolate contemporary social relations from the architectural and material cultural evidence.

THE STUDY AREA

Attempting to define the study area was something of an artificial process. Contemporary boundaries and political land divisions are not necessarily relevant to the seventeenth century so the definition of the study area was largely driven by both the geography of the region and the nature of the relevant and available evidence. Broadly speaking it includes the counties of Cork and Kerry, much of eastern Waterford and sections of southern Limerick (fig. 1). It does not include all of the present province of Munster. Clare, for example, was not part of the province in the seventeenth century and is consequently excluded here. Tipperary was somewhat different in a socio-political sense from the southwest and was not as grounded in the port dependant economies of the Atlantic seaboard. Many of its towns and settlements therefore only play a periphery part in this study. The

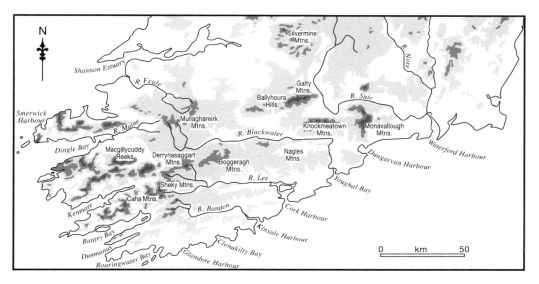

2 Physical map of the study area

large urban centre at Limerick is likewise not given equal coverage to Cork or Waterford simply for reasons of keeping the study to a manageable size and the influence a number of individuals exerted over the southwest and who were not influential as far north as the Shannon. The study is defined then by both geography and the politico-economic climate of the seventeenth century. Southwest Ireland was centred on the large port town of Cork with Youghal and Kinsale emerging as increasingly important towns. Waterford was undergoing considerable expansion and played a key role in linking the southwest with the eastern seaboard.

The physical area is one of contrast and difference (fig. 2). It is ringed by the Comeragh Mountains to the north of Dungarvan and the Knockmealdown Mountains north of Lismore running along the Blackwater Valley to Mitchelstown. The Galty and Ballyhoura Hills separate North Cork from south Limerick and east Tipperary. This area is predominantly well drained with good agricultural land. The Suir river valley borders the territory to the east flowing into Waterford Harbour while further south, in the central part of the region two river valleys dominate – the Lee and Blackwater, flowing into Cork Harbour and Youghal Harbour respectively. The region becomes significantly more rugged to the west. A number of mountainous peninsulas projecting into the Atlantic dominate, including the Dingle, Iveragh and Beara peninsulas. The land in these areas is often agriculturally marginal and consists mostly of barren and rocky upland. The

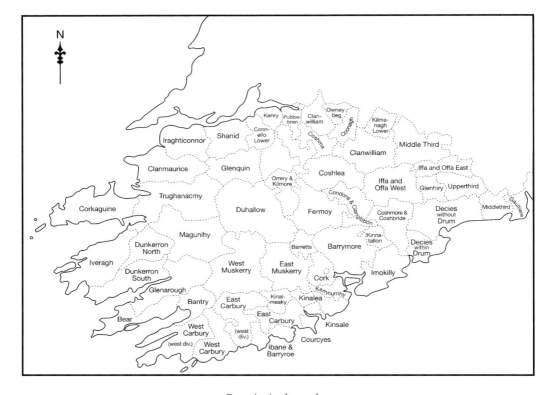

3 Baronies in the study area

sea was often a more important supplier of resources here with extensive fish and shell fish stocks. This was an extensive coastline, heavily indented with major sheltered harbours at Cork and Waterford with lesser examples at Kenmare, Bantry, Baltimore, Kinsale, Youghal and Dungarvan (fig. 3).

SOURCES

While this study adopts archaeological evidence as its primary data source a number of other evidence types are also integrated. Significant documentary information exists, much of it associated with the expansion of English interests across the region. The *Calendar of State Papers, Ireland* remain the primary source for the late medieval period supported by Tudor *Fiants* and the *Calendars of Patent and Close Rolls*. By the 1650s the so-called *Down* or *Civil Survey*, the *Books of Distribution*, the 1640s *Depositions* and the grants under the Acts of Settlement were valuable data sources on the nature and ownership of land-holdings in the middle of the seventeenth century and highlights the extent of plantation influence in the study area. Similarly, the Census of 1659, published in 1939 by Pender, was of value in examining demographics and landownership at the end of the Cromwellian period. There is a small but useful body of secondary sources available for the study area. A number of comprehensive historical studies have been published including David Dickson's 2005 masterful *Cork: a colony*, one of the most significant in-depth studies produced for any Irish county. The collection of essays contained in *Cork: history and society* (O'Flanagan and Buttimer 1993) contributes much in an inter-disciplinary vein. O'Flanagan's (1988) cartographic study of Bandon from a historical geographic perspective is an important introduction to this town. It is hoped that future proposed volumes of the Historic Town's Atlas for towns in the study region will appear in the near future.

The various county inventories have added greatly to our knowledge of extant monuments throughout the region. Published volumes include North Kerry (Toal 1995), the Dingle Peninsula (Cuppage 1986), the Iveragh Peninsula (O'Sullivan and Sheehan 1996), the various volumes of the Cork Survey (Power et al. 1992; 1994) and the Waterford Survey (Moore 1999). To these can be added the unpublished Urban Archaeology Survey, led by John Bradley, and the Industrial Archaeological Survey of Cork City and its surrounding area (Rynne 1999). A number of significant excavation reports have also been produced. Specifically, the large volume produced on the medieval Waterford city excavations (Hurley and Scully 1997) and the numerous monographs produced on excavations in Cork City. Indeed the initiative demonstrated by the City Corporation, UCC and various developers in Cork who funded many of these outputs deserve to be applauded. The difficulty of course with many of these projects from the perspective of this volume is that the excavations are multi-period. Indeed, many of the late medieval and post-medieval levels have been lost due to continual urban redevelopment and expansion. A number of themed projects looking specifically at aspects of seventeenth-century archaeology in Munster have been especially welcome. In particular Eric Klingelhofer's continued investigations into rural settlement in Munster are valuable (Klingelhofer 1999; 2000; 2005). Wiggins's (2000) study of the siege defences of Limerick is also important. Many relevant articles have appeared in both local and national journals including the *Journal of the Cork Historical and Archaeological Society*, the *Journal of the Kerry Historical and Archaeological Society*, the *Mallow Field Club Journal*, the *Journal of the Royal Society of Antiquaries of Ireland*, *Decies*, the *Journal of Medieval Archaeology* and *Irish Geography*. Full details of the relevant articles can be found in the bibliography.

4 Francis Jobson's 1589 map of Munster
(source: National Maritime Museum B8956/P/49)

A large number of historic maps and charts are available, most of which have been admirably studied by Andrews (1997) and more recently in a superb volume by Smyth (2006). Relevant maps include Mercator' *Angliae Scotiae et Hiberniae nova description* published at Duisberg in 1564, Goghe's 1567 *Hibernia, insula non procul ab Anglia vulgare Hirlandia vocata* and Boazio's *Irelande*, first published in 1599 although largely based on Lythe's previous 1571 map. The 1586 'Rough' map of Munster contains useful information relating to large settlements while Jobson's 1589 maps of the province contain an unprecedented amount of information (fig. 4). A number of relevant 'maps' are illustrated in the *Pacata Hibernia* including the siege of Dunboy, Carrigafoyle castle and town vistas of Youghal and Cork. The 1635 Blaeu map of Ireland entitled *Theatrum Orbis Terrarum*, subsequently republished in 1662, contains a number of features of topographic interest and includes various settlements and church sites. The first atlas of Ireland was published by William Petty in 1685, entitled *Hiberniae Delineatio*. Petty had previously produced a comprehensive set of maps and descriptions of the country generally called the *Down Survey*. Finally, the various editions of the Ordnance Survey six inch sheets, produced in the 1830s, 1860s and early part of the twentieth century are also an important cartographic resource for the study area.

CHAPTER 2

A Historical Context

In order to fully understand the complexities of the historical process in the Munster region during the seventeenth century we need to look back into the closing decades of the previous century. These years witnessed a number of significant nationwide upheavals, resulting in significant economic and political change throughout the study area. In particular, the collapse of the Desmond revolt in the 1580s and the onset of the Nine Years War paved the way for widespread plantation and intensification of economic practice. This allowed for the development and restructuring of settlement, both rural and urban, and began a process of significant change in the physical character of the landscape. These changes were built upon throughout the religious and political conflicts of the ensuing century, changes which gave rise to the advent of modernity and contemporary economic practice across the southwest of Ireland.

DESMOND REVOLT

Munster in the 1560s was a complex mosaic of politically ambitious lordships operating within an uncertain period of rule from London. The Old English Butlers controlled Ormond on the borders between Munster and Leinster while the earl of Desmond controlled the liberty of central Kerry as far as the Limerick border with outlying manors in Limerick and estates in Cork and Waterford (MacCathy-Morrogh 1986, 1). Other Old English families, direct descendants of the Anglo-Normans, included the Roches, Condons and Barrys with lands in Cork while a number of Gaelic lordships controlled much of the coastal territories of west Cork and south Kerry, including the MacCarthys, the O'Sullivans, the O'Driscolls and the O'Mahonys (fig. 5). Ormond and Desmond clashed briefly in 1565 over variant ambitions and this tension constitutes one of the underlying reasons why the Crown introduced a provincial council for Munster in 1569, designed specifically to undermine the power of the existing lordships throughout the province. In 1569 James Fitzmaurice, cousin of Gerald, fourteenth earl of

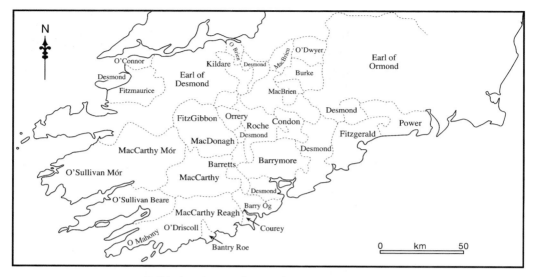

5 Political territories of sixteenth-century southwest Ireland

Desmond, initiated a small revolt against English rule in Ireland. This uprising was quickly countered by Sir John Perrot, appointed President of Munster in 1571, who moved across Desmond territory with some success, although Fitzmaurice succeeded in burning Killmallock (Hayes-McCoy 1976, 92).

Eventually the revolt was put down and Fitzmaurice subsequently left for the Continent in 1575 in an attempt to raise support for future rebellion, reflecting a general pattern of growing unease and resentment with the English amongst a number of Gaelic lords by the 1560s and 70s. There were a variety of underlying reasons behind this, including disillusionment with Elizabeth as a Protestant Queen, while many of the Irish lords were closely aligned to the teachings of Rome. What was seen as growing encroachment upon the traditional Gaelic system of land tenure and large land holdings of the Gaelic lords by new English arrivals also became a major bone of contention between the increasingly alien-ated sides. Invariably, individual ambition and politico-economic quarrels also lay behind subsequent uprisings but religious affiliation has been used continually as the justification for rebellion. Consequently, James Fitzmaurice, having spent a number of years abroad landed at Kerry in 1579, with a small invasionary force of European soldiers financed by Pope Gregory XII with support from the Catholic Philip II of Spain. This was an ill-fated expedition and Fitzmaurice was killed soon afterwards but Gerald, earl of Desmond was then, somewhat unwittingly drawn into the conflict, following his sack of Youghal in November of the same year. The so-called Desmond revolt ensued in Munster. The supporting Spanish

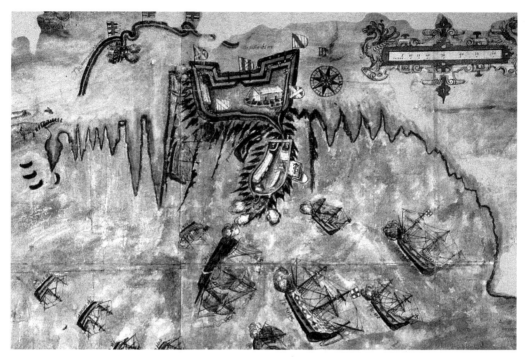

6 Detail of sixteenth-century map of Dún an Óir, Kerry (PRO, London MPF 75)

force that subsequently landed at Dún an Óir in Smerwick Harbour, Co. Kerry, in 1581 was almost immediately besieged by English forces and fell after two months with little mercy being shown to the garrison (MacCurtain 1972, 79) (fig. 6). Similarly, Desmond was not faring well. Lord Justice Pelham had taken the earl's Shannon castles and burnt much of his estates leaving Gerald to retreat to Kerry (Ellis, 1985, 280). Much of the Munster countryside was also now laid to waste by the English forces. There was widespread displacement of peoples and endemic food shortages, not helped by the English burning much of the 1580 harvest and driving off herds of cattle (Hayes-McCoy 1976, 107). Pelham himself wrote in 1579 that he had taken much of Munster's harvest resulting in widespread famine while Edward Spenser in his 1596 *A view of the present state of Ireland* wrote that 'in short space there were none almost left and a most populous and plentiful country suddenly left void of man or beast' (Renwick 1970, 104). In April 1582 St Leger recorded that 50 people were dying daily in Cork City while over 30,000 had died in the previous six months. He writes that there was 'such a famine among the people here, as it is to be feared this province, or the greatest part thereof will ere it be long be unpopulated' (MacCarthy-Morrogh 1986, 26; *Cal. S. P. Ire.*, 1582,

361–2). Rebellion had also broken out in Leinster under Baltinglass and O'Byrne but quickly collapsed through disorder and a general lack of support. By 1583 Desmond was marginalized and many of the original dissident lords had submitted to the Crown, including the MacCarthys, O'Sullivans, O'Callaghans and MacDonoghs (Hayes-McCoy 1976, 107). Gerald was assassinated in Kerry in November of the same year and the revolt collapsed. Wallop writes in the following year that Limerick and Kerry had largely been laid waste aside from small areas around Limerick City and Kilmallock while the people of Kerry had been 'consumed … chiefly by famine' (MacCarthy-Morrogh 1986, 29). The corn harvest of 1585/6 also largely failed giving rise to further suffering and population upheaval.

INITIAL PLANTATION

The English Crown now moved towards a strategy of subjugating Munster and preventing future uprisings. Schemes for planting the region with English adventurers were developed and Sir Valentine Browne and a team of commissioners were employed to survey the forfeited lands of Desmond and other dissident lords from 1584. In particular the surveyors were charged with establishing the ownership, value and areas of land as well as recording topography and economic resources. An earlier attempt at planting English subjects in the area had been suggested in 1569 when it was proposed to build a town at Bearehaven to combat the threat of pirates who were based there (MacCarthy-Morrogh 1986, 215). Warham St Leger and Richard Grenville leased land in Kerrycurrihy near Carrigaline and forwarded proposals for an ambitious scheme to develop a port town that would rival Cork. Now, in the 1580s the plan was to people selected areas of Munster with 'loving subjects of good behaviour and account none of the meer Irish to be maintained in any family' (MacCurtain 1972, 102). Specifically, John Perrott was charged with re-peopling the 'dispeopled' province of Munster so that its lands 'should be inhabited with obedient people' (Canny 2001, 128). Browne's subsequent report concluded that 574,645 acres of land, valued at £10,000 were available for settlement primarily in the counties of Cork, Kerry and Limerick (Ellis 1985, 292; Lennon 1994, 230). The survey generated some useful information relating to demographics specifically in Limerick where it was recorded that the majority of people lived in the east of the county and that much of its western portion was waste land (MacCarthy-Morrogh 1986, 9). The survey concentrated on the Desmond manors of Knockainy, Lough Gur, Askeaton, Shanid, Newcastle and Mayne in Limerick. Elsewhere the earl's manors in Kerry were concentrated in the northern half of the county and included Tarbert, Tralee and Castleisland. Towerhouses were recorded at each of these locations as being in ruins or 'broken'

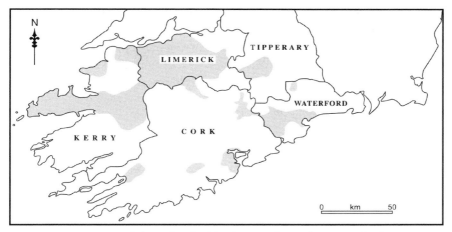

7 Location of the undertakers' lands across the southwest of Ireland

at this time. Desmond was also in possession of lands in Cork prior to 1583 including some in the barony of Kerrycurrihy, land around Youghal and the manor of Inchiquin. The earl's brother, John of Desmond, had lands along the River Bride, around Mallow and on the Cork/Limerick border. All of these lands were confiscated by the Crown along with other rebel lands including fitzGibbon's holdings at Kilmore, Condon's lands on the Cork/Waterford border and those belonging to Roche of Carriglemlery. Land confiscated from the Gaelic lords included O'Mahoney land in west Carberry and Kinalmeaky, MacCarthy sept land of Clandermot and Clandonnell Roe, O'Donoghue Mórs estates around Killarney and Teig MacCarthys lands at Mollahiffe Further west in the province. Confiscation was not then uniform across Munster but instead represents a mosaic of landholding (fig. 7). The larger towns remain largely unaffected while a number of Gaelic lordships in the southwest of Cork and on the Iveragh Peninsula retain their territories.

The initial plan was to bring over 10,000 settlers to Munster and plant them in 20–25 primary units of land called seignories of up to 12,000 English acres. Each seignory would be assigned to an individual undertaker who would 'undertake' to populate the seignory with settlers. By June 1586 Burghley records 43 seignories in eight regions but only 35 undertakers had been patented. The 1586 articles for plantation list the following undertakers – Sir Christopher Hatton, Sir Edward Fitton, Sir Rowland Stanley with the gentlemen of Cheshire and Lancashire for Limerick; Sir Walter Ralegh, Sir John Stowell, Sir John Clifton with the gentlemen of Devon, Somerset and Dorset for Cork; Sir William Courtenay, Edward Unton, Henry Oughtred and associates for Connello,

Limerick; Sir Valentine Browne, Sir William Herbert and associates for Kerry (SP/63/124/87). Most undertakers were in possession by the following year with the process completed in 1588. Thirty-five individuals had been granted a total of 298,653 acres, with fourteen in Limerick, ten in Cork, seven in Kerry, three in Waterford and one in Tipperary (MacCarthy-Morrogh 1986, 37). This process was not, however, without complications. A number of the claims were contested including that of the Clandonell Roe near Bantry. The Attorney General, Sir John Popham writes in December 1587 that this seignory was granted to his son-in-law Edward Rogers, who could not take his claim up as the land 'was wholly environed by the Irish ... and cannot be kept' (*Cal. S. P. Ire.*, 1587, 449). Rogers later took possession in 1588 but his problems continued. Popham again writes in 1588 about these issues: 'Edward Rogers was to have been placed at Bantry and finding there in all not passing 4,000 acres: the place being far off and dangerous, and all the rest thereabouts claimed by others of the Irish' (*Cal. S. P. Ire.*, 1588–9, 130–1). The earl of Clancar was much aggrieved at this grant and attempt at plantation and actively encouraged a campaign of harassment against the settlers over the next few years. In 1589 Sir Warham St Leger writes to Burghley that the earl of Clancar had dispossessed and threatened to kill the undertaker Alexander Clarke who held 25 ploughlands 'called Clan Donnell Roe' (*Cal. S. P. Ire.*, 1589, 208). The same document also refers to the earl's base son, Donnell McCartie, who had recently stabbed a person and was now playing at 'Robin Hood with 20 swords' (*Cal. S. P. Ire.*, 1589, 208). Elsewhere, both Roche and Condon engage in varying forms of resistance including boycotts in the Blackwater valley (MacCarthy-Morrogh 1986, 131).

Undertakers

The process of arrival of the undertakers is interesting not only from a political perspective but also in social terms. Some documentation and physical evidence survives that can be used to illustrate their material and mental approach to their plantations. William Herbert was assigned Castleisland in Kerry and essentially brought everything with him from England. He rebuilt the existing towerhouse and constructed a mill, brewhouse, kilnhouse and two stables. He also created a garden, hopyard, orchard and 'walks' around the castle (MacCarthy-Morrogh 1986, 125). This was a clear attempt to design a new landscape around his holdings in order to create an infrastructure for economic development and accommodate leisure activities. Herbert also brought a significant amount of material goods with him including tapestries, linen, bedding, pewter, brass, plate, jewels, cloth and foodstuffs. Work and defence are also catered for with his importation of iron and tools, body armour, hand guns, pikes, powder and two cannon. He was clearly

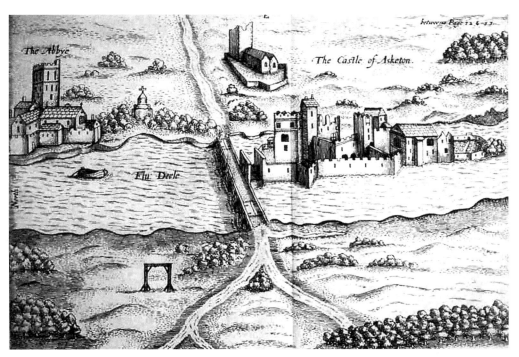

8 Askeaton castle (*Pacata Hibernia* 1633)

expecting some form of resistance and came prepared. Such weaponry is a repeated reminder of the still-unstable situation throughout the province. Both Henry Oughtred and Henry Billingsley arrived in March 1587 with 30 settlers abroad a 40-ton barque from Southampton. With them they brought, three tons of wrought iron, coal, wheels, harrows, harnesses, timber and nails, £660 in money, enough grain for one year and an array of arms including bows and arrow sheaves. Oughtred built what he describes as 'a fair house' while Billingsley occupied the towerhouse at Courtmatris. This reoccupation, or rebuilding/refurbishment of existing tower-houses, was a common feature amongst the undertakers. In Limerick the towers or castles at Askeaton, Corgrig, Rathurde and Lough Gur were occupied by the undertakers (fig. 8). Similarly, Killorglin in Kerry was occupied while Sir Thomas Norris built an elaborate house at Mallow on the site of the earlier building. Elsewhere, the undertaker Denny repaired of Tralee Abbey and subsequently lives there (MacCarthy-Morrogh 1986, 127). Sir Christopher Hatton spent £200 erecting a stone-built house and a malthouse kiln at Cappoquin.

It is clear that the original model of settlement was overly prescriptive and later changed as the settlements evolved giving the planters far more autonomy. The form of idealized planned settlement laid out by the settlement strategists was not immediately apparent on the ground although, as we shall see in later chapters, order is a central tenant of the new or re-established settlements. Bandonbridge of course epitomized this new sense of order but many of the other settlements established after 1600 also reflected this in their structure and morphology. Was then this sense of bringing order to a previously barbaric and untamed society the primary driving force behind these undertakings? In reality the situation was far more complex and there were a web of interconnecting philosophies and situations which led to the projects. The conquest and subsequent colonization of a troublesome region within the territories of the Crown has to be a major factor. The continued unrest across Munster, brought to a head by the Desmond revolt, required direct action by Dublin and London to quell this dissent. This became all the more important in the context of religious reformation when increasingly both the Old English and the Gaelic Irish identified with the Catholic political powers in continental Europe. To what extent this was a politically expedient alliance remains to be questioned but nevertheless dissatisfaction with a Protestant queen was citied as an issue of contention. These territories of Munster were also economically important with their fine agricultural lands, abundant woodland resources and highly productive fishery grounds. Such an asset could not be allowed to easily fall away. The suppression of revolt and the subsequent re-colonization of the attained lands became a political imperative.

Aside from the macro political framework there were also more subtle underlying social perspectives on the schemes. Contemporary writings clearly refer to a sense of ethnic and racial superiority held by the English over the inhabitants of much of Ireland. The undertaking schemes were then also painted in terms of bringing civilization to Ireland, essentially the transference of the emergence of polite and educated society into the reaches of a closed and barbaric traditionalist and unprogressive society. The sixteenth century was one of profound change in England with church reform, the introduction of new philosophies and investment in the arts and education. These combined factors lead to the emergence of a new confidence which expresses itself both militarily and politically and gives rise to the expansion of overseas territories and colonization schemes. Munster becomes one of the first centrally organized schemes and in doing so receives considerable attention from contemporary commentators.

NINE YEARS WAR

By the early 1590s there was growing unrest amongst the Gaelic lords particularly in Ulster. Much of this dissent centred around Hugh O'Neill in Tyrone who voiced concerns about the rise of English power within Ireland and the advance of centralized bureaucratic control from Dublin. Religion, again, was repeatedly citied as a factor in the increasing dissatisfaction with the spread of the established church. This period saw a number of internecine conflicts and smaller acts of resistance against English forces leading ultimately to O'Neill rising in 1594 (MacCurtain 1972, 83–8). His defeat of the English forces at the battle of Yellow Ford resulted in many other septs across the country joining the revolt. A number of septs in Munster had already come to be regarded as rebels. In 1597 Nicholas Browne in his account of the province of Munster lists O'Sullivan Beare and the 'McFynin duf' as among the leading Irish rebels in the region (Lyne 1976, 38). By 1598 much of Munster was in open revolt and many of the undertakers moved off their attained lands to the larger towns and cities. Many of the cities refused to join in open rebellion and continued to function within the economic sphere of London and Dublin. A number of the older castle sites such as Mallow and Askeaton became the central focus of these internal migrating groups, moving to find strength in numbers but also in the defensive nature of these places. A number of commentators have suggested that the plantation collapsed at this point (MacCarthy-Morrogh 1986) as a consequence of this displacement, conflict and subsequent downturn in economic viability of the estates. However, this was not a fatal collapse and the continuity in estate tenantship into the early part of the seventeenth century clearly shows that many leasees later returned and disruption to the enterprises was often temporary over a small number of years.

1601

George Carew, lord President, arrived in Munster in March 1600 and quickly subdued rebel activity in Waterford and Limerick. However, in the north, both O'Neill and O'Donnell had further strengthened their position. The earl of Tyrone had requested help from the Spanish king, Philip III, who subsequently dispatched a force under the command of Don Juan del Aguila from Lisbon in September 1601. Abroad these vessels were 4,464 soldiers but only 3,700 landed as Don Pedro de Zubiaur was separated from the main body of the fleet with eight vessels (Morales 2004, 93). The Spanish landed at Kinsale in late September and the English immediately begin to move their forces from around Ireland to try and counter the threat of this newly arrived force (fig. 9). Over 6,000 soldiers came together and formed an impressive siege around the town in October. This process allowed O'Neill to regroup his forces and territories throughout Ulster which ultimately led to him to begin a march southwards in support of the invasionary force. He managed to muster a force of over 2,500 men and 500 horse while O'Donnell raised over 1,500 foot and 200–300 horse (Morgan 2004, 104).

9 Detail of the siege of Kinsale *c.*1601 (*Pacata Hibernia* 1633)

O'Donnell now moves southward, evading Carew at Cashel and marched onwards to Bandon via both Limerick and Kerry while O'Neill reaches Munster largely unhindered. At the same time de Zubiaur had regrouped his small fleet and arrived in Castlehaven with six vessels and 650 soldiers in early December. He was soon engaged by an English fleet under the command of Admiral Leveson who succeed in sinking one of the Spanish vessels and causing a number of others to ground. Over 600 Spanish soldiers had already dizembarked and the garrison survived within one of O'Driscoll's towerhouses in the area allowing Zubiaur to play an influential role over the course of the Kinsale siege (*Pacata Hibernia* 1633; Klingelhofer 1992, 85). With the arrival of the Spanish off the southwest coast in 1601 a number of Gaelic lords, including the O'Driscolls, the O'Sullivan Beare

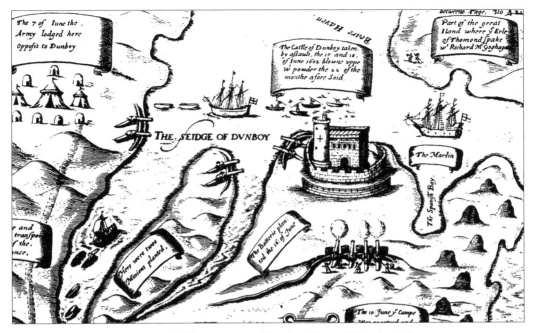

The 7 of Iune the . Army lodged here Oppofit to Dunboy

Beare Haven

The Castle of Dunboy taken by affault, the 17 and 18. of Iune 1602 blown: vppe w powder the 22 of the monthe afore Said.

Part of the great Iland where y Erle of Thomond fpake wt Richard M Goghag

THE . SEIDGE OF DVNBOY

The Marlin

The Spanish Boy

e and tranfpor f the. nce,

here were two Minions planted,

The Batterie plan: ted the 16 of Iune

The 10 June y Campe

10 Detail of the 1602 siege of Dunboy (*Pacata Hibernia* 1633)

and a number of MacCarthys pledged allegiance to them and put themselves at the disposal of the king of Spain. However, the Spanish found little support throughout the rest of Munster with Del Águila writing that the 'small towns and fortresses could have risen in arms ... but they did not' and instead supported the English (Morales 2004, 98). It is estimated that only 1,000 Munster men joined the Ulster earls and the additional 400 Leinster men brought by Tyrrell (Morgan 2004, 118).

The siege at Kinsale dragged on over a number of months. Both sides were suffering from poor supplies, with the Spanish in particular complaining of a near starvation diet and having to cope with the harsh Irish winter and environment. It was only in late December that the Irish eventually were forced into a confrontation with the English. It was to end disastrously with the Irish suffering heavy losses after being forced to fight in the open with far inferior cavalry and unprepared infantry more used to guerrilla style warfare. Following their defeat O'Neill retreated to Ulster while O'Donnell fled to Spain where he was to later die in 1602. Del Águila surrendered Kinsale leaving only a small force of O'Sullivan Beare followers left to defend Dunboy castle against a short-lived English siege (*Pacata Hibernia* 1633, 485). In April 1602 Carew left Cork with his forces for Dunboy and after a short campaign in west Cork erected siege works around Dunboy (fig. 10). On 17 May they overran the towerhouse and killed its defendants (*Pacata Hibernia* 1633, 577). Donal Cam O'Sullivan Beare was not in Dunboy at the time and engaged in a short resistance campaign against the English before embarking on his long march through Ireland to join up with O'Neill's forces in Ulster. O'Neill surrendered to Mountjoy at Mellifont and a peace settlement called the Treaty of London was signed in 1604. He later fled to Spain, where he was to die in 1616 (Byrne 1903). This whole episode centred around Kinsale was a major defeat for the politically aspirant Gaelic lords and was to severely damage their broader ambitions. It paved the way for a further intensive period of plantation in the first decades of the seventeenth century, relatively unhindered by Gaelic opposition. Edwards (2004, 282) argues that the English then pursued a policy of deliberate deGaelicization of the county led by Chichester through the abolition of Gaelic taxes and rents, strategies of encouraging division between septs and witnessing rising inflation which caused economic hardship for many of the sept lords. He suggests that the country was kept pacified through a government of military occupation which ruled with a garrison mentality.

Munster	*Commander*	*Martial law commission*
Limerick Castle	Sir Francis Barkeley	April 1599
Haulbowline	Sir Francis Slingsby	*c.*1602–3
Castlepark, Kinsale	Capt. Henry Skipworth	Feb. 1605
Dungarvan	Sir George Carey	1599 / 1600
Castlemaine	Sir Thomas Roper	Feb. 1605

Table 2.1 Munster garrisons, 1599–1605 (after Edwards 2004, 287)

Division was also encouraged amongst the lords in an effort to further destabilize any future Gaelic allegiances. In Munster, however, both the lordships of the MacCarthys in Muskerry and the O'Briens in Thomond manage to emerge from the previous decade of conflict relatively intact. They continue to play an important, if more subdued role, in the socio-economic structure of early seventeenth-century Munster.

RENEWED PLANTATION

The first decade of the seventeenth century was a confused time. Following the abandonment of the undertaker's estates in the 1590s there were now political questions over the commitment of a number of these people to the Munster settlement. The Crown had by now lost much of its original interest in Munster. The power of Desmond had been broken and interest had shifted to Ulster and the developing overseas colonies. A number of questions over ownership arise resulting in the return of some of the forfeited lands to their pre-undertaker owners. By 1611 over 30% of land forfeited in 1586 had been returned to their original owners (Dickson 2005, 11). A number of undertakers also stayed in England while others sold up. Raleigh's estates in Inchiquin were sold to Richard Boyle, then clerk of the Munster council in 1602 (MacCarthy-Morrogh 1986, 141). This sale marked the beginnings of a highly aggressive purchasing campaign by Boyle over the next three decades including the purchase of both the Nuce and Beecher seigniories in the Bandon Valley between 1613 and 1625 (Dickson 2005, 11). Other sales included that of Carrigaline in Cork, Ballymacdonnell on the Dingle Peninsula and Tarbert on the Shannon Estuary. Boyle ultimately purchased six seigniories and sections of four more. In the early 1600s the seignory of Clandonnell Roe was sold by Henry Goldfinch for £300 to Sir Nicholas Brown, a settler in neighbouring Kerry. Elsewhere in Cork, north of the Blackwater, Philip Perceval acquired the title to over 80 ploughlands by 1640. By the 1640s Dickson estimates that over 30% of county Cork and 20% of south Kerry was in New English ownership (Dickson 2005, 12), while 40% of west Waterford land was now mostly Boyle's property.

In 1607 the then bishop of Cork wrote that West Cork was still largely uninhabited by Irish (MacCarthy-Morrogh 1986, 149). While this statement may be reflective of continuing population displacement following earlier conflicts it has also to be seen in the context of re-emergent plantation and an increasing influx of English settlers after 1606. It suited contemporary commentators that large tracts of land were waste and open to colonization by the new arrivals. The subsequent 1611 commission into the Munster plantation, conducted largely by Sir Richard Moryson, lists 90 English undertakers and 483 tenants. 38 Old English tenants and 13 Irish tenants are also recorded leaving MacCarthy-Morrogh to estimate that the English population in the province was around 5,000 based on c.600 English households. What is especially interesting about this phase of plantation is the extent to which settlement occured outside the original seigniories of the 1580s. A number of Gaelic lords became involved in the mortgaging of land to new planters; Fineen O'Driscoll leased Baltimore and part of Collymore to Thomas Crooke, a more ordered town subsequently developed around the old castle site, which was in the possession of Walter Coppinger by the 1620s. By 1629 English tenants had built 60 new houses in the town (MacCarthy-Morrogh 1986, 154). In Bantry John Davenant obtained a 31-year lease of

Ballygobban beginning 13 April 1608 from Owen O'Sullivan following the fleeing of Donal Cam O'Sullivan Beare in 1602. Edward Davenant had also established a base on Whiddy Island by 1609 (MacCarthy-Morrogh 1986, 158) and was to remain there for the next 30 years until his death, becoming one of the major economic influences within the region. Similarly, Sir Thomas Roper obtained the lease of the Castleisland seignory in 1605 and established fishery stations at Crookhaven, Schull and Bantry in the 1610s and 1620s (*Cal. S. P. Ire.*, 1633–47, 156). Roper records that he planted hundreds of families at Crookhaven before he eventually moved to Wicklow. There is undoubtedly a degree of hyperbole here but nevertheless is an indication of the scale of ambition involved. William Hull, deputy vice-admiral of Munster, took over these settlements following Roper's departure. Much of the west Cork coastline witnessed similar ventures where fishing stations and small ports were established to exploit the extensive fishery resources of this area. They also serviced the burgeoning north Atlantic trade networks emerging at this time centred on Cork and Waterford, and focussed on the colonies and fishery enterprises in the Americas. Settlements were established at Dunmahon and Timoleague where Gookin had a fishery while Audley purchases land at Castlehaven and develops a settlement there (MacCarthy-Morrogh 1986, 158). Other settlements included 12 English families, mostly fishermen, at Galleyhead (TCD, MS 822, f. 177), 15 households at Kenmare and a smaller fishing village at Kilmakilloge. Robert Boyle also helped establish settlements at Enniskean, Ballydehob and Clonakilty. Each of these sites was now tied into an emergent formalized port system.

The position of the larger towns and cities was politically more ambiguous throughout this period. While in theory the citizens of Cork, Waterford and Limerick remained loyal during the conflicts at the turn of the century a number of commentators suggest that they did play a part in aiding rebel activity through the supply of arms and engaging in trading activity with them (Nicholls 2005, 116). Ultimately it appears that these centres of settlement, dominated as they were by mercantile activity, were playing a careful political game in maintaining economic interests. The populations of the large towns were overwhelming Catholic and played a fundamental role in the maintenance of the faith. However, while this religious allegiance to the rebels was present it was not enough to entice the urban inhabitants to rebellion. Instead, the merchants maintained their trade with the continent, monopolizing particular activities such as the hide trade in Cork during these periods of uncertainty. The dominance of the Catholic faith is amply demonstrated during the 'Recusant revolt' of the Munster towns in 1603 following the death of Elizabeth I in March. For a short period Protestant inhabitants of the towns were expelled and Catholic practices re-introduced into

11 Nineteenth-century view of the now infilled 'Castle Street' section of Cork port. Note the seventeenth-century front gable to the house on the extreme left and the vessel entering between King's and Queen's castle (source: Cork City Council).

the churches. This uprising was quickly put down by Mountjoy and Catholics again undergo a period of suppression in these urban environments.

The early decades of the seventeenth century saw significant economic change and readjustment. The port-town of Cork had petitioned for a charter in 1600 which they receive in 1608 establishing the town and its direct hinterland as a separate county (Nicholls 2005, 117) (fig. 11). The charter also reflects the increasingly centralized bureaucratic control exerted by the Crown on Ireland as customs on ship and goods tonnage had now to be paid directly to appointed customs officials. This new economic climate led to a large expansion in small town and village development across the province, and hence to the influx of increasing numbers of planters. It is likely that there were in excess of 10,000 planters, mostly English, in Munster by the 1620s. O' Flanagan (1993, 393) has identified three main axis of settlement growth in the early to mid part of the seventeenth century in the region; along the south and western parts of the coast, in the Bandon river valley and in the eastern section of the Blackwater/Bride river system. Numerous villages and smaller towns were now re-established or developed. It should be noted that while it has been previously thought that this period constituted the foundation date of many of Munster's smaller settlements this is not borne out in the archaeological record. As we shall see in later chapters almost invariably pre-existing settlement clusters were present at these sites in the later medieval period. What we do then see, in the early part of the seventeenth century, is a re-development, or reorganization, of these sites in a more structured or formalized manner. Significant development took place around the major urban centres while sites like Bandon considerably expand due to direct plantation-led investment. Throughout this the Gaelic Irish gentry, if we can use such a word, were increasingly marginalized by the new economic process. Repeatedly we see the mortgaging of Gaelic lands to the new arrivals, a process which slowly diluted Gaelic control and involvement in land management. It was easier for the lords to engage in such leases than try and attempt to manage and control their own tenantry, many of whom were either displaced or lost from the territories during the previous thirty years of conflict and associated upheavals. The arrival of the planters guaranteed a steady source of income which maintained their economic status to a certain degree. However, it also directly eroded their political standing and ensured a sustained period of marginalization.

Increasing conflict

Munster now witnessed a myriad of political and economic activity resulting in a widening division between the planters and Gaelic Irish, the mercantile ambitions of the urban patriarchs and religious tension between the Catholic and Established churches. Increasingly commentators recognize both the threat of internal revolt and external incursions. Pirate activity plagued the mercantile fleets operating off the southern coast while there were continual rumours and incidents of internal dissent. Sir Thomas Roper writes from Bantry in October 1624 that a friar was operating around Bantry and Bearehaven in an attempt to raise support for Spanish incursions (*Cal. S. P. Ire.*, 1624, 534). George Watts writes to Lord Dorchester in November 1631 that Irish plotters, including 'Mr. O'Sullivan Beer' planned to 'seize, burn and sack the new plantations in Munster' (*Cal. S. P. Ire.*, 1631, 634).

This regional uncertainty is reflected on the broader national scale. Various land reforms, religious tensions and the increased power of the Protestant English government in Ireland was undermining the political status quo, ultimately leading to the Ulster Rising of 1641 which spread to the rest of the country by 1642. In late 1641 and early 1642 officials attempted to compile a list of Protestant settlers and families living in Ireland in an effort to quantify injustices made against them. Canny (1993, 253) has identified 904 Protestant residents of County

Cork who filed depositions while across Munster a total of 1,414 depositions were taken. These depositions are important for a number of reasons. Firstly, while they are obviously not a complete record of planter society across the province they can be used to compile a general picture of landholding, demographics and settler distribution on the eve of rebellion. They also provide important economic data in terms of professions and the monetary movement and exchange. It should also be borne in mind that the depositions list the leading family member and are not a strict person-by-person census. It is therefore acceptable to regard many of the individuals mentioned as being married with children and possible further dependants. What the depositions clearly show is that planter settlement was concentrated in three primary areas in Munster; in the Bandon River area, in the Lee and Blackwater valleys and in the low-lying land south of the Shannon Estuary. Smaller concentrations of settlement can be seen along the southwest coastline and on the Dingle Peninsula. The highest concentration of respondents came from the Bandon area. These individuals were mostly artisans renting urban properties within the town of Bandon but also often leasing farms in the surrounding countryside (Canny 2001, 337). Canny (2001, 339) argues convincingly that there was a deliberate strategy in placing these settlers within targeted communities ensuring a sufficient skills base allowing the development of various industrial enterprises. The establishment of a number of fishing communities in the southwest is probably the most obvious manifestation of this strategy. These were often valuable and profitable ventures. The deposition of Whitcombe of Kinsale states that he lost £140 when his fishing palace was destroyed at Ballymaloe in east Cork while three Youghal-based partners lost 'implements necessary to [the] trade of fishing' valued ay £267 (Canny 2001, 340).

Other returns similarly supply important information for examining settlement morphology and other industry types. At Kilmacabea in west Cork Richard Christmas lost a tucking mill and a dwelling house. Henry Tatardall of Myross loses his tanyard, valued at £10, as well as a quantity of leather and tanned hides. A second tanyard is recorded under different ownership at Newcestown while textile manufacturing at Tallow, Co. Waterford, 'maintained above 150 people' (Canny 2001, 342). In Bandon Henry Turner records the loss of houses and garden plots in Sugar Lane near the North Gate which were deliberately destroyed to prevent them being used by the rebels. Seven further houses were burnt in the town valued at £30. Most settlers then appear to have been engaged in farming activity involving mixed tillage and stock rearing.

The depositions from the Barony of Beare and Bantry can be examined as an example of those returned and the important information that they contained.

Parish	Barony	Name	Place name	Occupation	Folio no.
Durrus	Beare and Bantry	Martha May and brother Nathaniel May	of Bantry	yeoman	823.76
		Nicholas Harvey	late Blackrock of	yeoman	824.211
		Ralph Oliver	Whiddy Island	yeoman	825.23
Kilmocomoge	Bantry	Thomas Moorecocke [Dromdoneen]	Dromanare	wheelwright	822.142
		Thomas Heyford	Bantry	gent	822.249
		Thomas Henry	Whiddy	yeoman	822.273
		John Browne	Whiddy	yeoman	823.23
		William Wood	Carie Inshikeene [Inchinariheen]	Joiner	823.55
		John Winter	Bantry	husbandman	823.87
		John Lak	Whiddy Island	husbandman	823.1
		Thomas Moorcock	Dromanara	yeoman	823.122
		Edmund McCarthy	Bantry	yeoman	823.143
		Valentine Gordon	Bantry (Scottish Protestant)	spinster	823.169
		Anthony Blunt	Bantry	yeoman	823.19
		Agnis Tucker	Whiddy Island	widow	824.149
		Katherin Heyford, wife of Owen Heyford	Bantry		824.223
		Christopher Speringe	Bantry	timberman	825.7
		William French	Kilmacom [Kilmocomoge]	tanner	825.264
		Robert Collins	Whiddy		
		John Smith	Gurtirow [Gurteenroe]	yeoman husbandman	825.318 825.301

Table 2.2 1641/2 Depositions from Bantry and Beara (Source: Canny 1993: 292, 295/6)

The records list six English families living on Whiddy Island and eight living at Bantry with others residing at Blackrock, Gurteenroe, Kilmacomoge, Dromanare and Dromdoneen (fig. 12). The numbers living at Bantry is especially interesting as the settlement here appears to have developed to a greater extent than the waterfront settlement at Blackrock where only one family is now listed. This would appear to indicate that Blackrock was now in decline, possibly due in no small part to the conflict, a sharp decrease in shipping coming into the area and a possible collapse in the fisheries. This is further substantiated by the fact that none of the individuals listed are referred to as fishermen. The majority were yeomen, or small freeholders, while a number of specialized trades are mentioned.

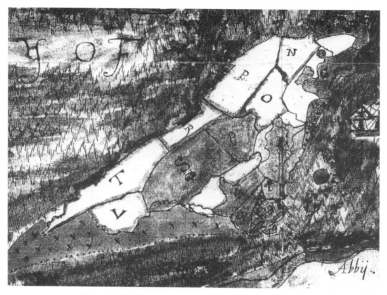

12 Detail of early seventeenth-century Whiddy Island
(source: East Yorkshire Archives DDCC[2])

Of course a number of them may have fished part-time in the same way as the wheelwright presumably also engaged in some agricultural and fishing activity. The same depositions for the Kenmare region list fifteen names. Of these six are named at Killmakilloge. Other than yeomen three are listed as merchants, three as smiths and one as a miner (MacCarthy-Morrogh 1986, 158; Kerry depositions, TCD, MS 828). Interestingly Valentine Gordon, who is listed as a spinster at Bantry, is the only person among the 1,414 settlers throughout Munster who is listed as a Scottish Protestant (Canny 2001, 308). The fact that Scottish nationality is mentioned is reflective of the fact that the vast majority of settlers into this area were English.

By 1641 the Mac Fineen Duffs held 'Glaunetrasny (Glantrasna), Dirinianvetick (Dereen etc.), Glanmore, Curraghereene, Nighanagh (Fehanagh), part of Agrovine (Ardgroom) and part of Dromclogh' (Lyne 1976, 42). The important harbour of Killmakilloge had by now passed into the ownership of Colonel Donogh Mac Fínín MacCarthy of Ardtully Castle, proprietor of the parish of Kilgarvan and other parishes (Butler 1925, 58–9). Their retention of their lands is interesting. It demonstrates that the old Irish order was holding on to some of their lands regardless of the incursion of the new settlers. The MacFineen Duff must have been engaged in a considerable amount of diplomatic manoeuvring to ensure that this was still the case.

1641

In April 1640 Scots armies were on England's borders threatening its national security. Charles I turned to Parliament for help but was rejected. The Scots entered the north of England and establish a base in Newcastle. Charles turned to Ireland and instructed Wentworth to raise a Catholic army in order to support him given the unwillingness of the English Puritans to offer any help. By 1641 Parliament was actively moving against the King and enacted legislation undermining his power. Ireland was placed in a delicate situation and brought to the verge of rebellion through a mixture of political intrigue, ambition and economic manoeuvring. The political context of the 1641 revolt in Ireland is complex. Historical overviews of the rising and the subsequent decade of conflict have been well treated elsewhere (Ohlmeyer 1995; FitzPatrick 1988) so I provide here only a brief overview of events in Munster. Ulster rose in October 1641 and Phelim O'Neill took a number of castles and towns including Newry, Tandragee, Carrickmacross and Mountjoy castle. A suspected move against Dublin castle was uncovered and martial law was introduced by the Council of Dublin. A direct appeal was made to the English Parliament for help in suppressing this supposed All-Ireland Catholic rising (FitzPatrick 1988, 131). The Gaelic Irish continually claim that the rising is in effect in support of the King and feared that Scottish Protestant forces would overwhelm the country and that their Catholicism as such was under threat. As a consequence by december much of the Old English in the country were almost unwittingly drawn into the conflict. In January the king called for their surrender but this was rejected. By the following spring of 1642 most of the country's Catholic elite joined the revolt and the island was in open rebellion against the Crown. By April a Scots army, under Robert Monro, arrived in Ulster and Presbyterianism was firmly established. In March the English Parliament act and Ireland was declared forfeit. Under the 'adventurers' act 2.5 million acres were to be set aside for English use at the end of the war, one million was to be raised in shares in the forfeited country and the Dublin Parliament was suspended. The underlying reasons behind the insurrection were varied. Nationwide the Catholic gentry certainly felt that their political and socio-economic position was being increasingly undermined, their property holdings were continually being eroded and their religion was subject to suppression. When the Dublin Parliament opened in March 1640 89 members were Protestant, 68 were Catholic Old English and six were Gaelic Irish (FitzPatrick 1988, 119). In south Munster Catholics held only eight of the 31 seats in Parliament (Dickson 2005), an indication of the dominance of the settler community in this region. Alarmed at further erosion of their holdings and status and a misguided and confused relationship with the Crown they revolted.

Munster saw only isolated incidents in the first few months of the rising, mostly concentrated in Tipperary. By December though the province moved towards a more general rising, the insurgents quickly took Cashel, Clonmel and Fethard with the Protestant inhabitants either expelled or killed. The Catholic gentry of north Cork, Limerick and Waterford, including the Barrys, Condons and O'Callaghans came together and began to form a Munster army. A number of the lordships of the south west also joined the alliance with intelligence from London in May 1642 recording that 'O'Suilleban Beara' and all of the Chief Lords of Munster supported the rebellion and were in arms 'resolved to die or restore the Catholic faith and freedom of the realm' (*Report on Franciscan Manuscripts* 1906, 134–5). Donal O'Sullivan Beare is subsequently listed as an outlaw in the period 1641–47 (Simington and MacLellan 1966, 336). In 1642 the English army in Munster was garrisoned at both Cork and Youghal. Murrough O'Brien, Lord Inchiquin, the commander of these loyal forces in the province began his campaign against the rebels in the summer of that year and recorded a solid victory at Liscarroll in August and a lesser success at Bandonbridge in November. However, by January of the following year his forces were in a weak state, suffering from poor provisions and a lack of supplies (Wheeler 1995, 46). They controlled the port towns of Kinsale, Cork and Youghal and much of north Cork but the remainder of the province lay under the control of the rebel forces. In the interim civil war had broken out in England in August 1642 between Charles I and his royalist forces and the Parliament's Puritan armies. This largely distracted Charles from affairs in Ireland and to a certain extent changed the direction of the Irish revolt. In October the rebel forces had come together at Kilkenny and created an oath of association and established a formal Confederation. This essentially provided legislative independence and allowed Catholics worship freely within Ireland. This confedration was never a truly unified force though and suffered throughout its lifespan from poor leadership and often an absence of a coherent direction. Charles instructed Ormond, now lord lieutenant of Ireland, to pursue a treat in January of 1643 (Lydon 1998, 188). Consequently by September a cessation of arms was agreed. The Confederates subsequently meet in Waterford in November and agree to concentrate their efforts on removing the Scottish Presbyterian army from Ulster.

In February 1644 Inchiquin went to England but was snubbed by the King and failed to obtain the presidency of Munster. These setbacks, combined with his frustration with Ormond in Ireland and royalist defeats in England, led him to switch allegiances and defect to the Parliamentarians. On his return to Ireland he renewed his campaigns against the Catholic rebels. In July Inchiquin expelled the Catholic inhabitants of Cork city who dispersed to Macroom and the

Mallow	Lord President St Leger	50 horse, 100 foot
Limerick	Sir John Sherlock, Captain Charles Price	100 foot
Cork	Captain Philip Wenman	50 foot
Waterford	Sir George Flower	50 foot
Roscrea	Sir George Hamilton	50 foot
Clonmel	Captain John Ogle	50 foot
Youghal	Captain Robert Byron	50 foot
Kinsale	Lord Baltinglass	50 foot

Table 2.3 Munster garrisons *c.*1639 (source: Edwards 2004, 288)

southwest. Cork was to remain a strongly garrisoned and loyal town for the next decade with similar expulsions taking place in 1649, 1651 and 1656. By 1645 the Confederates were beginning to achieve some success against him: Preston took Duncannon in March while Castlehaven overran the Blackwater valley by the summer, capturing Lismore, seat of the Boyles, along the way (Wheeler 1995, 53, Dickson 2005, 33). A reversal of fortunes occured in September when Roger Boyle, Lord Broghill, and Inchiquin's deputy in Munster, broke the two-month Confederate siege of Youghal resulting in a degree of dispersal and disunity amongst the rebel forces. They regained some ground in 1646 when they took Bunratty castle from the parliamentarians. In 1647, 4,500 reinforcement troops for Inchiquin arrived and he subsequently took Dungarvan in April/May and Cashel in September (fig. 13). In an important battle Inchiquin confronted Taaffe

Year	Protestant troop strength Munster/ Connacht	Catholic troop strength (Taaffe)
1642	2,000–6,000	3,000–5,000
1643	4,000–6,000	4,000–7,000
1644	2,000–3,000	5,000–8,000
1645	2,000–5,000	4,000–6,000
1646	4,000–5,000	4,000–6,000
1647	4,000–6,000	4,000–8,000
1648	4,000–6,000	5,000–7,000
1649	4,000–6,000	5,000–8,000 (under Ormond)

Table 2.4 Estimated troop strength in Munster 1642–9 (source: Wheeler 1995, 50–1)

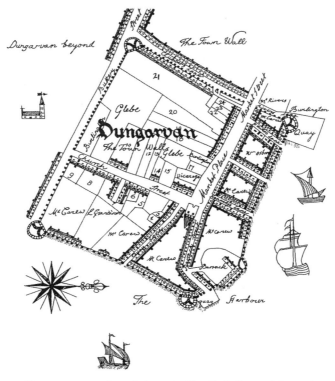

13 Dungarvan town in 1762 (source: Waterford County Museum)

at Knocknamuss near Mallow in November. The Confederate forces numberd 7,000 foot and 1,200 horse while Inchiquin had 4,000 infantry, 1,200 cavalry and three cannon. Inchiquin was victorious and routed the rebel forces which essentially marked the end of the Confederate army in Munster. He quickly moved on to take Limerick, Waterford and Clonmel. In May 1648 the second civil war breaks out in England. Inchiquin, in another twist to this complicated tale, once again changed allegiance and became a royalist, subsequently signing a truce with the Confederates.

The Parliamentarian Colonel Jones engaged in a series of successful campaigns against both the royalist and Confederate forces in 1647/8. This came at a crucial time for the rebel forces as they were now experiencing major financial and logistical problems. They had attempted to encourage continental trade and offset their economic woes through minting their own coinage but this was largely unsuccessful. Subsequent crop failures and plague brought them to their knees. Ormond negotiated a treaty in January 1649 between the royalists and Confederates. One month later Prince Rupert arrived from the Continent with twelve ships and established a base at Kinsale. He engaged in active harassment

14 Oliver Cromwell (National Maritime Museum, Greenwich)

against English vessels off the south coast in tandem with Irish privateers and attempted to block the supply routes into the English-controlled ports. These events provided a new emphasis to the now combined royalist/Confederate cause. The parliamentarian New Model Army was by now essentially in civil war against the forces of the Crown. By December the war was over and Charles I was executed in January 1649. With the King out of the way the parliamentarians renewed their interest in Ireland. By March Oliver Cromwell had been selected to go to Ireland with an experienced force of 12,000 soldiers and a substantial amount of money to support the war effort (fig. 14). Ormond, commanding the remaining royalist forces in Ireland, moved against Drogheda and Trim and advanced on Dublin in August. Significant reinforcements landed in support of Jones's forces and they routed sections of Ormond's forces at Rathmines. Inchiquin's previous return to Munster to protect the province did not help Ormond's position and contributed towards the defeat. His return though was instrumental in royalist's successfully defending Clonmel in May and Waterford in the autumn of 1649. The New Model Army under Cromwell arrived in August 1649 and the royalist garrisons at Cork and Youghal returned to the parliamentary fold then marched on Drogheda and ruthlessly destroyed the town's resistance. Rupert's royalist fleet had been blockaded at Kinsale since May but managed to escape to Lisbon in October. The parliamentary campaigns in Munster began in earnest in late September and early October when Cromwell's forces moved against New Ross and later attacked Waterford in November. They met little resistance at New Ross which surrendered on 19 October but the fort at Duncannon held out for longer before the Parliamentary forces broke their siege (Corish 1976, 324). They over-wintered for December and January in Cork encouraged by Broghill's defection resulting in the garrisons in Cork, Youghal, Bandon and Timoleague declaring for Cromwell. Dungarvan surrendered to Broghill in late November but portions of Waterford harbour remained in rebel hands. At the end of January the parliamentary forces moved from Youghal and into Tipperary where Fethard quickly surrendered. In late April Cromwell moved against Clonmel, whose defending forces were commanded by Hugh O'Neill. The rebel forces carried out a spirited defence of the town even after the parliamentarians had breached the walls, and sustained heavy loses. The defending garrison escaped but were unable to regroup. Limerick was surrounded in June and later besieged again from June to October 1651 when it finally fell. Cromwell had left for England in late May 1650 to counter the threat of a Scottish invasion in England and Henry Ireton, his son-in-law took charge in Ireland. Ireton established a civil administration appointing four 'commissioners of parliament', Edmund Ludlow, Miles Corbet, John Jones and John Weaver (Corish 1976, 353). Ludlow largely took control following the death of Ireton in 1651 by which time the country was effectively under parliamentarian control. Finally, Viscount Muskerry surrendered to Ludlow at Ross Castle in Kerry in the summer of 1652 and Munster was finally at peace (Dickson 2005, 38). The war had been devastating, with William Petty estimating that 616,000 individuals, mostly Catholic, had been killed, leaving a remaining population of 850,000 (Lydon 1998, 193), a figure which is probably a significant under-estimation. Many of these casualties may also be related to the outbreak of bubonic plague which reached epidemic proportions throughout southern Munster from 1649 to 1653.

The Cromwellian conquest of the country opened up a new phase of plantation. The new planters were initially in 1641 to be drawn from two primary sectors: the 'adventurers' who were involved in providing capital for the conquest, mostly merchants and parliamentarians and secondly, soldiers who had participated in the conquest and who had been promized land in part repayment for their efforts (Andrews 1985, 61). Following the ending of the armed campaign over a decade later much had changed and updated surveys were required. The 'Gross Survey' was established to map out the forfeited lands for distribution, including the mapping of topographical features, parishes and baronies. This became an overly complex exercise and the 'Civil Survey' was set up to list all relevant information relating to lands outside of the Strafford inquisition of the 1630s. The adventurer's were set aside confiscated land in ten counties while the remainder was to be given over to military personnel. The Surveyor-General, Benjamin Worsley, began to survey these lands in 1653, with both Worsley and William Petty undertaking a resurvey of the adventurers' land in 1656. Petty's 'Down Survey' began in early in 1655 and was essentially finished by 1659. The key component of this important survey was townland maps which showed important topographical features and differentiated between profitable and non-profitable lands. He later published an edited county atlas of his work, *Hiberniae*

15 Detail from William Petty's 1685 *Hibernie delineation*

Delineatio, in 1685 (fig. 15). These maps are a key reference point for examining landholding and the physical character of these lands in the middle of the seventeenth century. The maps, combined with the depositions and the later *Books of Survey and Distribution* are crucial to our study of Munster in this period.

Cromwellian change

Cromwellian settlements were to fundamentally change the nature of landholding in 26 counties of Ireland east of Connacht and Clare. All land now automatically became property of the government and was used to pay government creditors, soldiers who had fought for the parliamentary forces without pay and other individuals who had lent practical support in the form of money, supplies and other forms of assistance. Important resettlement plans were also put in place to move a number of the Irish families to Connacht. In effect many of the Old Protestant estates survive while large-scale displacement and upheaval occurs within the Catholic gentry. Many of the Catholic lower classes, however, were left in place to work the land and to continue the operation of the estates. The emergence of the Protestant ascendancy can clearly be seen to evolve at this time. In the first two years of the settlement the army effectively ruled the country and undertook the plantation. However, individuals like Boyle negotiated the political

16 Charles II as depicted in an
initial in a Plea Roll, 1661

scene well and managed to maintain their sphere's of influence. With the appointment of Oliver Cromwell to the role of Lord Protector Henry Cromwell assumed
responsibility for Ireland, becoming Lord Deputy in 1657, and lord lieutenant in
1658. Three years previously he had reintroduced civilians to the political stage
and increasingly moved away from absolute military control with the restoration
of local government and judicial systems in 1655 and 1656 (Corish 1976, 355). This
erosion of military power saw a coup undertaken by the officers of the parliamentarian army who were unsure of their future. Garrisons across the country
quickly supported them and once again the country moved towards an uncertain
political footing. The death of Oliver Cromwell in 1658 and the consequent
uncertainty had much to do with this new upheaval and led to the initiation of
arguments for the restoration of the monarchy and resumption of the Irish
Parliament. Charles II was subsequently instated in 1660 and in November
confirmed the soldiers and adventurers lands in possession in 1659 but excluding
that of the lands of 'innocent papists'. An act of settlement was published in July
1662 and some partial recovery of Catholic landholding took place (fig. 16).

The southwest of Cork is an interesting microcosm of the changes that occur
at this time. Bantry in effect witnessed two primary waves of planters in the
seventeenth century; the first wave arrived in the very early part of the century
associated with the pilchard entrepreneurs while the second group arrived during
the period of the Commonwealth and the initial years of the Restoration in the
1650s and early 1660s. However, this second grouping cannot strictly be termed
planters in that initially they did not have a major effect on the nature and form

of the landscape. This area only played a small historical part in the 1640s conflict as a whole and the only possible recorded event was in 1652 when Cromwell allowed defeated rebel troops depart from the port of Bantry (O'Carroll 1996, 162). Instead the primary effect they had was on the changing nature of landownership. Many of the land grants were brought up by individuals to create very large estates. These purchasers were for the most part English Protestants which in turn created a new landowning Protestant social elite. All of the lands of the Mac Fínín Duibh, for example, eventually passed to Sir William Petty who gradually acquired huge estates throughout Kerry while the O'Sullivan Beare had lost his lands in the 1650s. Daniel [Dermot] O'Sullivan Beare petitioned Charles II late in the 1660s in an attempt to get his former estates back which had been 'confirmed by Elizabeth and James' to his grandfather and father, Owen and Owen respectively, following their services at Dunboy (*Cal. S. P. Ire.*, 1669–70, addenda, 456). O'Sullivan points out that his estates had not been granted to an adventurer or soldier but that he had received letters ordering their restoration. Petty and others had taken the estates, deriving title from Walters who had received a large part of the petitioner's estate from Cromwell 'as a gratuity for transporting and selling your majesty's subjects beyond seas' (*Cal. S. P. Ire.*, 1669–70, 456). However, the petition was unsuccessful and Daniel is later recorded as a tenant of Petty at the Dereen estate (now extensive landscaped gardens), with five ploughlands, from 1672 to 1683 at a rent of £46 per annum (Lyne 1976, 45). This period essentially marks the end of the Gaelic Irish O'Sullivan Beare lordship as their power and lands are now gone. Elements of the family, do however, survive as chief tenants under the new elite.

PETTY AND THE SOUTHWEST

William Petty was largely responsible for the economic regeneration of the Glanarought/Kenmare territories. Petty had risen to the position of Surveyor-General in the Cromwellian army in Ireland, most significantly being charged with the Down Survey which formed the basis of the Cromwellian distribution of lands following confiscation in the 1650s. By the late 1650s he had acquired large tracts of land throughout Kerry and West Cork, acquiring 3,500 acres in Glanarought and bought 2,000 acres in the same area soon afterwards (Barrington 1999, 126). Following the Restoration Petty managed to win favour from Charles II, was appointed a knight, and proceeded to develop his lands and assets around Kenmare Bay. In 1662 he received 30,000 unprofitable acres in the area. He was not the only person who was in receipt of lands. Captain George Dillon received 615 acres at Loghnahane and 2,108 acres in Glanaroughty in

17 Kenmare River from Ardea Castle

January 1666 under the Acts of Settlement, while Thomas Compton receives part of Nedeen and Killowen in Glanarought totalling 1,410 acres in July 1667 (*Cal. Pat. Rolls*, Charles II, 1666–85). Sir George Carterett and William Petty were later to receive a further 7,787 statute acres under the same mechanism in December 1678 at an annual rent of £73. Petty was involved in two primary industries in the Kenmare region, fishing and iron-working (fig. 17). He had estimated that the pearl fisheries in Kenmare would yield an annual income of £1,000, pilchards would yield £1,250 per annum, £150 would come from salmon while £200 would come from train-oil extracted from the pilchards (*Osler MS* 7612 – W. Petty to George Carteret October 1666 and April 1667 – McGill University Library). Petty also makes comment on the fact that the woodland resource in Glanarought had the potential to supply surplus wood for barrel production. By 1667 Petty had commenced his iron works and 48 workmen are listed as part of the enterprise, three of whom were miners (Cowman 1993, 200). Two years later these works appear to have been faltering although his fisheries were improving with two seine boats having been readied with nets and 130 hogsheads of fish caught (*Petty Papers* vol. 14: J. Rutter to W. Petty 13 August 1672 – McGill University Library). By 1675 four seine boats were operating at Ballinskelligs and Killmakilloge (*Petty Papers* vol. 19: W. Petty to T. Crookshank 5 October 1675). Adam Goold is referred to at this time as clerk of the fish palaces at both locations and is recorded as marketing fish in Bantry. The operation of these enterprises was severely interrupted in 1689 with the onset of conflict at the start of the Williamite War (Wood 1934, 37).

Summary

The sixteenth century witnessed the gradual erosion of Gaelic power before a number of Irish septs were defeated following Kinsale and the siege of Dunboy in 1601/2. Large sections of Munster were initially planted by English colonists who leave their own cultural imprint on the area, which in turn begans to assume much of its modern form and character with more widespread change occurring after 1650. Much of the economic focus of these early planters on the coast was on the fishing industry while further inland it was agricultural production and trade. In this context they can be seen to be continuing the previous activities of the various Gaelic lordships albeit in a much more structured manner. The new arrivals formalized management systems over the countryside through fortification, enclosure and nucleated settlement. Industrialization in the form of iron-working is also in evidence which led to large-scale deforestation. However, it is only after 1650 that many of the Gaelic-Irish, including for example O'Sullivan Beare and MacFineen Duff, finally lost control of their lands. It is this later period that marks the collapse of Gaelic influence in the southwest region. Increasingly towards the end of the century landownership is dominated by an ever-diminishing number of people and the Protestant ascendancy is firmly established.

CHAPTER 3

Urban Settlement

This chapter examines the archaeology of the larger and more important urban settlements present in the study region. The assignation of importance could be viewed as being a arbitrarily subjective process in historical terms but it does appear clear that three or four of the large towns of plantation-period Munster were regarded as primary centres by both the contemporary population and policy makers and by later historical analysis. Specifically, the designation of the term large is dependant on a number of attributes – large and diverse populations, a wide concentration of social and economic activities, diverse functionality, contemporary recognition of the town as a central place, political and economic recognition of status, strong communication links and facilities and a well developed infrastructure. Three such sites in Munster are immediately apparent and include the towns, now cities, of Waterford, Cork and Limerick. Other places could of course also be included here. Both Youghal and Kinsale were important economic centres and established ports, often directly competing against or out performing the established Hiberno-Norse settlements. It should be noted that Youghal was also functioning as the outport for Clonmel. They may not have been physically as large as the other settlements but do, nonetheless, warrant identification as larger towns. Both Tralee and Dingle in Kerry and Dungarvan in Waterford should also be included as functioning ports, albeit on a smaller scale. Further inland a major new settlement is established at Bandonbridge (Bandon) in the early part of the seventeenth century. While it is now more recognized as a provincial market town it was originally established with a view to developing it as a major emerging economic and political entity. The investment in infrastructure, including walls and housing, are reflective of this aspiration. The historic town of Killmallock also experiences redevelopment at this time as do the medieval towns of Cashel and Fethard. This study will, however, concentrate on the coastal sites and the aforementioned towns of the southwest. Smaller towns and villages as well as dispersed and outlying settlement clusters will be dealt with in chapter five.

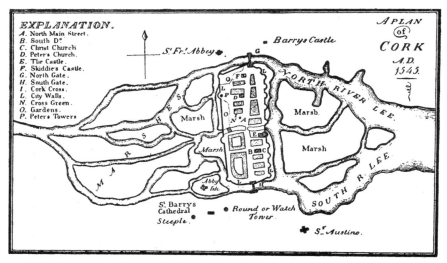

18 Cork *c.*1545

LOCATION

Even the most cursory cartographic examination of urban centres in southwest Ireland in the first half of the seventeenth century demonstrates how much the settlement pattern owed to town foundation and development during the Viking and Anglo-Norman periods. Certainly the major towns in the area, including Cork and Waterford with Limerick to the northwest, were Viking-period foundations which underwent significant subsequent development over the following four centuries (fig. 18). These were deliberately sited on the coast to function as ports and facilitate maritime communications and marine resource exploitation. In later centuries their influence grew and the resources of the hinterland and the access to it provided by a number of large river systems in this region became increasingly important. Much of the southwest, especially east Waterford, north Cork and south Limerick was productive agricultural land. The remoter parts of west Cork and much of Kerry were less profitable from a terrestrial perspective but did have access to extensive marine resources such as fish. Few of the large urban settlements prominent in the seventeenth century were developed then at greenfield sites with only a handful owing their ancestry to this period. The most prominent of the new sites was Bandon Bridge/Bandon. Richard Boyle was primarily responsible for the town's expansion but his reasoning behind such an investment remains something of a mystery. Bandon could never function as a port as it did not have navigable access to the open sea.

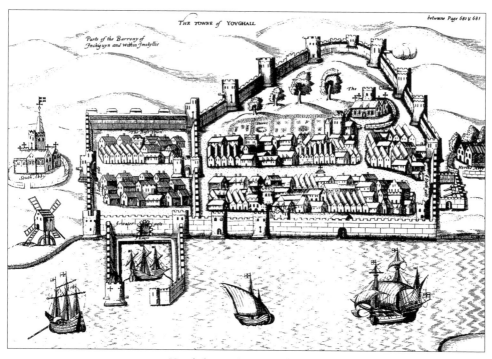

19 Youghal town (*Pacata Hibernia* 1633)

Neither was it in the centre of 'New English' activity, although a significant number of settlers came to live in its surrounding area. Granted it was relatively accessible on the terrestrial routeways of the time and was surrounded by good agricultural land but why Boyle did not invest further in Youghal, for example, is difficult to understand. It may be that in his efforts to maximizehis influence across the region he was attempting to set up a number of new settlements to function as direct rivals to the existing and long established sites. Certainly his attempt to establish a port at Carrigaline can be seen in the context of creating a rival for Cork. So while this rival port may have failed his ambitions for a settlement to rival Cork in size is evident at Bandon. The placement of the new site at Bandon would also act as a conduit between his territories in the east of Munster and his increasing interest in the west of the province.

TOWN WALLS

The enclosing walls of the towns under study here were complex and important constructs. The majority were of course constructed during the thirteenth century

20 Waterford town walls (Rory Quinn, UU)

when the Anglo-Norman administrators and emergent entrepreneurs invested heavily in the protection of their urban spaces and mercantile settlements. Strong enclosing walls served as a good defence in the prevailing warfare of the time when they adopted castle-like strategies of protection against light attack and sometimes long sieges. Over the following four hundred years they underwent almost continuous development and repair. It could be argued that on the eve of the seventeenth century, given the advent of artillery warfare, they were largely obsolete. Yet they continued to perform a number of roles. Defence was still their primary function and certainly during the conflicts of the later part of the sixteenth century the *Pacata Hibernia* illustrates Cork, Limerick and Youghal with intact and impressive walls (fig. 19). The walls would have had a key function in protecting these towns against Gaelic incursion, especially in the context that many of the Gaelic insurgents had little use or experience of artillery. Walls would also have had a role in regulating movement in and out of the towns. This was of central importance to an administration which laid heavy emphasis on the monitoring of goods and commodities and the associated collection of taxes and customs. Mercantile activity becomes increasingly centralized in both a physical and economic sense at the end of the sixteenth century and this clearly manifests

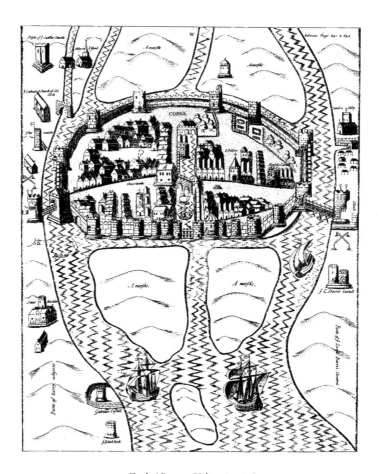

21 Cork (*Pacata Hibernia* 1633)

itself with these urban centres playing an ever-increasing role in social and economic affairs of both the region and the broader country. Walls then protected these areas and added a layer of prestige and importance to the urban centres. Marking the towns as important foci in the landscape and cementing them as central places.

Waterford's town walls were originally constructed in the Anglo-Norman period and enclosed a triangular area fronting onto the river (fig. 20). The primary phase of building was between 1220 and 1246 with further expansion taking place between 1290 and 1360 when a rampart was built. Between 1486 and 1597 the walls were continually redeveloped to encompass the area to the southeast of the town. These extensions were amongst the first defensive structures in Ireland to cater for artillery. Specifically, pistol loops were added to a number of the circuit towers including the three-storey French tower and the D-shaped tower to the north. There is also specific cartographic evidence that an internal rampart was built against the wall to absorb artillery attack. This would appear to have been removed in the early part of the nineteenth century to accommodate house and tenement building. An external ditch further strengthened the defences. The wall remained in use into the seventeenth century by which time it had 15 gates and 23 mural towers (Hurley and Scully 1997, 16).

Cork City's walls are poorly preserved above present ground level much of what we know about them is drawn from cartographic and historical sources but mainly from archaeological excavation. The walls were originally built in the thirteenth century using roughly dressed limestone and some red and green sandstone, laid in courses. It underwent continual repair and redevelopment over the following four hundred years. The *Pacata Hibernia* illustration of the town in *c.*1585 shows a complete circuit surviving around the core of the settlement (fig. 21). The town at this date had two main terrestrial entry points at the north and south gate respectively. A number of sea approaches are shown including the primary entry through the centre point of the eastern wall and a second watergate to the east of the south gate. A circular tower with possible cannon is shown immediately east of this feature. Cannon are shown on the towers of both the entry gates indicating a perception of threat from the land as opposed to the sea. The walls are shown crenellated with a wall walk or parapet with access steps and 16 towers of varying sizes. A later map of 1602 can be taken as being more structurally accurate than the somewhat artistic representation in the *Pacata* (fig. 22). Again the walls are shown as being structurally intact with 16–18 mural towers of varying form depicted. A wall walk with access steps is clearly shown but the towers must have had varying functions given their differing form. Some are shown as roofed while others are apparently uncovered and largely semi-circular form, indicating that would have been used primarily during times of conflict. The roofed towers may have housed garrisons and served other administrative functions. Again, both the north and south gates are well defended. It is clear from both these sources that the residents within the town still felt the need for the maintenance and upkeep of the walls during the Nine Years War. However, the following peaceful decade led to degradation as the Corporation of Cork in 1613 raise £500 in taxes to fund the 'erection of the walls of the city, now ruinous and ready to fall apart except speedily repaired' (Caulfield 1876, 44). Further expenditure took place in 1614 and 1617 when other sections of the wall were deemed at risk. In 1624 Robert Browne offers to fund the repair of sections of the west wall. He offered to 'make up and repair all of the western wall of this city,

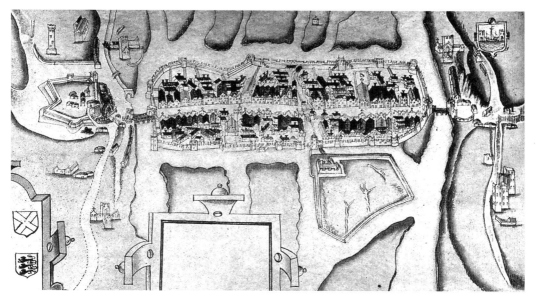

22 Cork 1602 (Hardiman Atlas, TCD MS 1209/45)

viz, from Thomas Morlyes house unto Droopsmill, lay it over above with fair large stones equal to the rest of the said wall' (Caulfield 1876, 116). Six years later in 1630 James Morrough, a former mayor, owed the corporation unused monies that had been earmarked for the 'building of bridges and the repairing of the walls of the city, then being fallen and brought away by the last water floods' (Caulfield 1876, 148). Again, in 1639, a plan was put forward to repair the bridges and associated 'castle' buildings which were in a state of disrepair after structural debris had fallen into the river.

It comes as little surprise that the walls required constant repair. They were originally effectively built on marsh and riverine gravels, a base not especially conducive to stability and good survival. Much of the seventeenth- century redevelopment of the wall utilized the core or base of the medieval wall as a foundation (fig. 23). A number of sections of this rebuilt wall have been uncovered during the course of excavation. Investigations at 81–3 Grand Parade demonstrated that the wall was rebuilt using ashlar masonry (Cleary and Hurley 2003, 176). Further ashlar rebuilds were found at Washington Street on the upper levels of the wall. The northeast section of the wall at Grattan Street was similarly rebuilt in the mid part of the seventeenth century following collapse while the wall section from Philip's Lane to Liberty Street was battered. This section also produced mortar bonding and rendering. Following the 1690 siege the walls were

23 Photograph of section of the Cork City walls at the Grand Parade

deemed no longer necessary and sections were demolished in 1694. Some repair took place subsequently but this seems largely associated with individual property boundaries and with the development of waterfront facilities.

The town walls at Bandon are important for a number of reasons. They were built in the first two decades of the seventeenth century and as such do not have the ancestry of the structures at the other urban centres. Such a construction date allows us to make a number of observations on both military and economic thinking. A deliberate seventeenth-century construct provides us with key insights into the reasoning behind such a building and provides a contemporary exemplar against which we can evaluate the redevelopment of other sites. There is some confusion as to the actual date of the erection of the walls. Richard Boyle claims to have started their build in 1620 with the commissioners of the Munster Plantation reporting in 1622 that 10% of the wall was standing to its intended height and a further 50% stood 4m high (O'Flanagan 1988, 2). Work was completed by 1627 with further work undertaken on the gatehouses in the 1630s. However, in 1616 a certain Captain Thomas Adderly is listed as having a house outside of the west gate indicating that some form of defensive structure was in place around the settlement at this time. A plan of Bandon Bridge made by Christopher Jefford in 1613 shows a wall, gatehouses and a number of bastions in

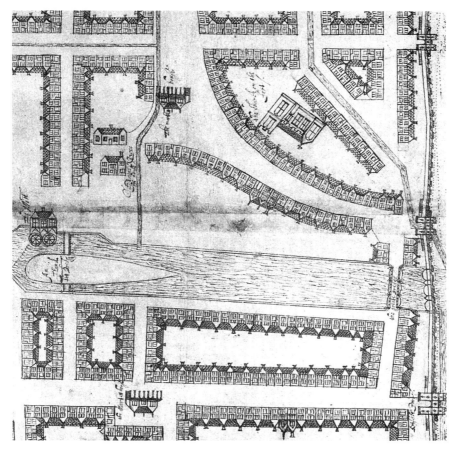

24 Detail of early seventeenth-century plan of the 'Towne of Bandon Bridge'
(TCD, MS 1209, Hardiman)

place around the settlement on the north side of the river (Trinity College
Dublin, MS 1209 [Hardiman], 39). While this was largely a conjectural plan or
a model for a proposed settlement the illustration of the gatehouses, coupled with
the historical reference, lends support to the existence of a defensive structure at
this time. It is likely that some form of earthen rampart with external ditch
protected by angular bastions was indeed in place prior to the construction of the
walls proper. Such an arrangement was common practice amongst the new settlers
at this time throughout the colonies. Boyle appears to have sponsored two further
plans of the town around 1620 (fig. 24). Both show the proposed walls enclosing
the town, depicted as a large rectangular settlement laid out in a grid, on both
sides of the river. The walls are illustrated with a wall walk and crenellations and

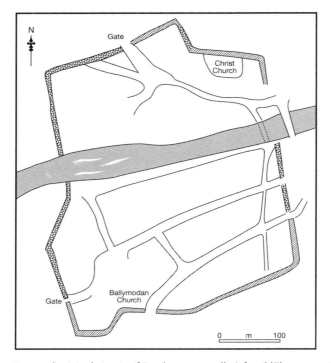

25 Proposed original circuit of Bandon town walls (after O'Flanagan 1988)

are defended by a series of circular and semi-circular mural towers. These are illustrated as accommodating guns, reflective of the increased use of artillery at this time. The reasoning why these were not illustrated as angular bastions, which was clearly the emerging preference for defence at this time, is unclear. It may be the cartographer was unfamiliar with this form of defence and/or they may have been mimicking the extant circular towers on both the city walls of Cork and those at Youghal, Boyle's primary urban interest. The illustration of town gates as high towered edifices would support this, given their similarity to the late medieval gates providing access to the older established urban centres across Munster. These plans must then be seen as a statement of intent by Boyle to create a settlement that would match the existing mercantile centres in size and appearance. They are reflective of Boyle's mercantile ambitions for Bandon but were clearly aspirant in nature as the walls ultimately took a different course and were not as regular as that depicted. O'Flanagan (1988) has traced their subsequent historical development, largely dictated by the natural topography, which shows them crossing westwards immediately behind Christ Church before dog-legging and cutting across North Main Street, through the Shambles building. They then appear to turn southwards at the rear of the old barracks and crossing the river at the weir (fig. 25). Across the river they angled slightly before running directly south to the base of Hill Street, immediately west of Ballymodan Church. They enclose the church and then head east in line with the Bridewell River before again turning north after Stanton's Lane. Boyle was clearly impressed with the walls and wrote in 1632 that the 'circuit of my new town at Bandon Bridge is more in compass than Londonderry, that my walls are stronger, thicker and higher than theirs, only that they have a strong rampart within, that Bandon Bridge wanteth … the castles with the turrets and flankers all being platformed with lead, and prepared with ordinance' (BL, Add. MS 19832, f.31). Aside from the omission of the internal strong rampart the wall appears to have served its function well. Bandon remained in English hands throughout the upheaval of the 1640s and Cromwell commented favourably on the town. By the 1680s it was largely still standing and was described as a 'handsome and strong wall of lime and stone, and fortified by eleven flankers and three of the stateliest gatehouses or castles in any one town in Europe' (O'Flanagan 1988, 4). By 1689 the region was again undergoing crisis and tradition records that Jacobite forces destroyed the wall in 1689. Significant sections of it remained in the eighteenth century but it was then used as a boundary feature and the full circuit was never rebuilt. In the nineteenth century Bennett (1869, 67) describes the walls as 'mainly composed or a thick, black slate. They were generally about nine feet thick, and varied in height from thirty feet to fifty. There were six bastions, one at each corner of the walls, one in the river, and one midway on the south wall'. Sections of the wall have been recorded in Casement Road and in Gully townland standing to a height of 1.7–1.9m and 2.47m wide. The wall face was rendered with a hard lime mortar.

Lesser town walls

A number of smaller towns were also enclosed with town walls. Dungarvan had a roughly square town wall enclosing the coastal town in the early part of the seventeenth century. No sections remain upstanding but its circuit is apparent from a number of cartographic sources and from the existing street pattern. It would originally have had two main gates, a water gate to the harbour and four corner towers. Excavations undertaken by Dave Pollock at Davitt's Quay in the town exposed sections of the wall which had been extensively constructed in the seventeenth century. Analysis further illustrated the presence of a D-shaped corner tower, mined at the end of the seventeenth century, and a further square tower at Quay Lane built on a shingle beach. Sections of the Youghal town wall circuit remain amongst the best preserved in the country (fig. 26). A murage grant of 1275 contains the first mention of the walls but by 1631 they are referred to as

26 Photograph of section of Youghal's town walls

'weak and ruinous … with no place to mount ordnance to defend the harbour' (Thomas 1992, 28). The useful *Pacata* illustration shows the town as having two primary wall sections, the first surrounding the central town area and the second encompassing Irishtown to the south. It would originally have had thirteen towers, a north and south gate and an important water gate providing access to the harbour. Sections of the wall survive to the north and west with three extant towers, two semi-circular and one circular, with a wall walk evident for much of its length. The wall was refortified during 1641–2.

Only a partial portion of Kinsale's northern section of the wall now stands. The town's walls were constructed in the medieval period and consisted of fifteen towers, four gates and an internal rampart and external ditch (Power et al. 1994, 284).

The walls appeared to have suffered some damage during the 1601 siege and again in 1960. They were largely removed over the course of the following centuries. No sections of Buttevant's walls now stand but in 1750 Charles Smith records that they were 'still to be seen the remains of a wall that surrounded the town; and that they also show traces of an outward wall which enclosed the other' (Smith 1750). Again in 1824 traces of the town wall were still evident with other house ruins (Thomas 1992, 28). Sidney records in 1587 that Clonmel was a walled town and well fortified. The walls enclosed a roughly rectangular area with seven to ten circuit towers, four gates and stood to a height of nine metres in places. In the seventeenth century further fortification took place; a fort was built on the friary site in 1625 and a circular tower was further strengthened. Excavations at Mary Street in the town, undertaken in 1930, uncovered a 2.5m thick earthen rampart faced on either side with a further metre of stone constituting further seventeenth-century constructional evidence for the town's defences against artillery. Sidney similarly refers to Dingle as a walled town and by 1599 it was described as the 'chief town in all that part of Ireland, it consisted of but one main street, … it hath had gates … at either end … and a castle also' (Thomas 1992, 68). In 1585 the Queen incorporated the town and granted permission for a stone town wall which was to measure 'three-quarters of a mile in compass'. Little survives of the wall but it was probably rectangular in shape. One possible section survives southwest of Main Street but this remains somewhat tenuous. Rosscarbery was probably walled in the sixteenth century but its seventeenth-century status remains uncertain. Finally, Kilmallock's walls were strengthened following the Desmond siege of 1571. They were heightened and many of the buildings within the town were improved. The walls had a 1700m perimeter length and enclosed 13ha. They were of an irregular rectangular shape and had four corner towers. External ramparts concentrated to the south were evident from 1654–6 by which time the town is referred to as being totally ruined and uninhabited (Thomas 1992, 133).

STREET MORPHOLOGY

Students of urbanization during the time frame under study here will be primarily interested in changes in street morphology and differing spatial relationships between structures in the townscape. The key comparison here is between those towns that were established in the medieval period and retain a tight, largely organic layout and those established by the planters to a much more formal and planned layout. Both Cork and Waterford's origins lie ultimately in Hiberno-Norse and Anglo-Norman developments and their emergent street pattern is reflective of gradual medieval growth with one or more main streets, lined by varying building forms. Numerous lanes run off creating an intricate web-like connection across the town. The towns expanded as time and conditions suited. Of course some form of control existed over expansion and building location and form but this was restricted almost on a case-by-case basis and was a decision taken by the city's fathers. By the late sixteenth century a far greater degree of uniformity appears, exemplified by the formal planned nature of Bandon consisting of a grid-iron pattern of streets linking blocks of development. This proposal is clearly represented in the relevant plans for the town dating to the 1610s. However, while a degree of regularity is maintained the eventual town was not as regularized as planned.

Other forms of planning are evident at other centres brought about by necessity in certain instances. The large-scale famines and widespread conflict of the late sixteenth century had resulted in the displacement of many communities. These now naturally moved towards the cities in search of employment and security. As a consequence periphery settlement grew up in certain areas outside of the town walls and so-called Irishtowns grew in size. This is especially evident again at Bandon but it is also to be seen taking place at Cork, illustrated by numerous small cottages and 'cabins' outside of the central area of the town on the various seventeenth-century maps. Youghal also had an Irishtown while Kinsale clearly had a similar internal division.

A number of key features survived the transition. The central area of the town remained the key economic focus. Here central mercantile areas existed along with the houses of merchants and shops (often one of the same thing), and primary administrative buildings including court and custom houses. Churches continue to play a centralized role with many sites remaining in active service and new sites, such as at Bandon, continuing to be positioned within the heart of the settlements. Walls are still used to enclose these central areas and provide a physical sense of security and demonstrate an overt sense of importance. The street pattern in the older towns remained largely unchanged aside from limited expansion and the closing of some lanes in Cork. A single street, now known as North and South Main Street constituted the main thoroughfare there but other smaller streets and numerous lanes fed off this primary artery. In 1582 Cork is described as 'being but one street not half a quarter of a mile in length' (Caulfield 1876, xvii). A further description from 1622 records that the city had its 'beginning up on the side of an hill, which descendeth easily into one wide and long street, the only principal and chief street of the city. At the first entrance there is a castle, called Shandon castle, and almost over against it a church built of stone' (Caulfield 1876, xxi). Youghal is described in 1681 as consisting of 'one fair street

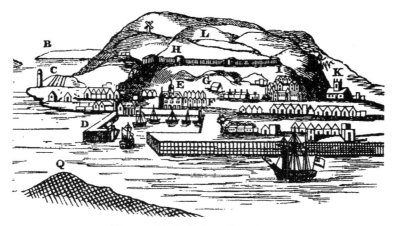

27 Thomas Dineley's vista of Youghal in 1681

continued from gate to gate, and afterwards through its suburbs towards the seaward. The houses are fair, built after the English manner, though low, not unlike those of Portsmouth in England' (Hayman 1879, 40) (fig. 27). As with housing plots we are fortunate in an Irish context that strong continuities exist in street morphology allowing an accurate reconstruction of their earlier forms based on existing morphology. The retention of street names is also valuable is ascertaining previous function. Bakehouse Lane in Waterford, for example, is first referred to in a survey of 1663. Ovens were subsequently found at the site during the course of archaeological investigation confirming this activity (Hurley and Scully 1997, 165).

URBAN BUILDINGS

The major issue that arises when it comes to the study of buildings in an urban context during this time period is one of survival. There are, in fact, few urban upstanding buildings, excepting church and military sites, dating to the early seventeenth century that survive in towns across Munster. There are a number of reasons for this. Unlike the earlier medieval period when we see extensive stratigraphy in urban contexts there tends to be limited surviving layers for the time period under study here. Where stratigraphy is present it is shallow. Part of this is the increased effectiveness and developing mechanisms for the removal of rubbish and waste material from the urban centres. There is no longer then a large buildup of debris which previously served to bury and protect earlier layers. There is also significantly more reuse of both standing buildings and their fabric. Such continual redevelopment or refurbishment has heavily masked many survivals and it is necessary that new research directions will begin large-scale analysis of many buildings in the urban cores and peripheries to see if there are earlier elements incorporated. Another consequence of the shallowness of surviving layers is that subsequent eighteenth- and nineteenth-century construction would have heavily interfered with pre-existing architectural forms. The picture is, however, not completely bleak. There is strong cartographic and some documentary evidence which detail housing form at this time. The spatial relationships of these sites also remain evident in the footprint of later house development. Indeed, one of the exciting findings from many of the urban excavations in the towns over the last thirty-year-period is the remarkable continuity in plot size, house footprint and usage. The survival of these features combined with the fact that many streetscapes retain a very similar morphology from their late and post-medieval forms ensures we can provide comment of urban form.

At the close of the sixteenth century Richard Stanihurst described Waterford as a city 'properly builded, and very well compact, somewhat close by reason of their thick buildings and narrow streets'. A number of buildings of architectural importance have been recorded in the city. A possible two-storey leper house, measuring 7.55m north-south, was located close to St Stephen's church. A chamfered lintel of limestone, bearing the date 1632, probably came from the former hospital but was incorporated into a brewery building in 1895. Further seventeenth-century features included a number of two-and three-light windows and a segment arched doorway. A 1661 inquisition found that the building was 'ruined, and the timber and materials thereof were taken away by Ensign Smart, Robert Woods, and others, and the same with the new House, a thatch house and a garden were set by the then Commissioners of Revenue to Col. William Leigh at forty shillings a year … masons, took away the tomb stones and paving stones that covered the graves of dead bodies in St Stephen's Church, and brought to Lott Leigh's house to floor his kitchen therewith, and also brought some of the said stones to John Morris' house' (*JWAHS* 1895). Two late sixteenth-century buildings have been recorded in Michael's Lane and Exchange Street. The former is a rectangular stone-built two-storey structure while the latter was a three-storey build with three bays and two fireplaces. A further seventeenth-century laneway was also recorded at Exchange Street and High Street where a courtyard, well, ovens and a drainage system were uncovered. One of the features of many of the towns post medieval houses was that they had cellars at the street front (Hurley and Scully 1997, 39), indicative of the multi-functionality accommodating mercantile and domestic usage. This dual usage was typical of the larger merchants' houses which also encompassed a shop or display area for their respective wares. The upper levels of the house were then for more private or family orientated affairs, a layout which again mirrors that of the earlier tower houses. Outside of

28 Tynte's Castle, Youghal

the town a two-storey house, built by Peter Aylward in 1572, has been recorded at
Passage East (Moore 1999, 238). The stone built house has a pointed doorway
with hood moulding and the Alyward family crest and date on its northeast
façade. A mullion and transom window is visible in the southwest wall.

Three Youghal buildings and complexes, in particular are worth examing.
Tynte's castle is a heavily altered sixteenth-century tower house located near the
waterfront in the town (fig. 28). It has a machicolation over its main door and has
two internal structural vaults. It is likely to have functioned as a merchant's
residence in the late medieval period and came into the possession of Robert
Tynte at the end of the sixteenth century. The town's council book records the
following in January 1626

29 Illustration of Myrtle Grove (source: *Dublin Penny Journal*, 1:48 25 May 1833)

Teigh Mourfie of Y., broguemaker, was admitted a freeman at large, on condition that he shall clear the passage and goute of water that is in the street and goes under *Sir Robert Tint's castle*, and to get an iron gate therein, and keep the same clear and running during his lifetime, granted on his own motion (Caulfield 1878).

Certainly the *Pacata Hibernia* map of the town does not highlight it as being unusual suggesting that this was a common form, or at least not an exceptional building, in the town. In later years it served as a garrison and military store and this must be one of the reasons accounting for its survival. The Almshouses were originally endowed by Richard Boyle, probably in 1634, for a number of protestant widows. This complex consisted of a number of two-and three-storey structures facing on to the street. How much we can actually saw about them is debateable as they were fundamentally altered a number of times and rebuilt in the nineteenth century.

Myrtle Grove, adjacent to St Mary's church, is a highly significant building (fig. 29). It is traditionally known as a one-time residence of Walter Raleigh after the 1580s but he does not appear to have built the structure. In 1616 it was occupied by Lawrence Parsons who received it from Boyle (Power et al. 1994, 283). Currently, it is a two-storey house with three transverse attic gables (fig. 30). It has been altered to the front, especially during the nineteenth century but retains many earlier features including internal oak panelling and a mantelpiece. The house retains a high degree of similarity to the late sixteenth-and early-seventeenth century gentry houses of southwest England, for example Newton Surmaville House in Somerset, 1608–12. These typically have three flat gables with windows

30 Myrtle Grove from the grounds of St Marys

becoming progressively smaller from bottom up. A doorway is centrally placed with an entrance porch and rounded arch, often surmounted by an armorial plaque. W.G. Field records an interesting and detailed description of Myrtle Grove in 1896. One of the kitchens had a wide-arched fireplace while the

> large dining room is on the ground floor, from which there is a subterraneous passage connecting the house with the old Tower of St Mary's Church … The walls are in great part wainscoted with Irish oak, which some former occupier sought to improve by partially painting in colour (Field 1896, xv).

The drawing room is described as having a fine dark wainscot, a deep projecting bay window and a richly carved oak mantelpiece standing to the height of the ceiling with a cornice containing three figures. Dutch tile which formerly adorned the fireplace had been removed and a stone chimney-piece 'inserted'. The adjoining bedroom had a mantel piece of painted oak with Dutch tiles remaining. A series of scriptural devices were found around the border. A small recess had formerly been found behind the wainscoting where a number of old volumes had been discovered including Comestor's 1483 *Historia Scholarstica* and a religious history

31 Thomas Dineley's view of the 'College', Youghal, 1681

printed in Mantua in 1479. The house has never been subject to detailed archaeological survey and one should be undertaken as a matter of urgency.

Boyle's own house, the former 'College' building, was originally founded in 1464 adjacent to St Mary's. The building suffered considerable damage during the later years of the sixteenth century and was acquired by Boyle who rebuilt it as a private residence (fig. 31). Two large garden terraces over 100m in length were added by 1612–14 and probably accommodated a series of knot gardens (Reeves-Smyth 2004, 124). In 1641–2 he 'added two large flanking towers ... built five circular turrets around the park and cast up a platform of earth, on which he placed ordnance to command the town and harbour' (quoted in Power et al. 1994, 282). He was to die there in 1643. Dineley describes the house as follows in 1681:

> the College, which I have drawn, was anciently a seminary for priests ... and was bestowed by Queen Elizabeth of blessed memory on her faithful servant, the famous Sir Walter Raleigh, of whom ye said Earl of Cork purchased it. This hath two courts, with a fountain in one of them, fair rooms with well wrought ancient chimney pieces. Its garden is extremely pleasant, being on the side of the mountain overlooking the whole town, College and Harbour, with walks one above another which nature itself hath contributed much to, and stone steps of ascent to each. The

uppermost walk hath also a spring at the end thereof, which it is said the Earl of Cork intended to supply fountains with below to form delightful throws of water (Hayman 1876, 41).

The interior of the house must have been equally impressive. Boyle's accounts refer to the purchase of a tapestry for the long chamber valued at £55, a green and gold bedstead, a second with parcel gilt, and one with black velvet (Townshend 1904, 47). The house underwent significant reconstruction in the eighteenth and nineteenth century and now little remains of the seventeenth-century construct aside from a chimney piece and two of the original towers.

Excavations undertaken by Rose Cleary (1997) uncovered the foundations of three buildings at Chapel Lane in the town. Structure 1 had walls averaging 0.5–0.6m wide and two internal drains. The first was flag-lined and covered with red sandstone flags. It measured 0.45m wide and 0.3m deep. The second drain was also covered with sandstone flags but the inclusion of brick material would date the structures to late in the seventeenth century or early in the eighteenth. Structure 2 was later in date and had an internal fireplace while structure 3 had walls that were 0.6m in thickness. While these buildings are later in date than the period under study here they warrant inclusion as so little is known of lesser buildings of this date and their survival rate with Munster towns is minimal.

In Cork City only limited late medieval architectural fragments survive. Aside from the church, monastic and military remains no upstanding buildings from this period survive in the town's central core. Excavations uncovered the foundations of Skiddy's castle near the North Gate Bridge, an urban tower house originally built in the middle of the fifteenth century. The investigations led by Dermot Twohig demonstrated the building had an internal length of 8.4m by 5.6m and was originally built on an oak raft foundation. A decorative mantle piece dated 1597 was recovered from the site and mounted on a nearby building in North Main Street. In 1603 the castle is described as 'a fort and a store house' (Caulfield 1876, xix). The 1602 map of the town shows its buildings in reasonable details. Their roofs, apparently slated, are coloured orange or brown while municipal and church roofs are coloured in blue. The buildings that line North and South Main Street have steeped crenellated gables reminiscent of early Dutch gables. This crenellated effect may also be an attempt to illustrate stone built tower house-like structures. Skiddy's castle appears to be illustrated in the vista and it is drawn in a very similar manner to the other buildings, albeit with a more tower-like appearance. Several buildings have single crosses mounted on their gables while a number also have attic dormers. The majority of the buildings fronting on to these streets are two to three storey structures but single storey buildings are evident to the rear of this main body. About 30% of the buildings are shown with chimneys with a number illustrated with up to three tall stacks. A clear attempt to illustrate property boundaries is shown in the internal western half of the town. Smaller single-storey Irish-type houses are illustrated lining the approaches to the gates at the north and south.

In 1622 the town's houses are described as being built of local stone and 'covered' with slate – 'but the greater number of houses are built with timber, or mud walls, and covered with thatch' (Caulfield 1876, xxi). This thatching was to have major consequences for the town in the same year as it was subject to a major fire. Contemporary reports state that 'near 1500 houses in the city and suburbs were consumed, and the whole city put in extremity of danger to be totally burned, which mischief hath arisen by thatch houses' (Caulfield 1876, 102). While this number appears large and probably also refers to a variety of other building forms as a consequence all future use of thatch was banned. The majority of the surviving historical records detail stone buildings. In 1609 John Roche fitz John built a stone house near the North Gate while a house 'built of lime, stone and tile' by the merchant James Morrowghe in 1610 was later instructed to be destroyed as it was built illegally. It had been built in a garden belonging to Henry Verdon near the South Gate on a routeway leading to St Dominic's Abbey. It is clear from this case that a series of pre-existing wall boundaries were in place separating properties. Lesser houses were also subject to dispute. Householders in four houses and cabins 'on the highway' to Knockrea in the town's liberties were ordered to repair fencing and enclosures about them in 1630 (Caulfield 1876, 149). A number of public buildings were in existence in the town throughout this period including a jail and court house (accommodated in the same building), a Tholsel, a hospital standing from at least 1616 and a pigeon house.

At Townplots in Kinsale a three-storey urban merchant's tower house, built by Fitzgerald family, survives. It was used as a magazine in 1601 and later as a prison (Power et al. 1994, 285). A string course and hood mouldings are probably indicative of refurbishment although it was originally a sixteenth-century construct (fig. 32). The Market house (Tholsel) in the town was originally built c.1600 but was extensively refurbished in the early part of the eighteenth century. No secular early seventeenth-century building survives in Bandon but the town is referred to as containing 'many slate roofed houses, stone built' in the mid part of the century (O'Flanagan 1993, 406). The expanding suburb of Irishtown is recorded as being dominated by 'cabins' outside the east gate. Dingle would appear to have a more late medieval character as its houses were described in 1599 as being 'very strongly built with thick stone walls and narrow windows like unto castles' (Thomas 1992, 68). This reference would imply a number of urban tower

32 Sketch of Kinsale tower house

house-type buildings were evident in the town at that time, none of which now survive.

The 1650s Civil Survey data for Macroom provides interesting information for establishing the hierarchical nature of settlement in the town. Cabins are listed as the least valuable housing stock, followed by thatched houses and chimney houses. Slate houses were often five times more valuable than chimney houses (O'Flanagan 1993, 406). Clearly then there was a variety of housing types within the towns. Many of the urban tower houses and stone buildings continued to be occupied from the late medieval period but it seems likely that other stone buildings were also in existence which had a number of the architectural traits of the towers. The new settlers brought new building forms with them and gradually the features commonly seen on mansion houses were introduced into houses of lesser value. Fireplaces became common, larger windows with mullion and transoms were introduced, often with hood mouldings and greater emphasis was placed on the internal use of space. The less well off continued to live in cabins, often mud and wood built structures with thatch roofs, but these were located on

33 Killmallock streetscape, *Dublin Penny Journal* 1:9, 25 August 1832

the peripheries. A useful illustration of the ruins of a seventeenth-century streetscape survives for Kilmallock (fig. 33). This illustration, although dating from the nineteenth century, clearly shows a sequence of buildings in ruinous condition but displaying clear architectural features of the period. Two-and three-storey buildings are shown with hood mouldings over both doors and plain windows. Late nineteenth-century photographs show the building on the left having transom and mullion windows at second floor level. Narrow doorways on the drawing are shown as both single and square arched. Dripstones are shown in the larger buildings, one of which has a string course above ground floor level. The illustrated street leads to a tower house, traditionally known as King John's Castle, which is a very different architectural form to that of the buildings shown.

HOUSE CONTENTS

A high level of artefactual material has been recovered from urban excavations showing the types of ceramics and other items present in these households. These became increasingly dominated by English ceramics and tablewares although a percentage of European imports remained in use. The dominance of ceramic material in the archaeological record is, however, a biased view of contemporary material culture and furnishings given the poor level of survival or organic material like cloth, fabric and timber in most Munster excavations. Little is then known of the types of furniture and furnishings houses of this period would have had. A number of wills from the period survive providing some indication although again there is a degree of bias here as these pertain to the households of the upper echelons of society and are not necessarily reflective of material content in lesser homes. One of the earliest inventories relevant to this study is that of

Patrick Ponche of Cork City compiled in February 1557 (Caulfield 1876, 1146). One silver cup, a brewing pan on an iron stand, five candlesticks, one basin, five pewter dishes, three chests of workmen's tools, one table, a gun and nets are listed among his possessions. The 1570 inventory of David Tyrry FitzEdmond, again of Cork, lists seven spoons, two brass pots, nine platters, five pewter cups, a pewter basin, six brass candlesticks, two quarts, two pints, a sword, three chests, one table, a pair of trestles, a Flanders table cloth with one new and one old Irish table-cloth, three towels, a feather bed and six flax beds. A number of inventories are informative on contemporary clothing with Daniel Conway of the City listing a cloak, a dublet of canvas, a shirt, a blue coat and a felt and a cassock of black worsted among his possessions in 1574. William Skiddy's household effects are indicative of a wealthy merchant in 1578. His inventory lists 4 table cloths, 8 pairs of sheets, 30 napkins, green, yellow, red and black silk, saffron, four tin drinking cups, 24 trenchers, 16 candlesticks, 5 brass basins, 5 silver cups, a saltcellar, 18 spoons, 4 beds, 6 blankets, 2 large and one small carpets, a brewing pan, griddle, 12 barrels of salt and a pipe of Gascon wine (Caulfield 1876, 1151).

The household effects of John Skiddy in Waterford city were recorded as part of the chancery Inquisitions of 1640 (Walton 1978, 99–106). These accounts detail the effects of Skiddy and his son, also John, from three houses they own in Trinity and St Patrick's parish. Skiddy was sherriff of Waterford in 1612–3, mayor in 1615 and again in 1635–6 before he died in November 1641. It is probable that the list is presented detailing each of the individual houses in turn beginning with Skiddy's main house in St Patrick's. His contents included a number of gowns and a scarlet coat, 10 pewter candlesticks and 10 brass ones, beds, a number of bed curtains – 3 red and green and 5 blue and yellow examples, Dutch linen sheets, 8 linen towels, a number of domestic towels and a series of cloth coverings, curtains and linen used to drape over furniture. The house also had a drawing table, bench, back table, 2 chairs with 2 big and 2 little stools, a side cupboard, a gaming board and 4 pictures. It is proposed here that the second house, that of his son John contained a bed with feather cover, blankets, a press, a table and cloth, a small box, a trunk, a great chest and one chair. A second room contained a bed, a drawing table and three stools. One of the rooms must have functioned as a working area as a set of scales and weights are recorded with a desk and bellows. Further domestic activity is indicated by the listing of a square table, wooden plates, knives and a chest. A trundle bed is also listed here. Extensive distilling equipment, beer and some wine bottles are recorded. Thomas Roninane, a Cork-based merchant and Alderman in 1641 had 7 bedsteads and 3 caddows or Irish rugs, used as throws and for bedding (Chinnery 2004, 208). He was also in possession of 24 pewter plates. The Kilkenny town-based merchant, John Roth

Fitzpiers of Rothe House, had a similar array of tapestries, curtains and hangings. The hall and chambers of his house were also covered in wainscot or panelling, similar no doubt to that surviving at Myrtle Grove.

Drainage systems

The opening years of the seventeenth century saw an increased interest in infrastructure associated with making urban centres cleaner environments. In particular greater investment took place in drainage schemes and urban excavations document a marked increase in the size and number of covered drains for this period. In 1625 Cork corporation issued directives for the improvement of existing mechanisms for effluent dispersal. Sinks and drains had to exit under the town wall or onto the slips surrounding the town. Anyone found digressing from this in allowing 'foul water or odour' onto the street was to be fined (Caulfield 1876, 119). Individuals were now also employed to clean the streets and carry out refuse disposal.

THE URBAN CHURCH

After Dissolution the Church in Ireland underwent significant decline. Following the Desmond revolt and the later conflicts many of the rural churches were in ruin and the Catholic structures of the parish system were under strain. This situation was mirrored in the urban centres where the established Church was officially supported and advocated and many of the Catholic houses faced financial difficulty and were under resourced. In 1604 Davies records 'The churches are ruined and fallen down to the ground in all parts of the Kingdom. There is no divine service, no christening of children, no receiving of the sacrament, no Christian meeting or assembly' (Maxwell 1923, 136). However, despite the official government line many of the towns in Munster remained pro Catholic despite the aggressive enforcement of established Church by the New English. The Boyle family now held the Sees of Cork, Cloyne and Ross (Dickson 2005, 8). There appears to have been both a regional and urban/rural divide in Catholic support. Cork City remained loyal during Nine Years War but the Aldermen and priests refused to recognize James VI in 1603. This short revolt was quickly suppressed by Mountjoy but support for the Catholic bishops continued to hold steady. By 1624 a Catholic Church opened in the north suburbs and four parishes were created in the 1630s. By contrast three parish churches were under Protestant control in the 1630s. Regardless of the official records of the Churches at this time, possibly a more realistic view of the church affairs can be gleaned from the physical state of the buildings themselves.

St Peter's, Waterford

Probably the most comprehensively investigated urban church site from an archaeological perspective is that of St Peter's in Waterford (Hurley and Scully 1997). Its seventeenth-century history is reflective of the general turmoil that effected the Catholic population of Munster throughout this century. Following the Reformation the reformed church began to take over many of the existing churches across the province. In Waterford this process was not overly successful as the new church was not able to collect many tithes and as a consequence it begins selling off church land and buildings and allows existing buildings fall into disrepair. Priests were now forced to conduct services in churches in a poor state of repair or in private houses. Some refurbishment was undertaken by the reformed church but this was limited. St Peter's was falling into ruin by the early part of the seventeenth century. In April 1609 Pope Paul V assigns the church of St Peter's, 'vacant and falling into ruin' to the Jesuits. Its chancel was in decay in 1615 and the rest of the building was in ruin. In the same year the Commissioners of Visitation report of Ministers' houses to the city's parish churches recorded that the archdeacon had a house near St Peter's (probably the priest house) that had fallen into decay due to lack of usage. Subsequently Bishop John Lancaster (1607–19) aided in this decay by removing timbers and other materials for his Episcopal residence. The grant to the Jesuits was confirmed by Pope Urban VII in 1629 but the fact that it was now a contested church over its status as a parish church and the role of the archdeacon it had 'completely fallen into ruin' by 1646 (Hurley and Scully 1997, 243). Some worship had continued to take place on the site throughout the 1630s when the roof was covered with a sail. The Jesuits took possession in 1646 and proceeded with refurbishment that was completed or at least abruptly ended by 1650 following the parliamentary siege. The excavators suggested that the crude and often haphazard nature of the refurbishment work undertaken indicates that it was carried out quickly (Hurley and Scully 1997, 242).

Following the siege the church was effectively abandoned although the graveyard continued to be used into the later part of the century. Extensive excavations on the site have exposed elements of this history (fig. 34). Stone buildings of the late and post medieval periods are poorly represented in the record due to the removal and reuse of stone foundations during the construction of new secular buildings in more recent centuries. Of the seventeenth-century work the western wall of a building survived (PS3), dated by gravel-tempered ware, with its eastern face consisting of well dressed masonry. The wall was bonded with a sandy mortar and had a wall trench, backfilled above its footing. The trench had a wooden pile foundation with loose shale stones (Hurley and Scully 1997, 187). A further late sixteenth/ early seventeenth-century building was located on the border of high

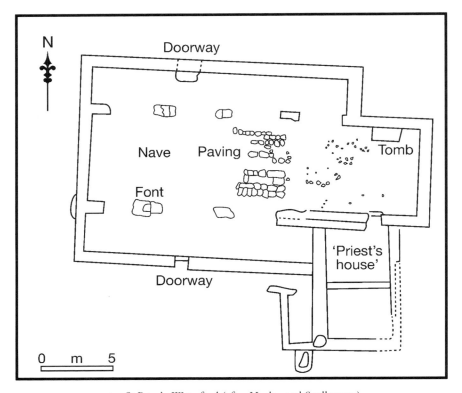

34 St Peter's, Waterford (after Hurley and Scully 1997)

Street and Peter street. Its south wall survived and had two dressed limestone
windows with a single light on south wall. The wall was constructed of roughly-
coursed shale and old red sandstone with some dressed limestone and Dundry
stone (Dundry Hill near Bristol) in the quoins and fabric of building.

In St Peter's itself two primary phases are of relevance to this study – Period III
consisting predominantly of late medieval burials and Period IV, dating to the
early to mid seventeenth century. The latter period sees the final renovation of the
church, the addition of aisles and the replacement of nave walls with arcading
(Hurley and Scully 1997, 216–18). Side aisles were added to the north and south
of the church, giving a width of 16.5m, while a section of the chancel north wall
was also rebuilt. Four arcades to the north and three to the south were constructed
with the north aisle measuring 18.8m long and 2.88m wide. The relevant floor
level was evident below the doorway on the north wall and consisted of a light
brown clay with purple slate and mortar. The south aisle was 16.75m long and 3m
maximum wide which abutted the 'priest's house' to east. The church at this date

35 St Mary's, Youghal, in the 1680s (source: Hayman 1879)

contained a font, indicative of its parochial function, and was made up of large roughly dressed and mortared blocks of limestone, sandstone and slate. The stones were faced with render. Limestone flags of irregular size paved the floor in the nave with upper faces punch-dressed in the interior with a border of smooth straight tooling. The chancel flooring was made up of medieval line-impressed and post medieval tiles, with the later tiles 0.23m² and 32mm thick. The building was likely roofed with slate, and also possibly featured low cockscomb crested ridge-tiles.

Significant evidence of burial activity was also uncovered during the course of this excavation. Graves of this period were rectangular in shape, suggesting internment in coffins. No evidence for gravemarkers was found. Within the church interior 33 period IV burials were uncovered with both earth cut and coffin burials represented. A tomb was located against the north wall in the chancel with slate capstones and a kerb of four dressed lengths of limestone. Four burials were found inside, clearly individuals of some importance or prestige. Following the abandonment of the church and the priest's house stables were built against the south aisle although burial continues.

St Mary's in Youghal is a thirteenth-century foundation built on an earlier ecclesiastical site and later served as a collegiate (fig. 35). It has a cruciform plan with an aisled nave and tower (Power et al. 1994, 282). The church appears to have sustained itself largely undamaged through the conflicts of the sixteenth century and becomes of central importance in the seventeenth century due to Boyle's association with it (fig. 36). In 1606 Boyle paid for the South Transept as a

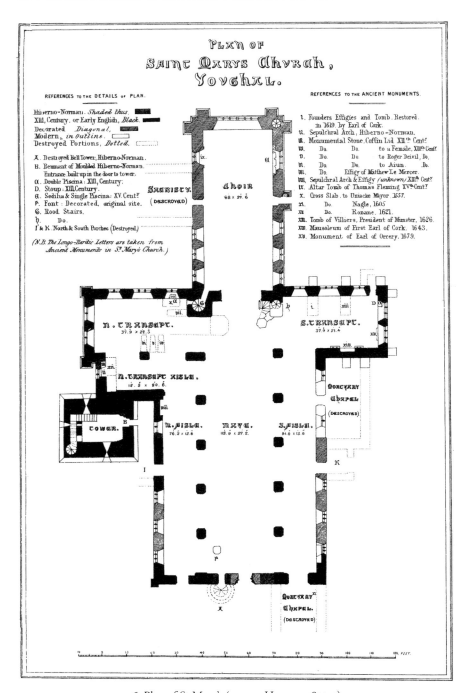

36 Plan of St Mary's (source: Hayman 1854–5)

37 Boyle monument in St Mary's (after Hayman 1879)

mortuary chapel for his family and two years later spent £2000 on church renovations (Hayman 1879, 15). The south transept, which was probably rebuilt or at least re-roofed at this date was re-edified by Boyle in 1619 'wherein the townsmen in time of rebellion kept their cows' and repaired the 'Founders tomb' and 'had their pictures cut in stone places thereon', a direct references to the location of a fifteenth-century grave slab during the renovation work. The south transept contains the elaborate monument to the Boyle family, built at this time, showing Richard Boyle centrally placed in a reclining position with both of his wives and their children (fig. 37). The feature was erected by 1620 by Alexander Hillis and is similar to the Boyle monument, erected in St Patrick's Cathedral in Dublin in 1632, in memory of his second wife, Lady Katherine. It features red, white, grey and black marbles and shows his first wife, Joan, dressed in a dark purple satin or velvet dress and wearing a ruff while his second wife is dressed in a robe of state with an ermine cape and a ruff (Field 1896, ii). The swords shown in the bottom right are representative of Boyle's power but also are symbols of justice and part of the armor of God (Ephesians 6: 10–18).

This monument is typical of the style of church monumentality spreading across Britain after the Reformation and heavily influenced by Renaissance ornamentation. Rounded arches with classical columns began to be adopted and figures were illustrated in a variety of forms including kneeling and reclining. The seventeenth century saw the continuation of this trend with more elaborate family groupings represented often in a grandiose Baroque style. In 1848 the Boyle monument was restored under the guidance of the church authorities (Hayman 1854–5, 122).

A number of dignitaries are buried in the transept including John Boyle, bishop of Cork and Ross in 1620, and Edward Villiers, lord president of Munster, in 1625. We know that the church was both slated and tiled at this date as a certain Robert Soddein is charged with the continuance of this work by the civic authorities (Hayman 1876, 15). Further work continues to take place including the creation of pews for the town's Corporation in 1625. By 1641 the chancel of St Mary's is reported as being in ruins although interments continued to take place including a number of the earl's children and the earl himself in 1643 following a further bequest for building work. Further renovations take place throughout the remainder of the seventeenth century. In 1681 Thomas Dienley records the following account of the church 'St Mary's is the chiefest, and in use though much out of repair … The first monument you reencounter at the entrance into the remains of the chancel … but without arms or inscription. Entering the church this way, and having passed under the ancient Organ loft, your left hand leadeth to a chapel founded by Richard Bennet and Elizabeth Barry his wife, as appears by this next monument and inscription set up at the charge of Sir Richard Boyle … [who] purchased the said chapel, and still keeps it in good repair … In the chapel opposite to that called the earl of Cork's vestry, and which forms this church into the shape of a cross … The Organ loft and division between the chancel and church hath been very rich and well carved, as appears by its remains doubly guilt, over which are painted the names of the twelve tribes of Israel. The roof of this church is admirable, of whole saplyns' (Hayman 1876, 36–9).

Bandon

Bandon is a unique town in the context of the Munster Plantation. It was dominated by the New English and, unsurprisingly, it is the established church

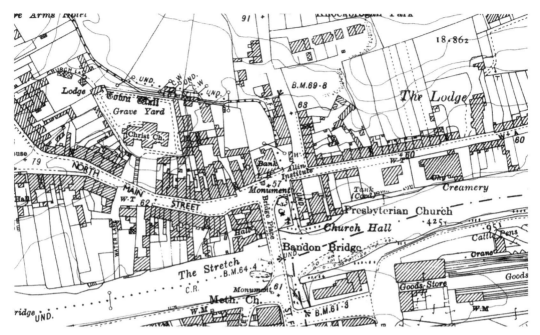

38 Location of Christ Church, Bandon (Ordnance Survey of Ireland)

which becomes pre-eminent during the early decades of the seventeenth century. The specific foundation of two churches within the town is a direct example of this religious affiliation. Christ Church was built about the year 1610 to a cruciform shape with triple light windows in the nave and transepts. It may have been established on the site of a late sixteenth-/early seventeenth-century fort as an 'old entrenchment' was found during refurbishment work in 1843 and a bastioned fort is shown on a 1613 plot of the town lying directly adjacent to the church's position to the east (Trinity College MS 1209 39). It was also referred to as the 'church on the fort' in *c*.1620. The actual line of the town wall eventually ran immediately north of the site (fig. 38). Its nave would originally have measured 20m in length by 9.5m in width with a tower standing over 25m in height. A stone plaque was placed on the external south wall bearing the inscription '1625 Memento Mori', a date when Boyle financed a number of important renovations including the creation of an entrance porch and possibly enlarged the church to include the chancel and transepts. In September 1628 Baptist Hassell was prebendary of Kilbrogan while three years later John Snary was prebendary and vicar (Bennett 1869). In 1634, the rectory of Kilbrogan was valued at £20 per annum, and the prebendary and vicarage at £37. Bennett (1869) is one of the first writers to draw attention to a brass tablet to the memory of Richard Crofte, one of the original twelve burgesses of the Bandon Corporation and provost of the town in 1617. The inscription reads Hic. JACET CORPVS. RICH^D. CROFTE VNS. LIBER BURGENS HVJVS BURGI DE BANDON-BRIDGE, AC QUONDOM. PREPOSIT EJVSDEM QVI OBIT. VIJ^{MO} DIE SEPTEMBERIS ANNO DOMINI ~1629. POSVIT ANNA EJVS MESTISSIMA CONJVX.

Boyle was also instrumental in funding the construction of a second church at Ballymodan in 1614. Originally its nave measured in excess of 13m in length and c.7m wide. A tower was constructed at its western end and stood 20m in height. A number of large windows were also placed throughout. The foundation of the church was prompted by dissatisfaction amongst the protestant inhabitants of this side of the town in having to worship in a chapel in the Irishtown area. This was felt to be an unsatisfactory situation as it was stated it was both degrading and inconvenient. Boyle records in September 1614 that he contributed a year's rent 'of my parsonage of Ballymodan, as a help towards the building of the new church at Bandon-Bridge'. Boyle was also later involved in expansion work at the church. Bennett (1869) provides a somewhat fictional description of the original church but it is worth repeating this in part to gain an idea of its interior:

> The enlarged building was a plain, unpretending structure; and was entered by a porch, over which was the date of the church's erection in 1614. Inside, it was gloomy and dark. The floors of the nave and transepts were covered by huge high-backed seats, large enough for the owner and his family to stretch at full length and take a comfortable nap, in case the homily was wearisome or too long. At the west window of the nave, and almost touching the ceiling, was the organ, in a galley set apart for it and the choir. Underneath this was another gallery, which formed a portion of the large galley which ran along the northern and southern walls of the nave. The transepts also contained a gallery each. Although to modern eyes this sombre, prim old edifice, with its box-stall pews and solemn-looking walls, would seem fit only to be occupied by a serious people, yet such was not the case. In the olden times this was our fashionable church. It was here the provost sat, with the insignia of his office lying on a scarlet cushion before him. In an adjoining seat sat the governor of the town; and in various portions of the building were the bright uniforms and the glittering accoutrements of the officers belonging to the various regiments that were quartered here.

The church was replaced in 1847–9 with a new and greatly expanded structure.

CHAPTER 4

Ports and Shipping

During the first decade of the fifteenth century Henry IV introduced a legislative differentiation between the ports that dealt with foreign trade and those that were licensed to deal with localized coastal trade. The larger, more important ports were now referred to as *Lez grantz ports du meir* while the smaller, local ports were called *petitz crykes* (Henry IV, 1402, cap.20). During the later part of the medieval period a more structured port system developed resulting in legislative formalisation by the seventeenth century of a three-tiered formalized port structure (Gras 1918, 99; Jarvis 1958, 459). This came about primarily through the increased dependence of many coastal ports on the dominant port of the area and through what could be termed a natural evolution of hierarchy. So while the three-tiered formalization is not necessarily evident legislatively during the fifteenth and early sixteenth century, it was in practice operational. By the late fifteenth century the port system had three primary officers: the collector, the controller and the searcher whose offices had been granted by the King or by royal patent (Jarvis 1958, 460). Collectors were, as their name suggests, responsible for the actual collection of the customs and for the recording of ship movements and cargoes (*Cal. Fine Rolls*, Edward 1, 1272–1307, 46). The controller essentially kept a counter roll of the collector's accounts and shipment records and acted as a check on his activities. Searchers had the responsibility for checking cargoes and ensuring that money, gold and silver were not being exported without a licence. Other officials included surveyors who were regularly brought in to check the operations as a whole, clerks who supported the officials and other port workers including weighers, cranekeepers, wharfingers and waiters (Gras 1918, 99). Waiters had the responsibility for supervising the port by day and night to ensure no illegal activity took place.

By Tudor times a three-tiered system had evolved based on the location of these officers of the custom. At the head of this system were the three 'great officers of the port' who controlled an appointed section of coast and who were directly accountable to the Exchequer. Secondary to these were the ports where deputies operated who had been appointed by the principal officers and were answerable to the larger port(s) (*caput portus*). Finally there were creeks where no officials were resident and no overseas trade could take place unless sanctioned by the patent officials (Jarvis 1958, 461). During the reign of Elizabeth I a statute was passed whereby it was only legal to engage in any aspect of the overseas trade at designated quays or ports where the Crown's officials resided or where they were specifically designated. In 1558 a book of 'Articles, Ordinances, Rules and Orders' specifically set out to build on port surveys and set out the extent of ports, designate the members of the head ports and defined the legal quays of the earlier statute (Jarvis 1958, 462). By the late 1660s the system was very clearly defined as head or chief ports, member ports and creeks (*Index Victigalium* 1670, 50–2). Head ports were defined as being under patent principals for fiscal purposes, member ports were under the authority of deputies of the patentees while creeks were ports where there was no official officer who was competent to deal with overseas trade (Jarvis 1958, 459). This was in essence the Tudor system that had evolved with very little change. The development of a customs system and formalized structural ports in Britain is paralleled in Ireland. In 1532 the earl of Kildare farmed out the customs of the Pale area and this situation remained unchanged for many years. Outside of the Pale customs officers were maintained but the situation is far less clear. The customs of Limerick, Baltimore, Kinsale, Cork and Youghal were granted to the earl of Desmond in 1497 (*Cal. Ormond deeds* 1413–1509, no. 261), while the customs of other ports alternated between local town merchants and various lordships.

A formal system of port hierarchy was now beginning to emerge. The actual terminology for a head-port system does not appear in Ireland until the sixteenth century but ports were already operating under this system by the fourteenth century, if not earlier. Certainly the customs returns of the thirteenth and early fourteenth century imply a recognized hierarchy. The staple system had in effect designated a series of major or head-ports in the fourteenth century. In 1438 Dublin was collecting tolls on imported city goods entering through the adjacent lesser ports at Howth, Baldoyle, Malahide, Portrane, Rogerstown, Rush and Skerries. In 1582 a Royal charter granted Dublin the rights of Admiralty between Arklow and Duleek and by 1612 Skerries, Malahide and Wicklow were incorporated as member ports of Dublin. Elsewhere Dingle's charter of 1585 incorporated Smerick and Ventry as members. Kinsale's charter of 1589 claimed jurisdiction over its member ports between the Old Head and Dursey Island, including Baltimore, Crookhaven and Bantry (*Cal. Fiants Eliz.*, no. 5334).

Definitions

The function and status of ports, creeks and landing places requires definition. Each has its own specific functions and morphology, which are established through topographic and socio-economic factors. Their status is defined by scale and location as well as by the nature of activities that are undertaken at the site. A port is the most important of the three within this hierarchical system. Ports represent a dynamic interface between the foreland and hinterland and are formally and universally recognized as such by the mercantile and political establishment. Ports were the largest maritime facilitator of boat and ship traffic and mercantile activity within a region and were recognized as an established landfall and a site where import and export activities, took place on a meso or macro scale, national and international scale. Ports would have been associated with areas of sheltered anchorage on varying scales. Most ports owe their origins to their physical ability to offer shelter, the primary governing factor in initial site selection and also one of the major factors in the subsequent success of the port. Areas of anchorage were no longer necessarily relevant with the massive increase in quay sizes and the rapid turn around of passenger and cargo vessels. Historically, however, areas of anchorage were necessary for long-term stays, as vessels may often have waited weeks for a cargo. Ports were physically recognized by the presence of a formalized or semi-formalized layout with waterfront structures catering for shipping activity. Quays would have been the most common structure type while projecting piers or jetties may also have been present. Buildings with a specific storage or administration function were also located at or near to the waterfront. The port was usually associated with a substantial settlement, with the size of the settlement being relative to its region. This settlement would have had permanent housing and an established street or road pattern. Administratively the port employed officers dedicated to the operation and maintenance of the site. These officers had to undertake a variety of functions ranging from boat and ship maintenance, cargo handling, administration, security and commercial roles. They were also responsible for the collection and charging of customs and tolls. Physical evidence for these administrative operations is less tangible and largely depends on the survival of documentary remains. However, the presence of customs houses and warehouses physically attest to their presence.

Ports were not a static entity; their size, status and morphology were constantly evolving with changing economic climates. There was a constant demand for upgrades and increased waterfront space. Ports had a general pattern of expanding outwards in a linear and perpendicular manner, reclaiming more foreshore to develop more quay space in order to accommodate larger and a greater number of vessels. In parallel to this they also had a tendency to expand in a landward direction in an attempt to develop more ground for storage, service and administrative purposes. Both of these expansive movements have the ability to mask or even destroy pre-existing structures. Within the broad category of ports, there are sub-divisions. Each region administratively had a head-port and possibly a number of subsidiary ports. Their designation as the head or lead port is not a temporal constant and ports will take on varying levels of control in different economic and political climates.

Creeks

Creeks were subsidiary in both status and size to ports. In a Munster context they were normally associated with small settlement sites. Physically the creek would have access to an area of anchorage in excess of three metres of water at high tide. Creeks would have had a firm shoreline capable of supporting a pier of jetty. Many of these piers and jetties are now characterized by parallel boulder lines on the foreshore associated with an area of beach clearance. Lines of timber posts can also define the former site of a jetty. This area should be large enough to allow a wide range of activities to happen, including storage, offloading and trade and exchange. A small narrow beach area for example, that is only accessed down steep rocks, will never be suitable for development as a creek. The shoreline would also have sufficient space to accommodate warehouses, or similar structures and provide ready access to the hinterland. There should also have been sufficient space to allow for the development of a small settlement. Evidence for many of these sites is now only characterized by the presence of tower houses. It should be noted that a number of tower houses and other house type-sites no longer survive and that these former sites would also have marked established creeks. These creeks played a minor economic role within the broader port framework and represent centres for local trade and communications which fed into the larger regional head port system. These centres were often the location for less formalized and even illicit trade, especially during periods of conflict between England and countries in continental Europe. Most would have had some form of waterfront structure, dependant on the coastal topography, normally a pier or jetty. The local towerhouse or fortified house could have fulfilled the dual role of port administration and storage. Port officers were occasionally based at the creeks but these were usually single customs officers as opposed to individuals with an administrative responsibility for the day-to-day operation of a port. Maritime activity was not constant and was controlled by the local lord or family.

Landing places

Landing places were for the most part natural areas, suitable for dragging a small boat ashore. They may have been associated with small settlements or single homesteads. It is unlikely that any form of formalized waterfront structure existed aside from beach clearance or the crude erection of a stonewall, which doubled as a pier and a boat shelter. Landing places are normally natural breaks in the foreshore bedrock or sandy beaches with unhindered boat access. Access to the hinterland is necessary but this might simply be provided by track-ways through relatively hospitable countryside. Large roads or comprehensive terrestrial communication networks were not necessarily associated with the site. Landing places, however, tended to be small localized areas, and it was this limited size that hindered their development. The construction of large waterfront structures or the expansion of a settlement at the site was impractical because of environmental limitations and topographical constraints. There was an absence of any formalized activity at the landing place aside from an occasional visit by a customs officer or merchant. Commercial activity at these sites was limited to localized fishing or the transportation of agricultural produce carried out by small local boats.

Stage	Form and usage
Informal stage	Informal use by small boats. No physical structures
Initial development stage	Site selection for development. Initial economic & communication activity
Development Stage	Established usage of site. Development of waterfront
Site Expansion	Formalisation and expansion of waterfront in line with increased economic activity

Table 4.1 Model for the development of *anyport* in Munster

Trade commodities

In the later years of the sixteenth century and early years of the seventeenth century the Munster ports were largely trading with southwest England and a number of French and Spanish ports along mainland Europe's Atlantic Seaboard. Interactions with visiting fishing fleets, largely from continental Europe prior to 1601, also played a significant part in the economic activities of the Irish port network. Post 1601 English merchants and fleets came to dominate the fishing market. Throughout this period Bristol was probably the leading external market player in this system. By 1516/17 Waterford controlled 19% of the Irish trade with

Ports	Creeks	Landing places
Large sheltered inlet	sheltered inlet	Absence of sheltered inlet
Associated anchorage/ deep water berths	Limited anchorage	No anchorage
Formal waterfront	Single pier or quay Structure	Beach/bedrock clearance
Port operation complex (incorporating warehouses & Customs)	Possible warehouse or administrative building	No administrative complex
Evidence for a number of medieval buildings	Single towerhouse	Absence of towerhouse
Large associated settlement	Associated settlement	Single settlement or clachan
Unhindered access to Hinterland	Access to Hinterland	Access to shoreline
Situated on established primary marine communication routes	Adjacent to established marine communication routes	No formal role in main communication routes

Table 4.2 Preliminary defining physical characteristics of ports, creeks and landing places in later medieval Ireland

Bristol and this had risen to 58% by the 1540s (Flavin 2004, 32). In the 1540s Cork only had 3% of the Irish trade with this port with both Kinsale and Youghal out performing it. Irish exports to Bristol in 1516/7 included hake (23%), herrings (15%), salmon (12%), with other fish (4%) giving a total for fish exports at 54% (Flavin 2004, 51). Other exports included sheepskins at 13% and mantles at 13%. This was a downward trend from the period 1478–1504 when fish constituted 78% (Flavin 2004, 64). Exports from Ireland to Bristol from 1541–6 included Cloth (42%), mantles, hake, herring (11%), salmon (7%) and sheep and lamb skins (13%) (Jones 1998, 36). Primary imports from Bristol included clothing (15%), saffron (16%), Wine (2%), iron and knives (11%) with cloth paying custom at 28% (Jones 1998, 36).

Port	1541/2	1542/3	1545/6	% total for 3 years
Cork	121	243	128	3.1
Dungarvan	126	42	111	1.8
New Ross	407	336	141	5.6
Waterford	3714	2114	3287	57.6
Wexford	86	85	226	2.5
Youghal	249	176	193	3.9

Table 4.3 Irish value of trade with Bristol in £ sterling (source: Jones 1998)

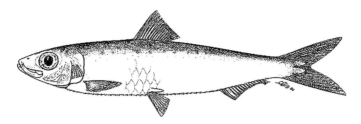

39 Illustration of a pilchard

By the seventeenth century agricultural products dominated the export trade of the Munster ports. Hides, sheep skins and wool represent the largest bulk commodities with only Dublin and Drogheda exporting more. In 1616–17 Waterford exported 165,750 sheep skins, Youghal exported 25,850 while Cork sent 25,600 abroad (Woodward 1999, 67). In the same period Limerick exported 19,260 hides while Cork exported 19,306. Youghal dominated the export trade in pipe staves in the same year exporting 256,000 and was second only to Wexford which exported 480,500. Youghal similarly dominated the Munster export in wool and sheep skins in 1621–2 when it sent 27,100 sheepfells in wool and 12,400 sheep skins abroad and also exported 299,500 pipe staves. In 1626 Waterford dominated the export market in cloth exporting 30,348 yards of frieze, 3,200 mantles and 1,544 rugs. No other Munster port came anywhere near matching these quantities. Other significant exports across the regional ports throughout the first three decades of the seventeenth century included wheat, timber and beef.

Fishery products also accounted for a significant portion of these exports. Herring, exported in barrels, pilchards and salmon dominated the fish types (fig. 39). Unsurprisingly the ports of west Cork and Kerry dominate this trade

Port	1616–7	1621–2	1626
Youghal	17	40.5	77
Cork	7.25	–	
Kinsale	161.5	–	792
'The West Parts'	833	55	–
Baltimore	–	–	794
Crookhaven	–	–	249
Bantry	–	–	1104.75
Kenmare River	–	420	

Table 4.4 Pilchard (tons) exports from Munster Ports (after Woodward 1999)

given their proximity to the most productive fishery grounds. Pilchard exports from the ports of the southwest including Baltimore, Crookhaven, Kenmare and Bantry accounted for 82% of their trade in 1617, 78% in 1622 and 75% in 1626 when they were valued at £29,000, with pilchards valued at £8 6s. 8d. per ton (MacCarthy-Morrogh 1986, 224). Bantry creeks at this stage are listed as Whiddy and Bearehaven.

A CUSTOMS SYSTEM

Information on the official ports in use in the first quarter of the decade can be gleaned from the lists of payments made to Munster customs officers (see below). Leed's District Archives contains a bundle of 81 debentures for the payment of custom salaries in the period 1 May 1614 to 22 April 1617 (Leeds District Archive TN/PO 7/1/25 (1)–(81)).

Name	Office	Port
Randall Brwyn & Thomas Jarry	Searchers	Youghal & Dungarven
Matthew Butler	Searcher	Waterford, New Ross, Drogheda, Dundalk & Carlingford
William Cayne	Searcher	Cork
Robert Cogan	Surveyor-general of all Irish Customs	
Charles Grimsditch	Searcher	Limerick
Edward Hinton	Collector	Waterford & New Ross
John Howe	Searcher	Kinsale
Edmund Hunt	Collector	Cork
Samuel Johnson	Controller	Cork, Limerick, Youghal, Dungarven, Kinsale & Dingle
Nicholas Lee	Controller & Collector	Waterford & New Ross
William Lewellyn	Customer, Collector & Receiver	Youghal & Dungarven
Robert Master	Controller	Waterford & New Ross
Edward Mottram	Customer	Waterford & New Ross
David Myagh	Customer	Kinsale
William Perry	Customer	Limerick
Gerald Trant	Collector & Receiver	Dingle

Table 4.5 Lists of payments made to Munster customs officers 1614 to 1617
(Leeds District Archive TN/PO 7/1/25 (1)–(81))

Woodward (1999) has documented the trade and customs statistics for the area during the period 1614 to 1641. While these revenue sources can be useful in examining the volume of trade coming in and out of a port they have to be approached with caution. Customs receipts only take account of produce that is officially declared. It does not account for false returns, dishonesty or negligence. Perhaps more importantly these returns fail to take account of the extensive illicit trading which would have taken place up and down these coastlines outside of the centralized bureaucracies of the Crown. In short they probably represent a significant under-representation of the true level of trading activity.

Port	1618–25	1626–31	1632–35	Total
Waterford	10,199.73	8700.8	6516.2	25,416.7
Dungarvan	804.7	413.8	596.6	1815.1
Youghal	7123.3	13,070.4	7116.6	27,310.3
Cork	6217.5	8607.6	6685.4	21,510.5
Kinsale	4247.6	5370.5	4308.6	13,926.7
West Ports	6031.9	–	–	–
Baltimore	–	1936.9	508.3	705.2
Crookhaven	–	1560.8	c.1282.9	c.2843.7
Bantry/Bearehaven	–	2195.4	c.1151.9	c.3347.3
Kenmare River	–	1287.7	531.13	1818.13
Tralee/Dingle	851.2	386.5	c.584.7	1822.4
Limerick	5670.5	7579.2	5794.4	19,044.1

Table 4.6 Munster Ports Customs Revenue 1618–25 (after Woodward 1999)

Port activity

The 1620s and 1630s appear to have been a prosperous time in the ports of Munster judging by the amount of coverage they receive in the records of the High Court of the Admiralty. This is a valuable source as not only does it detail economic activity but also gives important insights into how these activities were actually conducted (Appelby 1992). In one deposition before the court in 1632 and 1633 Robert Zachary, master of the 80-ton ship *John* of Dover, leased his ship to the merchant Bernard Mitchell in order to load a cargo of corn in Ireland and transport it to Lisbon. Hundreds of barrels of corn were loaded at Limerick quays where a dispute arose between the Captain and the merchant over quantities loaded and the vessel had to sail to Bunratty. Here the *John* sent boats up into the country to fetch corn to load the ship while corn was also '*brought out of the country on horse's backs, and some on men's backs, and brought aboard the ship'* (*Cal. Admiral. Exams.* 1632–3, 210–12). The whole process took three months during which time the ship's carpenter and master's mate Edward Whiting stole two sacks of corn and traded them with the locals for salmon. Eventually the ship left for Lisbon where it off-loaded the corn and took on a cargo of salt bound for Weymouth.

In 1626/7 the *St Peter* of Danzig, owned by Dutch merchants, sailed from Dublin to Tenerife with a cargo of 30 barrels of beef, 5 or 6 barrels of butter and 5 or 6 chests of candles. En route they loaded 200 hogsheads of pilchards at Bantry. In 1629 the Grace of Dundee loaded 164 hogsheads of pilchards at Bantry (*H.C.A.* f.133v.). Three years later a dispute arose over the *Samuel* of London which arrived at Bantry to load pilchards and salt (*H.C.A.* 1633 ff535–5v(531–1v)). After the ship had been loaded with salt by bushell rather than by barrel the master had run the ship ashore for graving but it became stranded and had to wait for the next spring tide to get off. During this time a large quantity of pilchards lay on the beach ready for loading. In 1638 James Browne of Kirkcaldy, Scotland, testified that the *Jane* of London had loaded pilchards at Bantry and was bound for Bayonne in France. The *James* of Kirkcaldy also loaded pilchards at Bantry as well as butter, tallow, hides and other goods for St Sebastian (*H.C.A.* 13/54 (1638–9). These references imply that the fishing was carried out locally and then packed and made ready for loading and distribution into larger visiting ships at the anchorages of Bantry and Bearhaven. McCarthy-Morrogh (1986, 226) notes that exports accounted for 84% of traffic from Bantry according to the customs accounts in 1632. Pilchards accounted for the majority of this percentage but other goods were also included. Imports largely consisted of salt, sugar and wine. A dispute arose in August 1624 in relation to a consignment of sugar which arrived in the *Hope* of Rotterdam and landed at Blackrock. Various people around Bantry received chests of sugar from the ship. Three chests were destined for the lord deputy, one for Sir William Hull (deputy vice-admiral at Kenmare), one for Edward Davenant, a number went to Bandon-bridge, Baltimore and Crookhaven while Henry Conway received three chests for the use of Sir Thomas Roper. In return the ship took on beef, beer, biscuits and shoes. The depositions in this case refer to a custom house under the care of Robert Burrage which recorded all of the transactions. This house must have been located within the vicinity of Blackrock. A year later in May 1625 the *Hope* was taken off Land's End by pirates and taken to Kenmare where the cargo of wheat and woad was distributed among local people including William Hull (*H.C.A.* 1626 ff136–6v.). Bantry was also listed amongst the ports engaged in the export of wool from Ireland between 1632 and 1641 under which a stone of wool was charged 8*d.* in customs dues (*Cal. S. P.*

Ire., 1641, 311). Analysis of these various references suggests that Blackrock served as the main area for anchorage in Bantry Bay and for the loading and offloading of cargo. This was where the customs house was and where many of the merchants appear to have had residences. Ballygobban/Bantry was primarily an artisan and fishing community and was located along the creek of modern day Bantry town. Support for this assertion comes from two examinations of Brian O'Hogan in 1627 before the attorney-general and Sir Roger Jones. In his testament he records that some of the 'rebel O'Gormlies have removed from Ulster to Munster and live at Ballagubbin in the County Cork, a fisher town, and wish to go to the Low Countries' (*Cal. S. P. Ire.*, 1627, 216).

PORT ARCHITECTURE

The seventeenth century saw the re-development and modernization of the major ports around the coast. Substantial stone quays were erected along the river front at Drogheda, Dublin, Waterford, Cork, Limerick and Galway. This century also witnessed the emergence of 'new' substantial ports including Londonderry, Belfast and Newry. Much of this development is still evident today incorporated into the modern line of the individual quays. In the absence of extensive investigative waterfront programmes of research in Munster cartographic sources remain our primary analytical tool for describing the morphology of past ports and harbours. The early depictions produced in the *Pacata Hibernia* and by individuals like John Speed and Thomas Philips remain especially valuable.

At Waterford the town took advantage of its position along the River Suir and constructed a series of quays along its northern section. A map with a possible date of 1673 shows extensive quayage along this waterfront including individual dock and quay areas (Hurley and Scully 1997) (fig. 40). A watergate, consisting of a low tower and timber-built dock was also constructed in the sixteenth century at the town's south eastern corner adjacent to John's River (Murtagh 2001). A number of archways supported the structure and gave access to boats from the northwest. The structure appears to have fallen out of use by the middle of the seventeenth century when a tannery is built at the site. The 1580s *Pacata* depiction of Youghal and the later 1681 view of Youghal are very informative (fig. 41). They show an artificially enclosed basin protected by a large entrance tower with cannon. There is a single entrance leading to a basin enclosed on three sides with quay frontage. A water gate was positioned in the town wall, providing access to the central urban area. A single vessel is shown in the basin and was tied to the fore and aft to the quays. Further vessels are illustrated lying at anchor off the structure. This structure was clearly built with defence in mind, indicative not

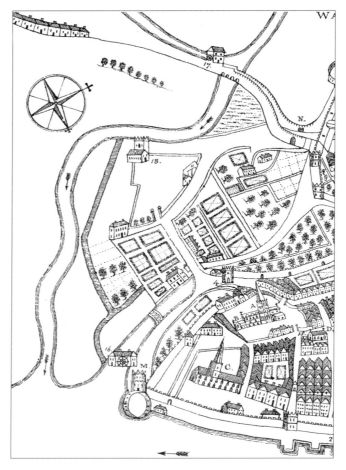

40 Detail of Waterford, c.1673 (source R.H. Ryland 1824)

only of the military and pirate threats the town experienced but also of the extent of mercantile trade that passed through this town at the time. The structure is also indicative of the localized seabed bathymetry. The creation of an artificial structure was necessary to mitigate against the strong tidal movement in the channel and was related to the generally shallow depth of water. A second water gate is centrally shown in the town walls facing out onto the foreshore. This would presumably have accommodated smaller scale activity leaving the harbour area as a focus for larger scale mercantile and military activities.

The earliest detailed map depiction of Cork's urban core, the *Pacata* plan of the 1580s does not specifically show a harbour structure. It does, however, clearly indicate that vessels could enter the city walls through a water gate, located at the

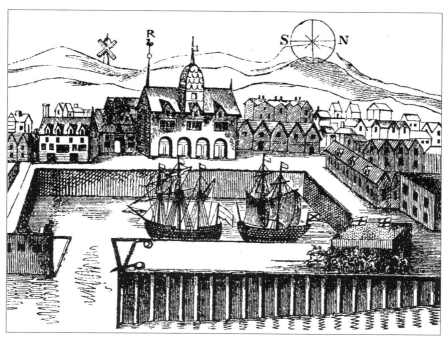

41 Detail of the port of Youghal in the 1680s (source: Hayman 1879)

Queen's castle which faces onto the contemporary Grand Parade. The creation of such an internal basin is unusual and is possibly reflective of the absence of suitable anchorage or a solid base on which to establish extensive quay frontage. A second possible water gate is shown immediately east of the southern entrance to the town. This feature is absent on subsequent sources. A map dated to 1602, and located in the library of Trinity College (TCD MS 1209, no. 45), again shows the existence of the centrally placed water gate but does not illustrate any vessels. The city's coat of arms is shown in the upper right-hand corner of the map. This shows a vessel centrally placed between the two entry towers and provides iconographic evidence of the entry of sailing vessels through a water-gate and into an enclosed basin. Speed's 1610 plan of Cork is also quite clear in illustrating the basin. At some stage over the following decades this basin was infilled, probably associated with increased sedimentation in the marsh area outside of the walls and increased investment in the land claim activities, particularly in the 'walkabout' area which had been a focus for domestic and industrial dumping. Certainly by 1690 the basin was no longer in use and quays had been established along the peripheries of the town.

The *Pacata* illustration of Limerick clearly shows a curved quay wall in the southwest corner of the town, integrated into an external section of the town walls

42 Detail of the late medieval waterfront from Francis Jobson's late sixteenth-century view of Limerick

and protected by a series of small mural towers. A centrally placed tower gate is positioned behind the quay frontage. A chain-like boom protects entry into the quay area which would have controlled access in the inner section. Larger vessels are shown in the Shannon where they presumably either waited at anchor for their turn at the berth or else were unloaded by smaller tender vessels. A number of other lesser gates are shown along the wall with associated towers and pier-like projections. Jobson's map of the city also clearly shows the curvilinear nature of the quay, the boom and ships lying at anchor in the Shannon (fig. 42). Excavations at Charlotte Quay in Limerick uncovered the remains of a seventeenth-century quay wall which ran parallel to the town wall and appears to have been built to provide boat access to the west watergate (Lynch 1984, 281). The wall survived to a height of 3.2m and ran along the river for 32.5m. It was built with a core of mortared rubble and faced with ashlar limestone blocks.

Away from the larger port sites smaller waterfront structures were also built to accommodate visiting boat and sometimes ship traffic. At Bunratty the remains of a stone quay wall are visible underlying the foundations of the arched bridge crossing the Owenagarney River. This quay, consisting of a series of horizontally laid large flat stones, lies beneath the tower house walls within the environs of the medieval borough. On Whiddy Island the basal remains of a stone pier associated with the early seventeenth-century pilchard fishery has been located on the foreshore in Trawnahaha townland (Breen 2005). A contemporary map of the inner Bay area clearly shows this structure and a terrestrial complex associated with it.

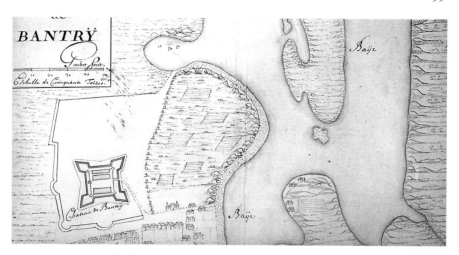

43 Detail of late seventeenth-century French plan of the settlement,
fort and inlet at Newtown (NLI MS 2742)

The remains consist of a rectangular feature measuring *c.*6m by 4m built with uncut sandstone boulders, averaging 0.4m in length, as a foundation. It is probable that this foundation supported a timber superstructure. A similar structure was located on the foreshore adjacent to the site of a mid-seventeenth-century fishing community at Newtown, located on the mainland across the inner bay from Whiddy (fig. 43). Philip's 1680s depiction of the town in his Bantry Bay vista shows two landing places at the extreme western end of this sector of the town. These are shown as projecting stone/wood composite features which extend from the foreshore out into the water in a northerly direction. Two small rowed vessels are shown lying at these features. Water depth within the inlet rarely exceeds 3–4m which militated against large seagoing vessels being able to approach the settlement. It was instead necessary for these vessels to lie at anchor in the sheltered Inner Bay area, where there was good holding ground, and use tenders to ferry people and goods in and out of the landing place at Newtown. The basal foundation of one of these landing places was located and consists of a linear stone feature running southwest from a soft sandy/shingle beach to below the low water mark and is made up of two lines of stones with occasional boulders running parallel to each other and spaced 2m apart in places. The space between both lines is infilled by sand and small stones. The feature is 22m long to its visible extent and is 2.5m wide on average. Originally this constituted the solid foundation of a stone pier with a timber superstructure. One chimneyed building is positioned directly adjacent to the landing on Philip's vista which also has a doorway in its eastern gable. The building runs parallel to the shore and is located

just above the high-water mark. It is tempting to view this as a waterfront administrative structure that facilitated such activities as customs duty, recording imports
and exports and controlling landing. It is physically removed from the main body
of the residential settlement and is directly associated with two buildings with no
chimneys which have well-built roofs and adopt the same orientation as the
waterfront building. They are shown windowless with gable doorways and must
be structures associated with storage or some other similar function.

BOATS AND SHIPPING

There are three primary sources for the types of boats and ships used in late
sixteenth- and early seventeenth-century Munster. The historical sources contain
many references to vessels arriving at the ports of the southwest but do not necessarily
contain any architectural information relating to them. A number of contemporary
cartographic sources contain illustrations of vessels which can be taken as broadly
representative of vessel types of this period. Finally, archaeological investigation
has taken place on a small number of sites which has added supporting physical
detail and material cultural information to our developing picture of the nature
of shipping at this time. Galleys – small, oared vessels which also carried a single
sail – appear to be the most common type of vessel used by the Gaelic Irish. A
number of illustrations of this vessel type survive but we, as of yet, have no
archaeological evidence. The later sixteenth-century map of Beare and Bantry, Co.
Cork, illustrates two oared galleys, without sails, being rowed up the Bere Island
Sound towards Dunboy castle, indicative of the type of naval galley operating off
the south coasts at this time. Two depictions of hulc-like vessels survive on the
sides of tomb chests in churches in Thurles and Cashel, Co. Tipperary. The
example from Thurles, which dates to c.1520, shows a bearded ecclesiastic,
presumably St Simon, holding a ship in both hands at waist level. The vessel has
a rounded hull profile with a pronounced after castle, which appears to be
incorporated into the hull. The vessel also has a single, central mast with two stays
running fore and aft respectively with a large, castellated crow's nests sitting on
top of the mast. At Cashel a similar clinker-built vessel with a single, central mast
is shown on the north side of a tomb chest dating to the first half of the sixteenth
century. A vessel is also depicted on the Youghal town seals, the earliest of which
dates to 1527 and continued in use into the seventeenth century (fig. 44). It shows
a double-ended clinker built craft with a single, central mast shown furled on a
yard. Three galleys are also shown on the Waterford town seals. On the charter of
Philip and Mary, dating to 1556, three wooden, clinker-built vessels are shown
with high curved bows and what appear to be square sterns with tents erected.

44 Municipal seal of Youghal (source: Caulfield 1876)

The vessels have a single, central mast with furled sails tied on yards. Eleven oar ports are visible on the sheer strakes of the vessels (Breen and Forsythe 2004). Three galleys are again shown on Elizabeth's charter of 1574. A later seal of Waterford Corporation, from a deed dated 1663, depicts three galleys with long, curved, slender lines, a pointed bow and a slightly raised stern castle section. Between 11 and 13 oars are shown protruding from rectangular oar ports on the sheer strakes of the vessels and the uppermost vessel is shown with two or three masts.

The majority of vessels plying their trade in the waters off the south coast were English or Continental vessels. A number of Spanish ships were wrecked off the southwest during the infamous Spanish Armada of 1588 (Martin and Parker 1988; Flanagan 1989). Of the many vessels lost on the western seaboard a small number were lost in the southwest. The *San Esteban* of the Guipúzcoan squadron was probably wrecked at Doonbeg in Co. Clare while the 703-ton *Anunciada* was scuttled near Scattery Roads near Kilrush. A pinnace, a small two-masted vessel of about 20 tons, was abandoned and fired near Tralee, while the merchantman, *San Juan* was lost in Blasket Sound in Co. Kerry, north of where another vessel was lost near Valentia. The wreck of the 945-ton *Santa Maria de la Rosa*, vice-flagship of the Guipúzcoan squadron under the command of Miguel de Oquendo, was located in Blasket Sound in 1968 by a team of British divers. The remains consisted of a large, tightly packed ballast mound of limestone blocks, 33m in length and 40m wide running on a north-south axis (fig. 45). Underneath structural elements from the lowermost part of the hull including a section of the scarf-jointed keelson was uncovered. A number of stanchions, which would have supported the orlop beams and a complex mast step with a surrounding wooden

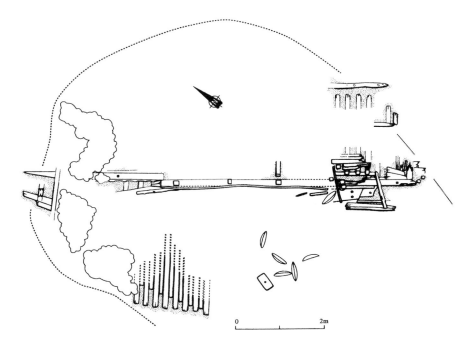

45 Site plan of the 1588 Spanish Armada shipwreck *Santa Maria de la Rosa* (after Wignal 1982)

box were also excavated. Lead ingots, shot, guns including arquebuses and muskets, two pewter plates, engraved with the name 'Matute', as well as the fragmentary skeletal remains of a mariner were recovered.

A number of vessels were also lost in naval engagements associated with Kinsale in 1601/02. A fleet of six Spanish vessels under the command of Don Pedro de Zubiaur was driven into Castlehaven in November 1601. In December an English squadron under the command of Sir Richard Leveson arrived at Castlehaven and proceeded to fire on the Spanish ships lying at anchor below the O'Driscoll tower house. The testimony of a captured Spanish solider records that one vessel, named as the *Maria Francesa*, was sunk by Leveson's *Warspite* laden with '300 quintales of biscuit and 400 barrels of wheat'. De Zubiaur's flagship appears to have been driven ashore and later lost its rudder.

Significant advancements in ship design took place in the early part of the seventeenth century stimulated by large-scale mercantile businesses carrying bulk commodities. Ship size greatly increased and vessels were now characterized by high sterns, three masts, a combination of square and lateen sails and complex rigging. A number of companies were also founded in Europe to develop

European trade with the Indian Ocean and the Far East. The English East India Company (EIC), established in 1600 by a group of London merchantmen, was one such company. The company developed a number of commercial interests, establishing a base at Dundaniel, Co. Cork, and a yard at Limerick at the beginning of the seventeenth century. A shipyard and ironworks were set up at Dundaniel. Three settlements Hope, Bandon and Bantham were established to house 300 workers and 22 armed guards. By 1613 Dundaniel had a dock where two vessels of 400 and 500 tons apiece were built. Houses, storehouses, offices, smiths' forges and an iron works were also built at the site to facilitate the works and accommodate the 300 English inhabitants. However, due to a variety of factors, mostly related to the political turmoil of the later 1630s, the settlement failed to reach its full potential and was abandoned in 1641. A vessel, *Pearl*, belonging to the company is recorded as being wrecked near Dursey Island in 1613. Wreckage from the vessel, including ship's oak ribs with treenails and cannon balls have been washed ashore at Trá na Phearla near Allihies in west Cork. To date just one wreck associated with the WIC has been recorded, a captured Spanish galleon, the *Santa Anna Maria*, taken into Castlehaven, Co. Cork in 1628/9 and subsequently lost in shallow water. Bronze and iron cannon were recovered from the site including one demi-culverine.

Finally, a vessel fitted with cannon has been uncovered at Duncannon, Co. Waterford, and tentatively identified by Connie Kelleher as the *Great Lewis*, lost during action against Royalist forces holding Duncannon fort in 1645.

CHAPTER 5

Rural Settlement

Following the Desmond Revolt extensive lands across Munster were confiscated from the Gaelic lords and granted to English settlers. It is important to note though that this was not whole-scale confiscation but rather piecemeal undertakings leaving a complex mosaic of changing landownership across the province. The Commissioners Report of 1584/5 shows that most of the attained land in Waterford was located between Cappoquin and Dungarvan in the Blackwater Valley region (MacCarthy-Morrogh 1986, 15). Ormond gains much of the escheated land in Tipperary. Significant sections of east and west Cork were similarly attained while much of North Kerry and sections of Limerick were now under English ownership. As a consequence of this gradual influx of settlers and landowners a variety of new settlement clusters are either established or redeveloped across the region. A note of caution needs to be introduced here about the nature and extent of earlier settlement at these locations. It would of course have suited the new arrivals to claim that they were establishing settlement on virgin uncontested ground where no settlement previously existed; this was often the case in the historical record and was used as a form of justification for their presence. However, it is clear from cartographic evidence and the limited archaeological data we have that this was clearly not the case. There were extensive groupings or clusters of Gaelic settlement across the landscape prior to the 1580s and it is simply untrue to claim that many of the undertakings were new builds or developments. One only has to look at the situation in Bantry and Beara, for example, to see the extent of such pre-existing activity (Breen 2005). Nevertheless what we do have from the mid-1580s onwards is an emerging body of historical and archaeological evidence for extensive redevelopment, enhancement or reordering of settlement in the region. This combined body of evidence can then be used to interrogate the pattern of expansion.

In Waterford Tallow is listed as having a population of 60 households by 1598 while Newtown, in Cuffe's seignory had 22 English households (MacCarth-Morrogh 1986, 118). Significant English settlements were also evident at Mallow in Cork, where they lived in thatch houses, and at Tralee and Killarney. Smaller settlements existed at Rathkeale and Newcastle in Limerick. Not all of the English arrivals lived in clusters. Norris writes that many of his English tenants live in 'remote and dangerous places in weak thatch houses' (MacCarthy-Morrogh 1986, 128), a reference clearly that more adventurous single tenants lived far beyond the central confines of attained English lands.

Mogeely

The majority of the existing evidence we have suggests that locating settlement at pre-existing centres was the favoured form. The concentration of settlers and their tenants at these locations provided security in numbers and the foundations of a new community on which to build. There was also the element of easing the process through taking over existing estates that may have been involved in land clearance and agricultural activity for many hundreds of years previously. It then made good economic and social sense to encourage this continuity of settlement location. There was of course a political point also being made with the displacement of the pre-existing Gaelic communities representing the arrival of a new political order. Displacement or replacement meant subjugation and the establishment of a new hierarchy of control. A number of these centres have been investigated archaeologically, most notably Eric Klingelhofer's work at Walter Raleigh's estates in the Blackwater Valley (Klingelhofer 1999a; 1999b; 2000). In August 1586 a set of regulatory measures for the tenants were laid down where 'no tenant belonging to the lands of Mogeely shall henceforth dwell abroad … in woods, bogs, glens and other remote places … but shall presently resort and dwell within the town or depart from those lands' (Klingelhofer 1999, 101). Furthermore the tenants were instructed to set their ricks of corn near the central castle area. Tenants were also ordered to 'dwell in town … keep their arms in readiness … [and] all upon the sound of the drum to repair to castle gate' (Klingelhofer 1999a, 170). These measures are reflective of prescriptive centralized control and of a new community not overly at ease in its surroundings. By bringing the community together and preventing new, and older Gaelic inhabitants, from living too far from the community's core Raleigh was ensuring the area could be adequately monitored and overseen. Henry Pyne leases part of Raleigh's estates at Mogeely by which time other settlements had been established nearby. Two households had settled at Kilmacowe, a tower house located between Curraglass and Tallow, where one plough, 100 ruther cattle, 60

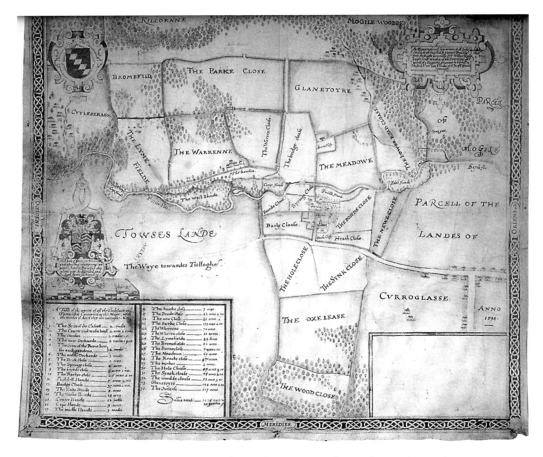

46 Manuscript estate map of Mogeely, County Cork, 1598 (NLI MS 22,028)

sheep and goats and swine were kept on 50 acres of fallow – a sizeable holding (Klingelhofer 1999b, 102).

The plantation settlement at Mogeely built up around the existing tower house site, another example of settling pre-existing sites. A detailed map of the area dating to 1598, produced for Pyne's lease adds to our understanding of plantation landscapes at this time (fig. 46). At the centre is Mogeely castle, a fifteenth-/ sixteenth-century tower house, with a church and an orderly settlement cluster surrounding it. A larger linear settlement is shown to the east at Curraglass where 19 houses line either side of the road. Historical records indicate that further houses existed beyond the boundaries of the map. An ordered group of houses line the roadway around the tower house. This symmetrical pattern is reflective of the later ordered nature of the plantation towns at Bandon or Coleraine and is

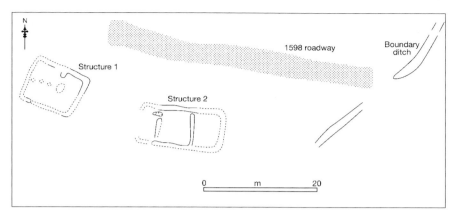

47 Carrigeen interpretative plan (after Klingelhofer 2000)

typical of English-type settlement activity – Gaelic-Irish clusters appear to have
been far less ordered and lacked the same sense of symmetry. The landscape is
mostly parcelled up into field enclosures and each unit is labelled. Woodland
dominates much of the northern section of the map and a cluster of Irish-type
cabins is shown on the margins of Mogeely wood. Excavations at the central castle
area uncovered the mortared stone foundations of a single storey late sixteenth-
seventeenth-century house with an internal measurement of 11.6m by 7.3m, on a
north/south orientation. The excavator suggests that this house was laid out using
the English measurement of 35 by 22 internally (Klingelhofer 1999b, 110) It was of
a timber-frame construction and located opposite the church. Contemporary
ceramics were dominated by red earthenwares with fragments of a Seville olive jar,
dating to the 1580/90s, also recovered. Both North Devon gravel-free and gravel
tempered-wares were present. Further north two houses were excavated in the
townland of Carrigeen (fig. 47). They were located in a green field site at the
location of a small cluster of four single storey structures shown on the original
lease map in an area of land referred to as 'The Warrenne'. Structure 1, uncovered
in Klingelhofer's trench B, measured 8m by 10m, was orientated northwest/
southeast, and had two bays (Klingelhofer 2000). Its walls were constructed using
stone and clay bonding with a central entrance to the north. Clay wall bonding
was also found at a late sixteenth-seventeenth-century structure at Glanworth
castle and during excavations undertaken by Klingelhofer at Kilcolman castle
(Klingelhofer 2000, 171). The Carrigeen site had right-angled corners, suggesting
an English form while cobbling was revealed in the interior. All of the evidence
suggested that the structure was only occupied for a short period. Structure 2,
found in trench D, was a timber framed building as evidenced by beam slots and
had an external width of 8m and length of 16.5m. A possible hearth was located

in the interior. Limited material cultural evidence was recovered from the sites but their survival represents an important contribution to the archaeological record or rural and vernacular housing of this period. There were a number of building styles present reflecting the introduction of new architectural styles by the English and the adoption or retention of some local styles. It was not possible to say on the basis of the recovered evidence to suggest whether these houses represented the dwelling places of English or Irish tenants with any certainty. The predominant English style of building coupled with their proximity to the centre of the estate and their presence on an established routeway would suggest, however, that they were English tenants. The houses were not occupied for any long period of time and were presumably abandoned by the middle part of the seventeenth century.

Following widespread unrest in 1598 Mogeely was garrisoned and managed to hold out against rebel aggression. Early seventeenth-century accounts, however, offer conflicting views of the state of the settlement following disagreements over the lease between Raleigh and Pyne. The latter had constructed a number of flankers and had installed windows, stairs and doors in the tower house, enclosed land and built a stone bridge (Klingelhofer 2000, 105). Extensive woodcutting for planks and pipestaves was taking place, an iron works had been established and 40 English tenants were living there. The reports that Mogeely castle had 'partly fallen down' seem then somewhat exaggerated.

TOWER HOUSES

The use and occupation of the tower house at Mogeely reflects a broader pattern across Munster with many other similar structures being either occupied by English arrivals or witnessing continued Gaelic occupation from late medieval times. The poet Edmund Spenser had obtained Kilcolman castle and over 300 acres in the 1580s (fig. 48). In the early part of the nineteenth century T. Crofton Croker, in his *Researches in the south of Ireland*, describes the site as being

> distant three English miles from Doneraile … The ruin itself stands on a little rocky eminence. Spreading before it lies a tract of flat and swampy ground, through which, we were informed, the 'River Bregog hight' had its course; and though in winter, when swollen by mountain torrents, a deep and rapid stream, its channel at present was completely dried up … Judging from what remains, the original form of Kilcolman was an oblong square, flanked by a tower at the south-east corner. The apartment in the basement story has still its stone arched roof entire, and is used as a shelter for cattle; the narrow, screw-like stairs of the tower are nearly perfect, and lead to an

48 Kilcolman in 1831 (source: *The mirror of literature, amusement and instruction,* 17:483, 2 April 1831)

extremely small chamber, which we found in a state of complete desolation. Kilcolman was granted by Queen Elizabeth, on the 27thJune, 1586, to Spenser (who went into Ireland as secretary to Lord Grey), with 3,028 acres of land, at the rent of 17l. 3s. 6d.; on the same conditions with the other undertakers.

Excavations undertaken by Eric Klingelhofer (2005) at the site uncovered a number of important horizons dating to the Spenser family occupation. Kitchen gardens were built to the east of the bawn with pleasure gardens located to the west. The bawn wall itself was largely insubstantial at the turn of the century, lacking bastions and a proper defensive framework. The small corner turret, still visible, is indicative of a late fifteenth-early sixteenth-century constructional date given the absence of the provision for artillery warfare in the design of the wall. This weak nature and constructional interference with the earlier wall was to have serious consequences for the castle when it was burnt in 1598 during the outbreak of conflict. (Klingelhofer 2005, 137) uncovered a structure he interprets as a parlour abutting the external southeast corner of the tower house. It had a probable timber floor and a plastered wall face 'fine textured with hair filler and coated with whitewash'. The walls were again clay bonded, over older mortared walls, and an internal hearth was present against the wall. A number of windows would originally have been present and paved with glass. The building was probably temporarily abandoned in 1598 and Spenser's son, Sylvanus, subsequently replaced his father's 'fair stone house' with 'a convenient English house' by 1622.

A majority of the standing tower houses in Waterford were occupied into the seventeenth century. Butlerstown South was in the possession of the Sherlock

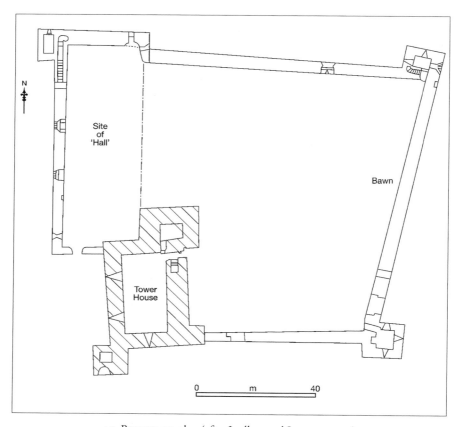

49 Barryscourt plan (after Ludlow and Jameson 2004)

family for much of the century while Ballymaclode was occupied by Lord Power of Curraghmore in 1640. Ballyclohy castle was owned by John Butler in 1640 and consisted of a circular tower within a trapezoidal enclosure measuring 66m in maximum diameter with an external ditch (Moore 1999, 220). This is probably a later defensive feature constructed in the later part of the sixteenth or early part of the seventeenth century.

In Cork evidence for early seventeenth-century activity was uncovered at Glanworth castle, during excavations undertaken by Con Manning in the early 1980s. Here a seventeenth-century bread oven was found incorporated into the west wall and the tower house was occupied into the eighteenth century. Barryscourt Castle, historic seat of the Barry family, has been intensively investigated (see Barryscourt Lecture series, Ludlow and Jameson 2004). Some debate surrounds its original construction date but the majority of its extant features would suggest a sixteenth-century date. Its current form consists of a rectangular tower block

50 Detail of the Ballincarriga tower house carvings showing the
crucifixion scene at the bottom of the image (DOEHLG)

with further towers incorporated into its southwest and northeast angles. A
substantial bawn is also present with towers at three of its corners and the tower
house itself in the fourth corner. A hall would have originally been incorporated
into the northwest range of the bawn wall (fig. 49). In 1581 David Barry 'defaced
and despoiled' the structure in advance of the arrival of English forces to prevent
it being used by them. He was subsequently regranted the tower and was involved
in a programme of renovation over the following two decades. A new doorway
was inserted and significant internal restoration was undertaken. The second floor
main hall was the focus of much of this work with a new fireplace inserted
bearing a mantle date of 1588 commemorating the marriage of David Barry and
Ellen Roche. These halls were public spaces where Luke Gernon records in 1620
that the Gaelic families' entertaining takes place. A second date of 1586 appears on
one of the widow frames. Work also took place on the bawn during this period.
While continued refortification of this feature was important it also served as an
enclosing element for a series of gardens. Barry remained loyal during the Nine
Years War and died in 1617. His grandson assumed his position but moved the
seat of the family to the mansion house at Castlelyons.

Timoleague Castle also carries a description commemorating Barry and Roche
through the inscription 'DB ET ER ME FECET', '1586 AUGUST 1'. This inscription

marks a refurbishment phase at this early sixteenth-century tower house. Gun loops were added on the ground floor and a number of windows were altered. Chimneys may also have been altered at this date. A similar inscription survives at Ballincarriga tower house, again a late fifteenth-or early sixteenth-century tower which underwent significant refurbishment in the 1580s. The inscription reads '1585 R.M. C.C.' (commemorating Randal Hurley and Catherine Cullane) and is located on the embrasure of the third floor. Further carvings include the probable depiction of Cullane and five rosettes (children?) on the first floor as well as religious scenes (fig. 50). Delle (1999) sees the religious figures as representing Gaelic resistance against the plantation and their carving emits a strong demonstration of Catholicism in the face of advancing Protestantism. Donnelly (2005) disagrees and instead sees their production as part of a long process of common medieval practice of depicting devotional images in a secular building. He goes on to argue that instead we should see the usage of IHS, found on four Limerick tower houses, as being a more convincing form of depictional resistance. Both arguments have validity but the survival of the depictions at Ballincarriga is important in a regional and iconographic context. As to whether this was an overt form of resistance by Hurley or an expression of continuing faith remains debatable, especially given the paucity of similar findings throughout the rest of the region. It is more likely that the carvings represent the continuation of tradition in difficult and changing times. If holding onto tradition is seen as resistance then so be it. The inclusion of a *Sheila-na-gig* on the tower house walls is of further interest and may link the building with a continuum of devotional activity over a number of generations. Kilbrittain was a fifteenth-century residence of the MacCarthy Riabhach which has undergone continual redevelopment and refurbishment over many centuries. It seems to have suffered heavy damage during a siege in 1641 and was later rebuilt a number of times. An inscribed stone originally from the house read 'AD 1596 DONALDUS CARTI ET MARGAERTA GERALD FECERUNT', a direct reference to redevelopment undertaken by Donal MacCarthy and Margaret Fitzgerald in 1596 (Power et al. 1992, 326). A number of features associated with the sites redevelopment at the end of the sixteenth century and into the seventeenth century survive including a turret with numerous gun loops and sections of a bawn.

Refurbishment or redevelopment did not always take place purely for aesthetic reasons. A bawn with corner towers is constructed around Carriganass castle near Bantry as a direct consequence of internecine conflict in the O'Sullivan Beare sept (Breen 2005). Dunboy castle, chiefry residence of the O'Sullivan Beares, was levelled to its first floor following the siege of 1601/2. It had been extensively refortified in the 1580s and 1590s to protect the site against artillery (fig. 51). A number of the O'Driscoll and O'Mahoney towers suffered a similar fate.

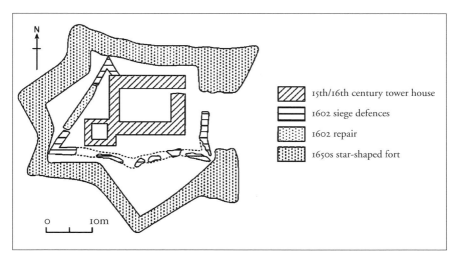

51 Plan of the seventeenth-century fortifications at Dunboy castle, County Cork

Blarney castle, chief residence of the MacCarthys in Muskerry, originally constructed in the fifteenth century underwent extensive renovations throughout the sixteenth and seventeenth centuries. This included the addition of large windows, defensive elements and a later mansion houses extension. This pattern of renovations is evident at a large number of Cork sites. The tower house at Ballea, outside of Carrigaline, was converted into a mansion house at the turn of the sixteenth and seventeenth centuries acquiring a new L-shaped plan and features such as mullion windows with hood moulding. The tower house at Ballymaloe was extended in 1602 by John Fitzedmund Fitzgerald and an L-shaped block was later added. Cahermone is a typical four-storey tower house with a late sixteenth- or early seventeenth-century annexe range built against the tower. The range contains standard features of the new architectural fashions of the time including large fireplaces, tall chimney stacks and a number of gun loops. The Fitzgerald tower house at Castlemartyr came into English possession in the 1570s and was later taken by the earl of Cork. A substantial mansion house was built immediately adjacent to the tower of which three large chimney stacks and a number of fireplaces survive. Indeed, each one of the Cork tower houses was either directly involved in or affected by the conflicts of the last decade of the sixteenth century and subsequent engagements in the seventeenth century.

Continued occupation into the seventeenth century is a feature of many tower houses in Kerry. Of the fifteen known tower houses on the Iveragh Peninsula each is associated with continued occupation into the seventeenth century and involvement with the conflicts of the first six decades of the century. Ballinskelligs

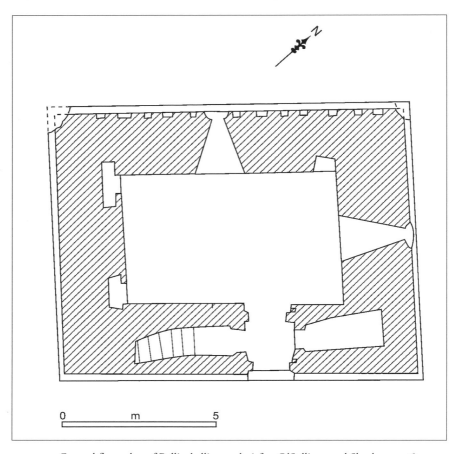

52 Ground floor plan of Ballinskelligs castle (after O'Sullivan and Sheehan 1996)

castle, excavated by John Sheehan (O'Sullivan and Sheehan 1996) is associated with the Sigerson family who occupied Ballinskelligs in the early part of the seventeenth century. In a list of people to be transplanted from Kerry in 1653 Richard Segereson of Ballinskelligs is listed as having 36 persons, over eight acres of summer corn, 21 cows, two yearlings and nine garrons (Hickson 1874). These records of transplantation also record other features in the landscape. In Glanarought Colonel Donogh Mac Fineen forfeited Ardtully in 1653 on which stood 'two good slate houses, a corn mill, a castle, malthouse, barn and tuck mill … iron mines and a silver mine' (Hickson 1874). Regardless, by the early part of the seventeenth century Ballinskelligs castle was closely linked to the nearby priory, garrisoned by English forces. The tower house itself was probably built early in the sixteenth- century and lacks any seventeenth-century architectural

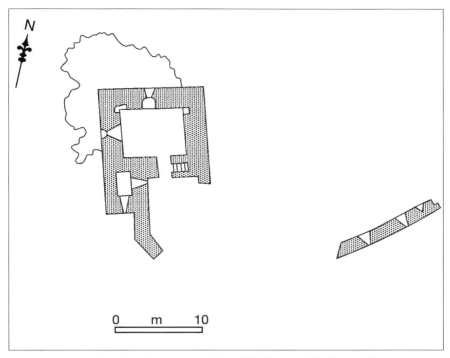

53 Plan of Dunkerron castle (after O'Sullivan and Sheehan 1996)

features. It was a small three-storey structure later used by Petty as a site for one of his fisheries as evidenced by the presence of beam sockets on the external northwest wall (fig. 52). Material culture from the excavations at the site was dominated by seventeenth-century English ceramics, most notably North Devon wares. Ballinskelligs would originally have been linked to the MacCarthy overlordship as was the tower house at Ballycarbery, overlooking Valencia Harbour, which was a MacCarthy More castle in 1594 (O'Sullivan and Sheehan 1996, 367). The undertaker Valentine Browne takes possession of the building in 1596 following the death of the MacCarthy earl of Clancar. Its subsequent history is little known but the tower and bawn were slighted by parliamentary forces in 1651–2. A third MacCarthy castle, Castleconway at Killorglin, was forfeited in 1583 and granted to Captain Jenkin Conway (*Cal. Carew MSS* 1587). A bawn wall was possibly subsequently constructed but both it and the tower house were attacked and burned in 1600.

A number of tower houses on the Iveragh Peninsula were O'Sullivan residences. Dunkerron was the chiefry residence of the O'Sullivan More (fig. 53). When Owen O'Sullivan assumed the title in 1580 he went onto build a manor house

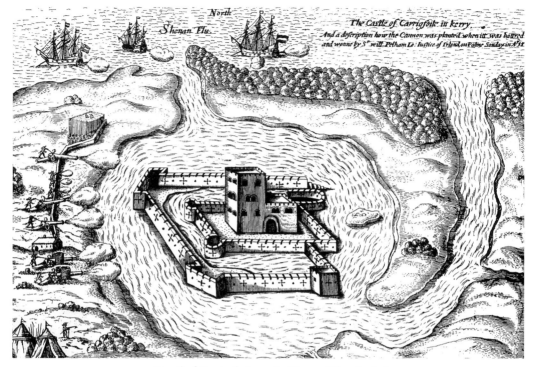

54 Detail of Carrigafoyle castle (*Pacata Hibernia* 1633)

adjoining the tower house (RIA MS 24 K 43). He retained this house until 1656 when it was acquired by William Petty. In the middle of the nineteenth century Du Noyer records an inscription stone from the site. It reads 'IHS: MARIA DEO THIS WORK WAS MADE THE XX OF APRIEL 1596: BY OWEN O SVLIVAN [&] SILY NY DONOGH MACCARTY RIEOGH.' This is a direct reference to the marriage of Owen, the O'Sullivan More and Sily MacCarthy. Only sections of the west gable of the manor house now stand but it would originally have been a three-storey structure with an attic. The first floor has a distinctive large and somewhat ornate fireplace, a common feature amongst mansion houses. The transference of O'Sullivan from the tower house to a mansion house is interesting and is again reflective of the adoption of new architectural norms amongst the Gaelic elite. Mansion houses were not then the sole preserve of the planter communities but were built across the ethnic spectrum.

Carrigafoyle Castle in North Kerry is probably a late fifteenth-century build but was intensively involved in the conflicts at the end of the sixteenth century (fig. 54). It was originally a five-storey structure with two internal vaults standing on an island and encompassed by a complex arrangement of curtain walls enclosing both the tower and sections of the foreshore to allow boats come into the enclosing elements. Geomorphological change has resulted in the sedimentation of much of the original lagoon the castle was contained in and it now sits in an area of marsh adjacent to the river. It was refortified in 1580 by John O'Connor against advancing English forces but was subsequently unable to withstand artillery bombardment and fell (Toal 1995, 275–6). In 1600 the tower house was granted to Charles Wilmot but was later retaken by Gaelic forces and was garrisoned during the Cromwellian period to protect sections of the southern shore of the Shannon Estuary. Other fortifications in this area were subject to changes in ownership at the turn of the century. Clogabeleesh was in the possession of the Cantillons which was subsequently besieged by Charles Wilmot in 1602. It was later occupied by loyalists during the 1640s and heavily refortified. A series of internal house foundations are evident at this complex and these appear to constitute the remains of a seventeenth-eighteenth-century settlement. Ballinruddery is an early sixteenth-century tower house that shows clear signs of renovation in the closing decade of the sixteenth century or early part of the seventeenth century. It was granted to William Herbert in 1588 following the Desmond revolt. It has a number of large inset fireplaces and has two surviving transom and mullion windows clearly illustrating renovation in line with contemporary developments in architectural fashion.

EARLY SEVENTEENTH-CENTURY PLANTATION SETTLEMENT

Following the upheavals of the Nine Years War a new phase of active plantation occured. This in many ways is a more intensive undertaking but the same degree of formality that was proposed for the earlier schemes does not appear to apply to the early seventeenth-century plantations. One reason for this is that much of the threat from Gaelic insurgents, a factor that hindered earlier settlement in the area, had now effectively gone. Much has also been written about the process of plantation and subjugation by the proponents of the earlier settlements (Canny 2001) but the later undertakings appear to be far more individualistic. The grantee(s) appears to have been able to operate without only limited political interference and was able to develop their scheme in a self-directed manner. This movement away from formalization is indicative of a broader conceptual movement away from recognized established centres of socio-economic power, a dominant paradigm during the high and late medieval periods, towards a much greater diversity of settlement in new centres and on the periphery. It is also reflective of increased diversity of economic practice and the leading role entrepreneurialism now played. A much looser and less controlled market had almost sub-consciously been introduced and individual activity and initiative was actively encouraged. This is essentially *laissez faire* in operation, evidenced by the establishment of 107 new markets in Munster in the 1610s (MacCarthy-Morrogh 1986a, 179). One of the direct consequences of this is that the actual morphology of the settlements in areas like west Cork is less rigid than that which was proposed for the earlier Munster settlements. You do not, see for example, the production of idealized plans of seignorys like those produced in the 1585 plantation schemes (PRO SP 63/121/55). It is also far less rigid than the ordered walled towns developed in Ulster at this time (Robinson 1984). This conformity of style is expressed in the spatial layout of towns like Coleraine and Londonderry for example, either established or redeveloped in the first decade of the seventeenth century (Curl 2000; Robinson 1984). The only example of such formalization in west Munster, as we have seen, was the development of Bandonbridge in Kinalmeaky with its surrounding wall and grid-iron street pattern (MacCarthy-Morrogh 1986a, 180). However, the majority of the new settlements set up in association with the previously mentioned markets were far looser entities with no formal planning.

SMALL TOWN DEVELOPMENT

It is probably necessary to briefly define what is meant by small towns in the context of this regional study. Previously many historians and geographers have narrowly defined towns as settlements with charters (for example, Nolan and Simms 1998, 10). This legalistic definition fails to recognize the multi-faceted nature and function of many small- to medium-size settlements during the early seventeenth century that did not receive or maybe even seek charter status. It is probably more appropriate to here identify a small town as a settlement with a reasonable population (probably in excess of 25 leading household members who are engaged in a diversity of activities other than solely agriculture) and a nucleated concentration of dwellings with some associated farm-land. The settlement had individuals who had defined trades and specialisms but did not exclusively have to be employed in these singular activities. Trade and exchange probably took place at this location primarily through the presence of a marketplace. People in the locality must also have recognized or perceived this place as a centre of activity and settlement in the area and identify with it as a central place. Within the place then there is likely to be buildings with specialist and non-residential functions. These could include buildings for administration, storage, meeting places or mercantile activities. Communications are an important part of the definition and the towns will normally be recognized as a node within a wider network. A variety of other settlement forms also existed ranging from nucleated settlement clusters to isolated farm or homesteads. The so-called clachan type settlement is evident in a number of cartographic sources but we have only limited tangible archaeological evidence for this form during the study period.

The 1610s and 1620s saw extensive investment and changing ethnic profiles in small towns and villages across the study region. O'Flanagan (1991) refers to this period as an 'urban revolution' across the region. Again, while there is a noticeable intensification of settlement activity by the planters we cannot forget that this landscape was already littered with late medieval settlement clusters. Luke Gernon, writing in the 1620s, states that 'The [Irish] villages are distant each from the other about two miles. In every village is a castle and a church, but both in ruin. The baser cottages are built of underwood, called wattle and covered some with thatch and some with green sedge, of a round form and without chimneys, and to my imaginations resemble so many hives of bees around a country farms' (Harrington 1991, 106). We may not have extensive historical records associated with these sites but there is an increasing body of archaeological material reflective of this change. Regardless, by the second and third decade of the seventeenth century economic and political conditions pave the way for new arrivals and investment. O'Flanagan identifies 40 villages in the country of Cork at this time with a population of 100 people or more, one of his crucial elements constituting urban settlement (O'Flanagan 1991, 396). Canny (1991), using the 1641 Depositions builds a similar demographic picture across the county. Of the 904 deponents from Cork, 309 are from ten parishes, indicative of a number of notable settlement concentrations of planters. Significant numbers settled in the valleys of the Blackwater and Bandon rivers, along the coastline and in the existing large urban settlements. The largest cluster comes from around the town of Bandon where they are mostly artisans renting houses in the surrounding towns and leasing farms – in particular the towns of Clonakilty, Castletown, Mitchelstown, Newmarket, Kanturk and Mallow are especially well represented. These settlements served varying functions including port and fishing activities along the coast and artisan centres in the hinterland. Certainly the small centres of Ballydehob, Newcestown and Tracton would have had specialized artisan activity supplemented by agriculture. The garrisoning of soldiers was also important with significant centres known at Crookhaven, Newtown, Ballyclough, Buttevant and Liscarrol. The earl of Cork was heavily involved with the majority of these sites but other landowners also played a part including St Leger at Doneraile and Condon at Kilworth.

Coppinger built a mansion at Rosscarbery by 1631, at which time there was possibly up to 80 households in the town with a further 27 at Cove outside of the town, most of whom were English. Petty later described the town as having two short and narrow streets, four or five substantial houses, numerous cabins, and a corn mill (Flanagan 1991, 393). William Hull based himself at Leacom and took out a lease on the town of Crookhaven by 1616 where a pre-existing settlement is known to have been in place. Prior to 1641 there many have been 200 houses at the town with MacCarthy-Morrogh estimating that maybe 80 of these were English households (1986, 157). In Kerry settlements were known at Castlemaine and Kenmare where fifteen households were present in 1641 and an inn, destroyed in 1627. Smaller fishing villages were also present on the Beara Peninsula at Castlehaven and Kilmakilloge. It is Richard Boyle who led much of this invest-ment by the 1620s. He had obtained 86 ploughlands and the three manors of Ballydehob, Clonakilty and Enniskean by 1620. Clonakilty was an unwalled town incorporated in 1613 where 'some one hundred English families' were living (MacCarthy-Morrogh 1986, 163). A large English settlement was also present at Enniskean. These were essentially market towns facilitating agricultural pro-duction and trade. The 1659 'census' records Castlelyons having a population of 891 while Buttevant had 836 (Flanagan 1991, 396).

Bantry and Beara

While the earliest plantation schemes in the area took place in the late 1580s and early 1590s there was a more significant and successful phase of plantation after 1608/9 when Owen O'Sullivan Beare begins leasing out his lands to new arrivals. Entrepreneurs like Davenant and Roper arrived and established fishery enterprises at Bantry and on Whiddy Island. Detailed information on the nature and extent of the early seventeenth-century plantations in the study area is scarce. Aside from the documentary evidence, there is one informative map of the Inner Bay area, which appears to date to the 1620s, and significant archaeological data from excavations undertaken by the author at Blackrock, in the grounds of the demesne of Bantry House. The map was located as a loose item in the East Yorkshire Archives (item DDCC(2); reproduced in Breen 2001b, 32) and was initially ascribed a late seventeenth-century date on the basis that it was a later copy of the Down Survey (Donovan and Edwards 1997, 272) It has been shown elsewhere that it clearly dates to c.1620 (Breen 2005). Two key settlements are illustrated on the map including Blackrock, a plantation town founded at a pre-existing Gaelic settlement cluster and Ballygobben, the modern town of Bantry. Blackrock is shown as a linear settlement running along the southern shore of Inner Bantry Bay, in what are now the grounds of Bantry House. There appears to have been two separate components to the site including a number of closely spaced houses to the east, with a large structure adopting a central position, and a group of eleven less substantial structures shown running along the inlet below Abbey. Ballygobben is illustrated as a linear settlement located on either side of the narrow inlet below contemporary Bantry. It is referred to as a 'fisher town' in the documentary sources in the early part of the seventeenth century and the uniform illustration of its houses as small single-storey structures would support this reference. Three pilchard fishing stations are shown on Whiddy Island. The basal foundations for a pier survive on the foreshore in the townland of Trawnahaha associated with one of these stations.

Blackrock Excavations

Excavations at Blackrock in 2001 (excavation licence no. 01E0648) provided an opportunity to verify the information contained on the map and examine an undisturbed seventeenth-century site. Following the site's abandonment in the later part of the seventeenth century no further cultural activity was undertaken. One of the immediately identifiable aspects of the site was the direct continuity it demonstrated with earlier activity. The late medieval village and house site located at Blackrock have been discussed elsewhere (Breen 2005) and it is clear that the planters simply moved in and took over this location for the development of their new settlement. It has already been shown that one of their first acts was the erection of a substantial palisade around the site. Early in the seventeenth century a decision was made to remove this palisade, or the structure was destroyed, and its trench was backfilled in a single instance. The removal of this feature must reflect a renewed sense of security on the settlers' behalf and the removal of perceived threats. Both the artefactual evidence and the historical and political evidence suggest that this act took place sometime in the first two decades of the seventeenth century.

A house was then built in the area that directly overlaid the back-filled trench. Excavations revealed a rectangular structure orientated roughly east/west on its long axis with an external measurement of 5.2m in length and a width of *c.*3.8m, giving an internal area of *c.*18m². It had a stone foundation platform on its western gable made up primarily of three large sandstone slabs averaging 0.8m by 0.29m in length and width (fig. 55). The southern end of the foundation consisted of a platform of smaller slabs and filling stones. A row of cobble-like stones (averaging 0.1m by 0.1m) abut the western face of this feature and acted as packing. The foundation was compacted into the glacial sub-soil which has a natural clay-like consistency that negates against the use of artificial bonding. The opposing gable end consisted of a cut trench feature, rectangular in profile with rounded bottom edges, measuring 4.9m in overall length and 0.81m deep. Two large stone-lined post holes were set at either end of the trench, measuring 0.2m

55 Excavations underway at the seventeenth-century house site at Blackrock, Co. Cork

wide by 0.15m deep and 0.23m wide by 0.18m deep respectively. These would have held substantial posts given that the overall buried depth of the uprights would have been in excess of a metre in each case given the depth of the foundation trench that they lie in. No indication of the nature of the side walls survive but these undoubtedly must have been of a timber-framed construction supported on sill beams. The flat nature of this level would further support the presence of sill beams. Support for this interpretation comes from the density of iron nails that were found within the stratigraphic contexts contained in the house. Ninety-six nails were recovered, the vast majority of which were found in secure contexts. In fact nails were singularly the most common find on the site.

This general form of box-framed structure at this date is distinctively English and is a common feature of many sites in England (Newman 2001) and of the plantation sites of North America (Deetz and Deetz 1998). Houses using earth-fast posts in their construction appear to have been more common amongst the Irish as evidenced by the structure at Movanagher (Horning 2001, 391; O'Conor 2002, 197–8). Interestingly the Bantry site represents a fusion between earth-fast structures and timber or box-frame buildings. Certainly a western gable in Bantry would have been required to be the strongest on a house given the nature of the prevailing south-westerly winds. The earth-fast nature of the eastern gable may have been a further local adoption to ensure the structural stability of a box frame house in this region. The structure clearly had glass windows as 33 fragments of thin green typical early seventeenth-century window pane glass were recovered along with 46 sherds of thin white glass, although much of the latter came from later contexts. A flat base stone, located 1.2m in from the northwest corner on the northern side of the structure, may mark the location of the doorway. Certainly an opening at this position onto the waterfront, where the main focus of economic activity would have taken place, would make sense in the overall context of the settlement. The building was roofed with local slate that had been shaped in a very uniform rounded shingle form. Each slate measured 0.25m in overall length with a maximum width of 0.13m at its rounded head. Many had single surviving nail holes. The sheer density of slates contained in the surviving deposits of the structure suggests that it was either abandoned or forcibly taken down very quickly or during the course of a single event. Historically this was most likely to have taken place during the political turmoil of the 1640s. The artefactual evidence would support this in general but the continuity of pottery usage throughout the seventeenth-century complicates this picture. However, all of the clay pipe fragments that have been recovered predate the 1660s indicating that the house was indeed partially destroyed by the turmoils of the 1640s or 1650s.

Both the physical location of the structure and its morphology suggest that this was a high-quality residence. It is suggested here that it was the residence of a merchant or trader who was living in the settlement at Blackrock and that this building represents one of the houses shown on either side of the 'central' building shown on the early seventeenth-century map of the area. All of the artefactual evidence recovered from the building supports a domestic function. Forty-four clay pipe fragments were recovered along with six sherds of black glass from wine bottles. Seventy per cent of the pottery sherds recovered were domestic English wares including blue rim porcelain, North Devon gravel-tempered and gravel-free ware as well as tin-glazed earthenware. The majority of these were platters, milk pans etc. A quantity of European ware was also recovered including Germanic stoneware, tin-glazed maiolica and Italian tin-enamelled earthenware highlighting the extent of trading and inter-change that was going on at the site. One fragment of a tin-glazed Albarello drug-pot was also recovered. The assignation of the term drug does not necessarily mean that these items were used for storage by apothecaries, rather that they could have served this function as well as been used for the storage of paint, food-stuffs etc (Noel-Hume 1971). These finds along with the recovered window glass are indicative of a high-status residence or structure.

Isolated settlement

A number of further isolated settlements require mention. Isolated in this context refers to house sites outside of small towns and urban type settlements. They may consist of individual farmsteads or small settlement clusters. A series of Gaelic clusters have previously been recorded on Dursey Island and the Beara Peninsula (Breen 2005). A similar cluster at Bray Head on Valentia Island has been extensively investigated by Alan Hayden (Hayden 1995, 1998, 1999, 2001; Walsh 1995). Here in the later medieval period a street of houses was built over underlying medieval field systems and continued to be occupied into the seventeenth century. House 1, a rectangular stone built house measuring 4.6m by 7.6m, was associated with a number of small fields. It was a two-phased structure initially consisting of a drystone and sod construction and later being replaced by drystone walls and internal flooring with internal hearths and drains. A small bank and ditch enclosure surrounded the structure. In county Cork an important complex was uncovered at Ballinvinny South by Eamonn Cotter (Cotter 2003). Here three later seventeenth-century domestic buildings were excavated. The houses were identified by shallow foundation trenches which may have held wooden sill beams. One building measured 11m by 5m and had large rooms either end with a smaller central room. A hearth was identified in the east gable wall and the entrance would appear to have been centrally placed in the south wall. A smithy complex dated to the late seventeenth/ eighteenth century was found close by.

MANSION HOUSES

One of the key architectural developments of the early seventeenth century was the emergence of mansion houses across the countryside of Ireland. These site types have traditionally been referred to as fortified houses (Sweetman 1999; Barry 2000) but detailed examination of their role and function within society clearly indicates that they had only a limited defensive role and were rather elaborate expressions of new or continued wealth. Few were built to cater for artillery warfare and most lack the key defensive features of military forts. Many do contain elements of defensive ability including the inclusion of pistol loops and smaller windows at ground floor level but these must surely be aimed at protection against robbery as opposed to a long sustained siege or effective military attack representing sensible small-scale defence against limited attack. Even the addition of a surrounding bawn wall would have been largely ineffective against artillery. The presence of bawns at these sites can instead be seen as an extension of the need to create a defined private area. Many of the bawn walls may also have enclosed kitchen and leisure gardens and had more to do with planting and fashionable design than defence. Three bawn walls survive in association with mansion houses in Cork while Kanturk has additional evidence of an enclosing element. Mossgrove also has small circular corner towers with slit pistol loops. Mansion houses were adopted by many landowners across the social spectrum and represent an important response to a changing or transformatory socio-economic and political climate. The houses show a deliberate movement away from the monumentality of the late medieval period towards new traditions reflecting style, a degree of elegance and the emergence of larger and more open private space.

Mansion houses in an Irish context were usually symmetrical commodious buildings with three storeys and an attic, with decorative features that included large chimney stacks, stylized windows, often with mullion or hood mouldings, and numerous large fireplaces (see Kerrigan 1995, 65–7; Sweetman 1999, 175–92; O'Keeffe 2000, 55–6). Many of the doorways are equally elaborate but share common features with tower houses including yet-holes and a variety of arched forms. These structures were following earlier established trends in Renaissance architecture concerning designs of formal and symmetrical plans where their occupants were looking for increased luxury (Sweetman 1999, 175). Machicolations (projecting stone or wooden structures supported on corbels on outside walls used for dropping items on attackers), and bartizans are also often present (Sweetman 1999, 175). The majority of houses across the study region were constructed between 1615 and 1640 and have a similar distribution to the main centres of plantation activity in the Blackwater and Bandon valleys, and along the coastal fringe. There is a clear sense of ordered functionality running through these buildings. The ground floor is mostly a domestic space used as a kitchen or for storage with bread ovens and plain fireplaces located there. Ightermurragh in Cork has a date of 1641 on its groundfloor fireplace lintel. The first or second floor, depending on the size of the house, often functioned as a public space with private apartments accommodating large open rooms and elaborate fireplaces and decorative arrangements, at Mountlong in Cork for example, decorative plaster-work showing hunting and biblical scenes is evident internally on the second floor. In some way these spatial arrangements are directly reflective of earlier tower houses that contained very similar arrangements of space. It seems probable then that their emergence owes as much to the architectural fashions in England as to the houses of the disposed Gaelic lords and merchants of the previous century.

The mansion houses in Waterford share a number of common characteristics and are largely concentrated in the west of county, mostly controlled by Boyle (Moore 1999, 231). Each is two to three storeys in height with attics, with two to three large chimney stacks, and a series of large windows with external moulding. The houses are often t-shaped in plan with frequent fireplaces and internal wooden staircases. Ballyduff Lower appears to have been built in 1627 by Andrew Tucker. It was a rectangular structure incorporating three bays and three storeys with an attic. The windows have three to four lights with square hood-mouldings and a string course over a section of the first floor (ibid.). Sleady castle is recorded as having been built a year later and is also a rectangular structure with three bays, three storeys and an attic. It has a square bartizan incorporated into its northeast angle and also features a series of gun loops. Tikincor Lower is again a rectangular structure built over three floors and an attic. It has four bays with a two gable façade. The upper floors have a number of simple rectangular windows with square-hood mouldings but they are certainly not as elaborate as other houses. Smaller windows were placed at ground floor level and musket loops are evident. Nine fireplaces have been recorded internally and the house would originally have had wooden floorboards. A stringcourse can be seen directly above the second storey level and below the attic.

Little survives of the original medieval castle at Lismore. It was damaged during the Desmond Revolt of 1579 and had come into the possession of Walter Raleigh by 1590. Boyle had obtained the site by the first decade of the seventeenth century and subsequently became involved in significant alterations to its fabric. From 1614 works included the addition of family crest and arms, decoration and glazing work by the stairwell and in 1622 the study, bedchamber and nursery were coated with a 'Spanish white' (Townsend 1904, 126). Internal furniture included a number of large chairs and stools covered with a

> crimson velvet and fringed with silver and silk, an another set were of red, embroidered in black velvet. There were gilt bedsteads and quilts of needle-work or of Indian embroidery. The dining-room walls were hung with tapestry. On the floor was a foot Turkey carpet and the window seats were covered with velvet cushions. The dinner-table was loaded with plate. (ibid.)

The gardens were amongst the most impressive features of the site with three acres enclosed within a rectangular enclosing stone wall with turrets added in 1626. They consisted of a raised walk area with a series of terraces, stairways and a central path aligned on the town's Cathedral (Reeves-Smyth 2004). Musket loops and wall-walks were structural features on the small towers. Terracing in the garden with paving stones was also a feature. Lismore is described as being in ruins in the 1650s but some refurbishment took place late in the century. Smith's 1746 *Ancient and present state of the county and city of Waterford* provides a limited description of the castle but includes a valuable illustration of the site (fig. 56). The entrance is approached by an 'ancient and venerable avenue of stately trees. Over the gate are the arms of the first great earl of Cork, with his humble motto "*God's Providence is our Inheritance*". Most of the buildings remain in ruins since they were destroyed by the fire in the Rebellion. The several offices that make up

56 Lismore (source: Smith's 1745 *Ancient and present state of the county and city of Waterford*)

the two sides of the square are kept in repair. At each angle is a tower, the chief remains of its ancient state' (Smith 1746, 56). The castle was extensively rebuilt in the nineteenth century and only a number of basal sections of the structure can now be interpreted as being seventeenth-century in date. Again, a detailed contemporary archaeological survey would be valuable.

The inventories of county Cork list 22 mansion houses spread across much of the county with the exception of its central part. A number of different forms are present including those with four angle towers, (Monkstown, Mountlong and Kanturk), cruciform (Ightermurragh and Kilmaclenine), T-shaped (Reenadisert) and a number of other forms (Sweetman 1999). We need to be careful when examining these sites that we do not group them together as a single homogenous unit. There appears to be a 60-year-period when these mansion houses were built across the region. This, as we have seen, was a tumultuous period which witnessed significant political and architectural change. The influences and building charac-teristics evident in the later part of the sixteenth century would be somewhat different from those built in the middle part of the following century. There is also a degree of ambiguity about the ownership and original building dates of the mansions as we have remarkably little historical evidence associated with them. We need then to caution against an automatic assumption that these houses were linked to the new planters. Closer examination reveals that many were in fact built by the Gaelic lords or old English, demonstrating their readiness to change with the times. Coppinger's Court is one of the finest surviving examples of one such site (fig. 57).

Building conversion work at medieval Mallow castle had commenced prior to 1597 and was completed before 1610 when it was owned by the Jephson planter

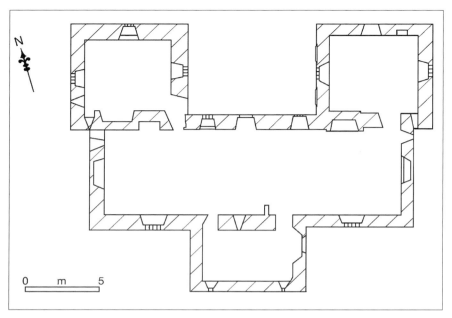

57 Ground floor plan of Coppinger's Court

family making it one of the earliest mansion houses in southern Ireland. It has a basic rectangular plan with three storeys and an attic. Two four-storey polygonal angle towers project from the southwest and northwest while two further angled towers project centrally from the mid sections of the east and west faces. Numerous windows with varying numbers of lights are present with a number of transoms and mullions. A sequence of pistol loops is also contained at ground-floor level. The early date of the castle made some form of defensive accommodation necessary given the recent ending of open conflict and war. Kanturk remains one of the more controversial of the houses (fig. 58). It appears unfinished and stands three storeys high with a possible fourth floor or attic, with a central block and four corner towers. The house has an elaborate doorway which is raised above ground level and would have been approached using steps (fig. 59). A second doorway has an arched entrance typical of those placed in later medieval tower houses. This presence of two distinct architectural styles is reflective of the complex negotiations the Gaelic lords underwent within the new political order. The main doorway is outwardly expressing participation in the new styles and economic process while the presence of the second doorway grounds the residents and visitors in a continuum of Gaelic traditions and activity. There is some conjecture as to why the building is unfinished but it appears to be related to the loss of MacCarthy lands after 1628 in the area and a downturn in their political

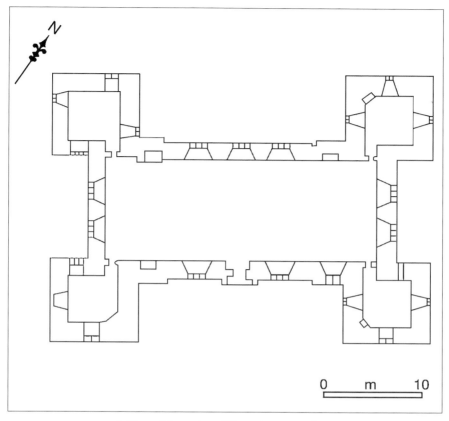

58 Ground floor plan of Kanturk mansion house

influence. As with many of the Cork houses it has pronounced string courses at each level.

Dickson (2005, 24) assigns the building of Monkstown to Anastasia Archdeacon in the 1630s and was later to pass to the earl of Cork's cousin after 1650 (fig. 60). A fireplace on the first floor contains a carved date of 1636 which may either be a foundation or refurbishment date. It sits on a prominent height overlooking the town of Monskstown and southwards towards Haulbowline Island and Cork Harbour. It is strongly built with four angle towers at each corner and small central space. The building had four storeys in each tower and an attic with three storeys in the central structure. Bartizans are evident at each corner and these features along with the generally smaller window size and number of pistol loops would indicate a greater awareness of security than other houses of the period. Sections of walling to the north, although incorporated into early modern out-buildings, would appear to be traces of an original bawn wall, a further security

59 The main entrance doorway at Kanturk mansion house

feature. Mountlong in west Cork, while sharing the same form, has similar loops but lacks bartizans. Coppinger's Court is one of the best-known examples of a mansion house in the county. It consists of a central rectangular block with square towers at its northeast and northwest angles. A third tower-like projection is centrally placed in the south facing wall. It was a three-storey building with an attic with numerous mullion and transom windows with hood mouldings. A series of loops are present on the ground floor and five machicolations were evident.

A number of mansion houses were built in the first quarter of the century by Gaelic lords throughout West Cork. The O'Driscolls built a house at Baltimore at this time while the MacCarthy Muclaghs built a house at Gerahameen (Power et al. 1992, 332). These houses were clearly representative of the political survival of a number of the Gaelic elite. In adopting these new house forms the Gaelic lords were doing a number of things. They were demonstrating externally their ability to adapt to the changing political climate and their ability to take on the emergent social norms under a new political order. The Geraldine knight of Kerry writes in 1642 about the 'fortified house' he had built in North Kerry that it was constructed 'for peace, it having more windows than walls' (McCarthy-Morrogh 1986a, 181). To some extent they were also marking a break with the traditions of the past in moving out of their tower houses in some instances and investing in this new type of residence. There is the potential to exaggerate this process too much though for as we have seen the spatial format of the mansion houses owes much to those of the tower houses. Fenlon (1996, 34) has also convincingly argued that they were expressing themselves as landowners in the English style and were essentially demonstrating their loyalty to the English administration and crown.

60 Early nineteenth-century drawing of Monkstown castle
(Henry Hill, Cork Public Museum)

Owen O'Sullivan built a mansion house at Reenadisert, outside of Bantry, in the first few decades of the seventeenth century (fig. 61). The house was built over looking a small, shallow, sheltered inlet, a position reflective of the decreased role O'Sullivan now played in this landscape. Its position, effectively in a small defined hollow is in marked contrast to the overtly centralized position previous O'Sullivan Beare tower houses adopted in the landscape. The house was T-shaped in plan with five pointed gables, three of which are mounted with elaborate brick mounts. Externally a series of squared windows with mullion divisions and dressed stone surrounds survive on the south wall. Bartizans are present on the southeast, and northwest corners of the east arm and on the southwest corner of the west arm. Other defensive features include machicolations with drop holes positioned in the base of the structures between the supporting stone corbels. In the context of seventeenth-century warfare these were ineffective. They lack pistol loops which further reduces their effectiveness.

The primary role of the building must have been in the provision of an elaborate and impressive English-style domestic residence for Owen O'Sullivan. Certainly the first-floor of the house is evidence of this. Aside from the well-lit nature of the rooms the elaborate fireplace on this floor in the west arm is indicative of this. While the fireplace is of a plain style, in comparison to others from both Cork and Kerry (Sherlock 2000), it is nonetheless an impressive

61 Detail of corner machiolation at Reenadisert

structure. It stands over 1.5m high, is in excess of 2.5m wide and is undecorated but lintelled. This is one of two surviving fireplaces in the west arm, the second positioned on the ground-floor level. The differences between both are stark. The first-floor example is well built, centrally placed, and is a dominant architectural feature at that level. It is clearly the primary fireplace in the main public chamber or long gallery of the owner. In practical terms its functions included the provision of heat but was also another physical expression of prestige and wealth. The fireplace on the ground-floor served a very different function. It was primarily a domestic entity and was probably the main cooking place within the residence. It is very large, standing in excess of 2m in height and is *c.*3m wide. This is a very plain stone built structure and it clearly lacks the centrality of the first-floor example. Its functionality is further demonstrated by the large projecting flue and chimney, 0.7m deep and 3.35m wide, which is so obvious on the external face of the north wall of the west arm. The presence of this large fireplace on the ground level strongly suggests that this level was the domestic level, used for storage, cooking and other similar tasks.

In Kerry the house at Tailor's Row in Castlegregory, possibly built by Gregory Hoare, a tenant-in-chief of the Desmonds, in the later part of the sixteenth century has been destroyed. However, a number of architectural fragments survive from the original house. Two inscribed arched sections, a gun loop and a dripstone have been found and mounted on a gateway in the main street. While the castle/mansion house constructed or refurbished by the Welshman and undertaker William Herbert at Castleisland no longer survives its owner left a detailed inventory of his possessions there in 1590 (Chinnery 2004, 201). Herbert arrived well provisioned with military equipment for over 30 men including small arms, armour and other fighting equipment. A garden, recreational walks and a hop yard for a brewhouse were created. The larder of the house was stocked with meal, malt, butter, chesses, bacon, bread, beer, soap, starch, 'spices of all sorts' and a variety of seeds including onion. Internally the house had three field bedsteads made from walnut, each with three pairs of bedsheets and hangings or curtains in red and yellow, green say and yellow dornix. Furniture included long table-board, square table-boards, bedsteads, cupboards, chests, stools, tables made from spruce, leather chairs, and a close stool with two pewter pans.

CROMWELLIAN DEVELOPMENTS IN SOUTHWEST CORK

With the onset on the political troubles of the 1640s the O'Sullivan Beare sided with the Irish rebels in a move that was ultimately to see the end of Gaelic land-ownership and power in the area. Little documentary information survives relating to the effect that this conflict had on the study area. The primary phase of Cromwellian activity in the Bantry and Beara region occurs after 1651/2. Cromwell had left Ireland in 1650, leaving the control of his forces with Henry Ireton, with the country essentially subdued (Prendergast 1865, 12; FitzPatrick 1988, 204–5). Gaelic power had been broken and the uprisings of the 1640s had been comprehensively put down. The Cromwellian confiscations of land and subsequent re-granting of it to soldiers and undertakers loyal to the Parliament was to have a fundamental impact on the nature and ownership of landholding throughout the country (Prendergast 1865, 78–89, 116–19; Aalen, Whelan and Stout 1997, 62, 67–8; Smyth 2000, 163–70). Bantry and Beara were no different. All of the lands of the O'Sullivan Beare were confiscated and were never returned. This, it is argued, is in effect the end of the later medieval period. Physically this change is manifested in the development of a number of new fortifications within the region, the founding of a number of new planter towns and the development and intensification of industry on the Beara Peninsula. The primary catalyst for these developments was the Anglo-Dutch war of 1651/2. Little activity seems to have occurred in the area during the main phases of the actual Cromwellian campaigns in Ireland apart from a local tradition that Bantry was used as a dizembarkation port for defeated rebel troops in 1650 (Carroll 1996, 162).

Newtown Town

This new town (Newtown) must have been established very soon after the foundation of the fort of the same name. Petty's Down survey in the mid-1650s

62 Thomas Philip's *c.*1680 vista of Bantry Bay (TCD MS 1209 (24))

shows *Bantry Town* and *Bantry fort* at Newtown and *Ballygubbin Towne* (at the site of modern Bantry) to the south (Hourihan 1985, 86). The town appears to have been set up in direct competition with Ballygubbin and was focussed on the exploitation of the fisheries of the Bay. In 1659 the Census of Ireland lists 67 settlers in the parish of Kilmacomogue (the parish which included Newtown and Bantry), while the garrison at the fort consisted of 113 foreigners (Pender 1939, 228–30). Newtown had a population of 119, of whom 34 were colonists while the townlands around Balligobane (Ballygubbin) had 74 persons, 16 of whom were foreigners. On 29 March 1661 Charles II wrote to the Lords Justices on behalf of Col. George Walters (*Cal. S. P. Ire.*, 1661, 283). Walters had settled his own and other English families at Bantry and intended establishing an English settlement there. The King recommended that he be granted the governorship of the fort at Bantry which had been

> erected there by the late usurper and in which there is a garrison. He shall be paid 5s. a day or less, as you think right. Should you think it well to withdraw that garrison, you shall put him in possession of the fort for his own safety and for that of the other English who shall plant there (ibid.).

Six years later on 18 December 1667 George Walters is recorded in the Irish Staple books as being from Whiddy and was then in debt of £340 to the staple towns (BL 15,635 f.211a). A number of plans survive of the town site including a vista of the location recorded by Thomas Philips in the mid 1680s (TCD MS. 1209 (24)) (fig. 62) and two French plans of the town, possibly recorded in 1689/90.

A number of letters written from Newtown in the 1660s testify to Orrery's presence at the site. On 4 February 1661/2 Thomas Walcott wrote to Orrery concerning money he owed relating to the grass and tithes of Robertstown and the Abbey (MacLysaght 1941, 19). He apologized for non-payment when Orrery was at *Newtowne*, and promized immediate payment on production and surrender by Sir (St) John Broderick of the written agreement concerning the letting. On 5 May 1663 Orrery wrote to Clarendon from Newtown (*Cal. Clarendon State Papers*, 1663, 312). Thirteen days later Orrery wrote to Ormonde from Charleville about the possibility of a French invasion and recorded that there is a small garrison at Bantry fort (*Cal. Clarendon State Papers* 1660–1726, vol. V, 544; Bodleian Library). On 25 August Orrery wrote to Secretary Bennet from *Newtowne* about affairs of state and the recent trial of the marquis of Antrim (*Cal. S. P. Ire.*, 1663, 224). The earl again wrote to Secretary Bennet from *Newtown* saying that he had been 'burning of fever for four weeks' and was writing for payments from the King. He had also prepared three greyhounds for the service of the Secretary. Unfortunately a 'mastif running through the streets [of Newtown ?] which flew at men as well as dogs, the brace of shagged dogs fell on him and killed him. Some think the mastiff was mad, and two of the three greyhounds being bit, I am forced to physic them to prevent the worst' (*Cal. S. P. Ire.*, 1663, 291). The Lord Chief Baron Jo. Byrsse wrote to Orrery from Dublin on 24 November acknowledging Orrery's letter of the 17th and expressing gladness he had recovered from his sickness. The letter was in relation to a petition from Orrery dealing with a debt he appears to have been falsely charged with in relation to lands at Killmuckey. The letter is addressed to Newtown, Co. Cork (MacLysaght 1941, 35).

The occupation of Newtown appears to have been short lived and its demise seems to have been brought about by direct economic competition with Bantry. In 1671 Arthur, earl of Anglesey, obtained a grant of 96,284 acres of the forfeited estates of the baronies of Bere and Bantry under the Act of Settlement. These lands included Ardnagashell and Ardneturrish, 2,247 acres at £7 p.a. rent; Comeholly [Coomhola], 1121 acres; Kilcaskan 1197 acres; Glangarrufe and Island (Island-J-Cullin) [Glengarriff], 6065 acres at £20 pa rent; Berehaven, 2215 acres at £7 pa rent; Derehin, 1480 acres; RossMcOwne, 1356 acres; Loughanbegg, 306 acres at £1 p.a. rent; Argroome, 2212 acres at £1 p.a. rent; area of Coulagh 2014 acres; Ballydonogane 1180 acres at £3 p.a. rent and 8 acres of Abbey Land (*Cal. Pat. Rolls*, Charles II, 1666–1685, 23). The earl had essentially received all of the lands of the former O'Sullivan lordship and was to hold them for the next century. One of the few other individuals who received part of the former Gaelic territories was Edward Adams, a London merchant, who received 446 acres in the northeast part of Carriganass in December 1666 (*Cal. Pat. Rolls*, Charles II, 1666–85, 21). Anglesey later procured a patent dated 15 March 1679 for holding fairs at Ballygobban on 29 and 30 May, 10 and 11 August and 4 and 5 October.

Markets could also be kept on Wednesdays and Saturdays. John Davis acquired a patent on 10 March for holding a fair on 2 November and the day following at Bantry (Newtown) (Bennett 1869, 337). It appears that this competition between Ballygubbin (Bantry) and Bantry (Newtown) spelled the end of the prosperity of the settlement. In July 1688 Decrees for the King were brought against the corporation of Newtown in the Four Courts. In 1689 the settlement at Newtown ('old town of Bantry') is described by John Stevens, who landed with the Jacobite forces at Bantry in May following the Battle of Bantry Bay, as lying half a mile from Bantry and 'is much like the new [town]' (Durrell and Kelly 2000, 16). This was not an overly complementary statement as he describes Bantry as a 'mizerable poor place, not worthy the name of a town, having not above seven or eight little houses, the rest very mean cottages' (Durrell and Kelly 2000, 15). He describes the fort, the building of which he ascribes to Cromwell, as being on a hill above the town and creek which had by then gone into decay but was 'never of any considerable strength'. The extent to which we must trust historical eyewitness accounts like this needs to be questioned. Stevens's statements on the nature of the town are in direct contrast to the prosperous-looking settlement shown in Philip's vista three or four years earlier. It appears to be a question of perception and what was a small 'mizerable place' in Stevens's eyes was most likely a standard small town in the southwest of Ireland at this date. Certainly the range of artefacts recovered from the trial trenches would support the view that Newtown was a relatively prosperous typical late seventeenth-century settlement.

Newtown is situated 1km north of modern Bantry town in a small eighteenth-century demesne. Now a green field site, it is dominated by Newtown House, a late eighteenth-century house, overlooking the shallow sheltered inlet of Gurteenroe c.200–300m wide at its mouth and leads to Dunnamark waterfall at its head. Sixty per cent of the inlet dries out at low water leaving the freshwater channel from Dunnamark flowing into the inlet. This river is a constant source of freshwater. A number of springs are also present within the Newtown estate, one of which was centrally placed within the former town site. Two very different plans of the town survive from the 1680s. In Philip's vista of Bantry Bay the village is shown in an inter-drumlin hollow overlooked by the fort to the west (fig. 63).

A number of general geographical factors can be inferred from this plan. Shelter was a primary consideration as demonstrated by its low-lying position in the hollow and by the fact that it is north facing and sheltered from the south-westerly prevailing winds. The physical focus of the settlement is on the sea which reflects its primary function as a fisher site. From a spatial perspective there appears to be six units contained within the town. Much of the western town appears to be an industrial quarter, indicated by the presence of only one building

64 Excavated finds from Newtown

and the absence of mortar or bonding of any kind would support this assertion. The presence of a number of iron nail fragments, a fragment of green glass and some slate all contained in secure datable contexts would instead argue for a timber-frame construction built on basal wooden sills with a slated roof. This interpretation is somewhat complicated by the presence of the stakeholes in one corner. No evidence of a stone footing or dwarf wall was uncovered and its seems that the basal sills would have been placed directly onto the ground in this very shallow trench, a process which of course would have left the structure susceptible to rotting (Grenville 1997, 34). It may be that the stakes were used to pin the sill-beam to the ground or represent some form of repair. Small fragments of burnt bone, again in secure contexts in the structure, would argue for a domestic function and this is further supported by the absence of materials relating to industrial processes.

The location of the house site is significant. It is clearly located on the periphery of the town as defined spatially by the cartographic evidence. However, it appears to be a house built for or by an English person. The structural character of the building is clearly English and the material culture, as defined by a number of pottery sherds which are all English wares, would also support the assignation of an English ethnic identity for the occupants of the building. Its presence then on the periphery in the town which has a higher Irish population than that of the English settlers, as defined by the 1659 Census, would argue against ethnic divisions within the town and argue instead for an integration and lack of division between the two groups. The upper disturbed layers of the trench did produce a number of sherds of Irish earthenware which also argues for the close proximity and integration of local material culture into the town. The artefactual evidence is still totally dominated by English wares though possibly demonstrating the dominance of English socio-economic structures.

Newtown is clearly the largest mid seventeenth-century settlement in the Bantry and Beara region. This is substantiated by the Census figures of 1659 which lists 119 individuals at the site, as previously noted (Pender 1939, 228–30). Remembering of course that this 'Census' only lists individuals who paid tax at a higher rate and the number of families with Irish names in each barony, the actual number of people in each settlement will be significantly higher. Other probable settlements of note at this time include 'Berehaven' with 82 people, 16 of whom were English and 66 Irish; Ardgroom with 33 people, four English and 29 Irish; Blackrock was still occupied with 44 people listed, nine of whom were English and 35 Irish. Ballygobban on the other hand seems to have experienced a downturn as only 11 people were listed, four of whom were English and seven Irish (Pender 1939). This possible fall in the numbers living at the site must be related to a movement of people to the newly established settlement at Newtown.

THE RURAL CHURCH

Following the Dissolution of 1536–40 the majority of monastic establishments and many churches within the English-controlled areas had either fallen out of use, were subject to limited usage or had been taken over by the Established Church (Watt 1972). Those in Gaelic areas fared little better and suffered from limited investment and disappearing tithes. A sixteenth-century commentator records that

> Some sayeth that the prelates of the church and clergy is much cause of all the misorder of the land; for there is no archbishop, ne bishop, ne prior, ne parson, ne vicar, ne any other person of the Church, high or low, great or small, English or Irish, that useth to preach the word of God, saving the poor friars beggars (Watt 1972, 182).

In 1571 the adventurer Edmund Tremayne writes, while travelling across Munster, that the Christian faith amongst the Irish has generally declined and that many of the churches lie like 'stables' (FitzPatrick and O'Brien 1998, 111). Edmund Spenser similarly comments that the ruined churches of Ireland need to be built up and repaired as they mostly 'lie even with the ground', while Sir John Davis writes to Lord Deputy Cecil in 1604 complaining that 'the churches are ruined and fallen down to the ground in all parts of the Kingdom' (*Cal. S. P. Ire.*, 1603–4, 143). Ecclesiastical visitations in 1615 to the south-west region recorded that a large number of the churches were now in ruin (Lunham 1909; 19–27; Power et al. 1992). In the diocese of Elphin the Catholic bishop recorded in 1631 that there were formerly 65 churches but only 5 remained and were used by Protestants (Cotter 2006, 266). A number of churches had then been subsumed into the new Established Church with Kilmocomoge, for example, belonging to the deanery of Foneragh in 1615 and the church was 'up and thatched' but the chancel was 'down' (*Archivium Hibernicum* II, 189). It was undergoing repair in 1627 but had been reduced to a state of ruin by 1667 (Brady 1863, vol. 1, 163). Daniel O'Wollohan is rector of Kilcatherine Church in 1591, while 'O'Linshigan' is listed as Vicar of the same church (*Cal. Papal Letters*, vol. 8, 424). Farnahoe in Inishannon was in repair in 1615 and again in 1639 but was extensively rebuilt in later centuries (Power et al. 1994, 299). The Royal Visitation of 1615 further records that the church at 'Killoconnenagh' was in a state of repair (*Archivium Hibernicum* II, 210). Larger centres were in a similar state of disrepair or were now being adopted for secular purposes. A number of agricultural buildings were constructed at Bridgetown Abbey in the late sixteenth or early seventeenth century. These were probably associated with the granting of the site to an undertaker. Iron working also took place at the site at this later date.

On the Iveragh Peninsula a number of churches became centres for Protestant worship. In the dioceses of Ardfert Kilcrohane was recorded in a 1622 list of its parish churches while Rathkieran was described as in good condition. The Royal Visitation of 1615 records that Cahersiveen church was standing and under the patronage of Edwardus Spring as was Killinane church, Glebe (O'Sullivan and Sheehan 1996, 352–5). Knockane was similarly standing and its minister was Willmus Lane in 1633. Thomas Harris was listed as incumbent minister for the parishes of Cahir and Glanbehy. On a larger scale, extensive excavations under-taken by Fionnbarr Moore at Ardfert Cathedral uncovered evidence for late medieval burial throughout the study period. The South transept was also extended into a pre-existing cemetery in the seventeenth century. A probably late medieval doorway level was found at the northeast doorway. Three post-medieval statues, roof slates and ridge tiles were also recovered.

Internal memorial monumentality is a feature of a number of seventeenth-century churches across Munster. Boyle's monument in Youghal has been discussed already but less well known are the monuments in Cloyne Cathedral and Kilcreadan church. At Cloyne both Sir John FitzEdmund Fitzgerald and his son Edmond are commemorated in a monument located in the northeast corner of the north transept (Harris 2002 171). Sir John was a leading landholder in Imokilly and was made mayor of Cork in 1570 and later knighted in 1602. He died in January 1612 and his son was to die in March of the same year. The monument consists of a plain altar tomb with a mural backplate, framed by single columns of the Ionic order. A coat of arms is illustrated with an inscription below which is a cadaver effigy of a skeleton lying on its side. A winged hourglass is present illustrating the passing of time while the skeleton grips a scythe as a symbol of death and the grim reaper. The tomb's panels show a variety of implements including a shield, sword, dagger, halberd, spear, musket and a vizered casque. Two kneeling male effigies were formerly part of the tomb but now lie apart from it. At Klicreadan Sir Robert Tynte, third husband to Spenser's widow Elizabeth, whom he married in 1612, is commemorated in an elaborate tomb dated 1636 (Harris 1999). Tynte is shown lying recumbent and dressed in armour with a sword. Two female effigies, apparently his two wives, kneel either side of him with the figure at his feet dressed in a bodice with lace decoration at the breast and with ribbon ties. The monument has incised ornamentation including an armorial shield and a series of implements including a drum, musket, a helmet and swords as well as a variety of other items. The inscription records that Tynte of Somerset 'caused this church and monument to be (built), by the providence of Almighty God, in the year of our lord 1636'. Tynte died in 1643. The church was built on an earlier foundation and consists of a rectangular building measuring 17m in length and 5.5m in width with a round arched doorway to the west and a lintelled doorway on the north wall. A second monument commemorating the Chief Justice of Munster Sir Edward Harris and his wife Elizabeth in evident on the north wall. It consists of two kneeling figures facing each other but is in a poor state of preservation.

POST 1660

The conflict of the 1640s, Cromwellian interventions in the 1650s and the subsequent Restoration brought about significant change across the Munster landscape. The dwindling power of many of the lordships was finally eroded with the Cromwellian confiscations and subsequent regranting of lands. Cox's survey of c.1680 paints a changing picture of settlement patterns in the study area. He divided urban centres into three primary groupings: towns, villages/ petty villages and decayed/ ruined villages. The character of the landscape has changed with many towns including Middleton, Doneraile, Charleville and Castlemartyr having parks surrounding them (Flanagan 1991). Improved communications are a central feature of the preceding decades with roads being constructed into Kerry and the more rural parts of Cork and many new bridges being built – Fermoy and Mallow in 1666. In 1639, immediately prior to the conflict, proposals had been put forward to substantially rebuild the North Bridge at Cork 'with sound and good timber … and be well paved over with stone, gravel and sand' (Caulfield 1867, 196–7). The South Bridge was also to be redeveloped with a 'like pavement'.

One of the most significant changes was the emergent dominance of a small number of landowners, reflected not only in their political power but also in the new forms of houses and monumentality they constructed in the landscape. Barnard (2004) has documented the material culture of these individuals. In particular he notes the importance of the mansion house at Charleville built by Orrery from 1661 with subsequent expansion over the following two decades (Barnard 2004, 50). This house was built in a new, almost palatial style, but retained the 'little old fashioned flankers such as most noble men and gentlemen's houses have to this day in Ireland'. It was extensively furnished with hangings, carpets and curtains, its most obvious display of wealth and prestige.

CHAPTER 6

Fortifying the Landscape

Conflict played a major part in the shaping of the region's cultural landscape in the period under study. This was a defining era in the geopolitics of western Europe with renewed warfare and empire-building ambitions by the major players on the European stage including England, France and Spain. The almost continual conflict between these nations both directly and indirectly affected Ireland through proposed invasion attempts, support for uprisings and England's developing view of Ireland as being of strategic importance and as a source of provisions for its war and colonial efforts. The widespread adoption of artillery changed the physical practice of warfare and the appearance of military sites. Elaborate siege works were now erected and armies became increasingly professional with full-time garrisons being deployed across the countryside. Conflict was not just confined to perceptions of external threat but also took place between the Gaelic Irish septs as both individuals and family groupings took alternate views of England's colonial efforts, variously engaging in resistance and economic collaboration. This invariably led to internal disputes within the septs and a re-evaluation of their inter-relationships, expressed physically in increased usage of defence mechanisms in their places of residence.

Changing approaches to warfare and defence
Approaches to military strategy and defensive structures begin to change radically in Ireland in the second half of the sixteenth century. These changes in approach and attitude are led primarily by the widespread adoption and increased usage of artillery warfare. Traditionally, defence in an Irish context was achieved through large castle structures with substantial walls in well-chosen topographical positions. The Gaelic Irish did not invest heavily in these larger castles and preferred the temporary security offered by tower houses. Inter sept conflict was mostly fought in fleeting engagements using the natural landscape for cover and manoeuvring. Movement was a key factor in this strategy so a familiarity with siege and large-scale warfare was not part of the Gaelic mentality. This absence of an expertise in

the type of warfare coming to dominate Europe at this time is well reflected in the use of French and Spanish soldiers during the course of the Nine Years War and the inherent advantage the English forces had, having experienced this form of conflict over the preceding decades. One of the earliest physical impacts of this new warfare comes in 1580 with the fortification of the Dún an Óir site in Kerry. The landing Spanish forces constructed an earthen embankment with demi-bastions at either end of the structure, each supporting single cannon, on an exposed headland on the western shores of Smerwick Harbour. A further spear-shaped gun emplacement is illustrated on a contemporary plan projecting into the bay while a series of tents and huts are shown in the central area of the fort (Jones 1954–6, 40). This possibly marks the earliest occurrence of this type of fortification in Ireland and it therefore comes as little surprize that it reflects the continental origin and experience of the fort's garrison. These types of forti-fication, exemplified by the star-shaped fort, emerge as direct defensive solution to the use of cannon in warfare. There are a number of key components to the defensive capabilities of these structures. The ability to withstand sustained attack from direct fire results in large embankments being constructed with both internal and external ditches. The internal ditches could constitute secondary lines of defence in larger forts and could also function as covered walkways where the defenders could move freely around. The banks were fronted by sloping earth banking designed to absorb the impact of cannon fire. Angled bastions were also created to allow for interlocking fields of fire, a direct move away from the limited sphere of view from a tower house window for example. These bastions were primarily designed as gun emplacements as well as accommodating infantry fire.

In the years following the failed Smerwick landing conflict with both France and Spain led to a number of initiatives to further protect the coast. In October 1587 instructions were issued to fortify Waterford harbour due to its perceived strategic importance (Kerrigan 1995, 41). A blockhouse was constructed at Passage East while a series of gun emplacements and other earthwork defences were initiated and largely complete by May 1590. Similar concerns relating to possible invasion and pirate activity were expressed about the ports of the southwest coast including Glandore, Castlehaven, Baltimore and Beara.

Plantation defences
The arrival of the undertakers across Munster from 1586 onwards was met with a variety of responses varying from economic engagement and encouragement to periodic resistance. The levels of engagement that the new settlers took part in is reflective how they structured their settlements and to their perceived sense of threat. At the Beacon/Goldfinch sponsored settlement at Blackrock in the inner

Bantry Bay area the early English settlers erected a palisade, standing over 4m in height, around their houses in response to the threat that the displaced Clandonnel Roe posed and the fact that McCarthy Reagh engaged in a lengthy campaign of harassment against the settlers (SP/63/132/39; 158/46; Lambeth, *Carew MSS* 625, f. 36v; McCarthy-Morrogh 1986, 86). The foundation trench for this feature was located during the course of excavations of the site. It averaged 1.2m wide and was *c*.0.4m deep with a square profile with a slightly rounded bottom (Breen 2005). Two postholes of original palisade timbers were located within two small sections excavated across the trench. The first posthole was circular in plan, measuring 0.27m in diameter and 0.25m deep, with stone packing on three sides. The second post was of an irregular shape and measured 0.28m in maximum width and was 0.18m deep. A large quantity of wood-charcoal was found in this post suggesting that it had been burnt down.

Gaelic responses

Three major factors played a role in the development or refurbishment of the tower houses and primary residences of the Gaelic Irish lords throughout the southwest: the arrival of the English settlers, the outbreak of various conflicts in the later part of the sixteenth century and a series of internecine disputes. Refurbishment and refortification of tower houses and often the associated erection of enclosing bawns or other forms of defence can then be interpreted in different ways including resistance against the new settlers, defence against both internal and external threats as well as expressions of confidence in both a socio-economic and political sense.

Bawn walls

The late construction of bawn walls is a feature of a number of tower house sites across Munster. In North Kerry the extensive defences surrounding the island tower house at Carrigafoyle were refurbished by John O'Connor in 1580 in defence against English forces under the command of William Pelham (Toal 1995, 275). A 21m-long section of part of this enclosing element survives to the west of the central tower. At Castleconway, on the Iveragh peninsula, a bawn was likely constructed around the tower house in 1583 when it was granted to Captain Jenkin Conway (*Cal. Car. MSS* 1587), although no above-ground trace of the structure survives. Excavations at Kilcolman castle in north Cork uncovered an interesting sequential development of the bawn wall in the later part of the sixteenth century (Klingelhofer 2005). It is probable that at the time of Spencer's occupation of the site the internal area of the enclosure almost doubled in size when it was extended northward. However, the excavator suggests that this

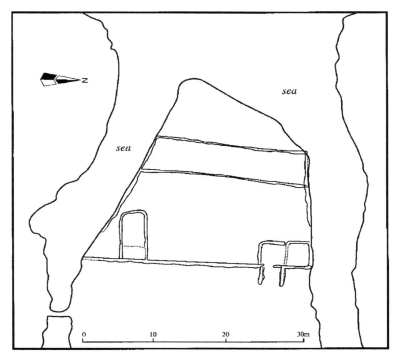

65 Dursey Island fort, Co. Cork

extension was not necessarily defensive and was possibly more likely associated with the creation of a walled garden. Such a development is indicative of an increased sense of security felt by some of the English arrivals, in direct contrast to the turmoil evident amongst other groupings.

At Castlefreke or Rathbarry Castle a bastion which originally would have accommodated cannon survives in a section of the enclosing wall. The bastion contains arched opes and is semi-hexagonal in shape. This is probably a later feature than the refurbished bawns of the later part of the sixteenth century and is likely related to the eight-month long siege of 1642. A substantial bawn wall measuring 65m x 50m survives at Castlemartyr in east Cork (Power et al., 1994, 223). Extensive refurbishment work took place at this tower house site in the seventeenth century following its acquirement by Richard Boyle, most notably through the erection of a new building complex incorporating the bawn. While there is an element of defensive construction to this feature the refurbishment was mostly related to the building of an elaborate building range along the south wall, now characterized by three substantial chimney stacks and a number of surviving windows with mullions and hood mouldings.

Dursey fort and the siege of Dunboy

Elsewhere in the southwest branch's of the O'Sullivan Beare responded to both the internal conflict and external threat from English forces during the Nine Years War in a number of different ways. Don Philip O'Sullivan Beare in his *Compendium of the history of Catholic Ireland*, published in Lisbon in 1621, refers to his father Dermot building a fort on Dursey Island in the later part of the sixteenth century (Byrne 1903, 156). The fort was built on a small headland on the southeast corner of Dursey Island directly overlooking Dursey Sound (fig. 65). It is currently a rectangular enclosure encompassing all of the apex of the promontory currently with a stone-built enclosing wall measuring 32.5m east/west by 24m north/south, giving an internal area of 780m². The walls are on average 1–1.2m in width and are built using coursed uncut small sandstone slabs. The east-facing section of the fort cuts off the promontory and is the most defensive portion of the site as its remaining three sides consist of steep vertical cliff faces. Its entrance feature consists of a short, formerly walled avenue, 3m long, leading to a 2.5m wide entrance with a square guard hut structure, measuring 3.5m by 3.5m, lying immediately inside the entrance on its northern side. An internal rectangular building, orientated east/west, measures *c*.3m x 6m in width and length and may have served as a domestic-type residence, officer's quarters or block house. The *Pacata Hibernia* (1633, 564) refers to an inner and outer fort with gun emplacements for 'three iron pieces of Spanish Ordnance' placed at the eastern end of the headland (ibid.). This site is important for a number of reasons. It is a good example of the transitional military thinking the Gaelic Irish were undergoing at this time. On the one hand they are selecting a remote location to store cattle and supplies and hold hostages (*Pacata Hibernia* 1633, 565); on the other hand the presence of artillery at the site marks a significant departure for the way the Gaelic Irish now conduct their defence and is clearly representative of continental influence in their strategy. Spanish gunners were employed to work the guns while the Irish engaged in more traditional forms of engagement. Artillery defence marks a significant movement away from the guerrilla-type warfare that the Gaelic-Irish had been engaged in over the last number of centuries where the defence capabilities of natural landscape and hit-and-run tactics had been used to good effect. This engagement with artillery is also amply reflected in the mechanisms employed to defend Dunboy during the post-Kinsale siege (Breen 2005). In 1601/2 Donal Cam began to redesign the defences of Dunboy castle with Italian and Spanish soldiers in advance of the arrival of English forces under George Carew. In May 1602 Carew writes to the Lord Deputy describing the siege fortifications at Dunboy stating that the castle was 'ramparted-round with [a] barbican 18 feet in thickness as high as the top of the barbican and thereupon have raised a parapet of earth; upon this rampart they have placed their artillery and have taken down the castle to the vault which is a pike length above the barbican' (*Cal. S. P. Ire.*, 1601–03, 240). The siege fortifications were also recorded in the *Pacata Hibernia* as follows

> the Barbican whereof being a stone wall of sixteene foot in height, they faced with soddes intermingled with wood and faggots (above four and twenty foot thick) for a defence against the Cannon; they had also sunke a low Plat-forme to plant their Ordnance for a counter-battery, and left nothing undone, either within or without the castle, that in their opinions was meet for defence (*Pacata Hibernia* 1633, 520).

Excavation work undertaken from 1967 to 1973 (Gowen 1978, 1) and 1989 (Klingelhofer 1992, 89) exposed these siege works. The sub-rectangular barbican with an external rampart of earth and sod to protect against cannon was located closely positioned against the tower house walls. A section of this wall was subject to an immediate pre-siege alteration which strengthened it. Bastioned angles were also incorporated into the overall defensive mechanism to allow for the strategic positioning of gun emplacements.

Subsequent feuding resulted in Donal Cam O'Sullivan disputing his uncle Owen's claim to the title and territories of the O'Sullivan Beare (Breen 2005). As a direct result of this conflict Owen erected a substantial bawn wall around his tower house at Carriganass, north of Bantry, in order to protect himself from internal sept aggression. The bawn also constituted a more formal statement of intent by Owen, physically demonstrating his capability to erect a defensive stronghold to match the primacy of the O'Sullivan Beare chiefry site at Dunboy, and presented a direct architectural challenge to Donal Cam's claim to the sept title. The bawn is roughly rectangular in shape with four spear-shaped corner bastions located on the northern bank of the River Ouvane and an internal area of 882m^2. A number of gun loops are present with lintelled splayed embrasures on its walls and visible in three of the bastions but there is no evidence of larger gun emplacements. This was clearly a structure built with defence against local aggressors in mind given the lack of consideration for artillery and the fact that internally it was set up to house a garrison with its domestic or office quarters built along the southern range and the provision of a fireplace in the southeast bastion. Owen's intentions were put to the test in 1602 when Donal Cam attacked with the site with Don Philip O'Sullivan recording that he 'reduced it [Carriganass] partly by raising a rampart, partly by towers, mantlets, sows and gabions, and partly battering it with brass cannon' in 1601/2 (Byrne 1903, 152).

However, with Donal Cam subsequently defeated at Dunboy, Owen went on to largely maintain his position and later move from Carriganass to a newly built mansion house at Reenadisert. Similar defences were built at the MacCarthy Reagh tower house at Kilbrittan. The southeast circular corner tower of the enclosing bawn had up to six gun-loops in its ground floor walls. Significant repair and refurbishment work has taken place at this site and much of the original bawn structure is now gone.

Kinsale siege works

It has already been demonstrated that the siege of Kinsale was a defining event in the history of seventeenth-century Munster. The occupying Spanish forces were immediately at a disadvantage in the low-lying nature of the town. Its original medieval physical focus was on the sheltered harbour and the opportunities this presented for maritime based trade so it mattered little that this sheltered hollow was surrounded by low hills and would later be so susceptible to besiegement by artillery. In order to keep the entrance to the port open the Spanish also occupied Castlepark, where a large star-shaped fort was to be built shortly afterwards and Rincurran on the eastern shore, the location of the late seventeenth-century Charles Fort. A gun emplacement and observation post appears to have been placed on Compass Hill, south of the town, while the defenders also constructed a series of parallels running from the north western sector of the town as well as to the south and southwest.

The English in response constructed an elaborate siege around Kinsale. The Lord Deputy's camp was established on the main Cork road directly north of the town above the 200m contour mark, probably at the place now known as Camphill. On a map published in Stafford's *Pacata Hibernia* in 1633 this fort is shown a large rectangular structure with four corner bastions (Morgan 2004). Two further bastion-like structures are shown on both the north and south walls while a rounded gun emplacement in shown centrally placed on the north wall and a more elaborate bastion-like structure placed centrally on the south wall. It is unclear as to the structural nature of the fort but it was likely to consist of a surrounding trench with an earthen embankment, possibly topped by a fence or palisade. The earl of Thomond's siege camp was initially positioned on Ballinacubby Hill but was later moved closer to the South Gate of the town (Shiels 2004, 343). Two further small earthen work forts were established to the southwest to close off this access to the town and provide cover for ordnance on high ground between Thomond's camp and the Bandon River. Thomond's camps were again rectangular with variously shaped bastions while the two sconces were irregular in form. A series of elaborate parallels linked each of these defensive positions. A battery was placed below this just north of the Abbey. Three batteries were established at Scilly and on the eastern side of the Cork road. Two further batteries were located at Ardbrack and Forthill respectively. Finally a naval blockade was put in place at the entrance to the harbour. In 1940 O'Neil undertook a survey of the fortifications associated with the siege but only found what he interpreted as elements of 'Sir Jaratt's Horseis' scone 'some 210 yards west south west of Cappagh House … most of its outline is just traceable as a hollow in the fields on each side of the road and its eastern bastion exists as a formless lump in the field. It seems to have been 90 to 100 yards square' (O'Neil 1940, 114).

STAR-SHAPED FORTS

Star-shaped forts were enclosed structures built of earth and/or masonry and were used to mount and resist cannon (Hogg 1970, 110–21; see Kerrigan 1995, for overview of star-shaped forts in Ireland). They worked as defensive fortifications through the strategic placement of cannon on salient angles or bastions which aspired to command a full 360° line of fire around the fort (Klingelhofer 1992, 93). Each bastion was roughly spear-shaped and projected from each of the salient angles on the fort. The walls of the fort were fronted by low thick-profiled ramparts, 4–6m thick, built of earth and sods and revetted with stone, which were built to absorb the impact of cannon. The ramparts were in turn surmounted by a parapet, access to which was gained by a series of steps or ramps from the interior. The forts were also almost exclusively surrounded by a deep external ditch. The size and sophistication of each fort was governed by a wide variety of factors. Strategic positioning was obviously of primary importance with many of the forts positioned to protect harbours, sea-lanes, communication routes and significant settlements (see Gowen 1979). Local factors also influenced location and design. Topographic suitability was an over-riding concern. Forts had to be positioned on well-drained soils as sandy soils were subject to sliding. Well-drained soils also mitigated against damp and flooding which was of especial importance to a fort designed specifically for artillery. An elevated position with commanding vistas was an important military requirement as well. Financial resources, personnel, building expertise and tools would all have played a role in determining the nature of the structure (Gowen 1979). Many of these factors fluctuated so forts periodically fell out of usage while others were re-established or re-fortified.

The combination of all of the defensive and aggressive characteristics of these forts points to structures that were fundamentally different to the tower houses built in the study region over the previous centuries. Star-shaped forts were exclusively military structures built to house a garrison of professional soldiers and to engage in artillery warfare. They had no other major role to play within society other than the protection of the surrounding land from hostile forces. This mono-functionality is reflected in the short-term occupation of many of the sites and their subsequent abandonment and decay once a period of conflict ends. Only the larger sites associated with urban settlements or important ports appear to have been occupied for any length of time.

Post-1601 defences

In the immediate aftermath of the Kinsale siege the English initiated a number of building programmes to prevent a further recurrence of the taking of such an important port. Paul Ive designed and constructed a large pentagonal bastioned fort, over 200m in external diameter, on a pre-existing tower house site at Castlepark (Kerrigan 1995, 55). By October 1604, at a cost of £675, it was finished but a central complex was later built between 1608 and 1611 in recognition of the fact that the original fort would require a large garrison of over 500 soldiers to defend it successfully. The outer fort consists of a pentagonal structure with five angled earthen-built bastions each linked by an earthen embanked curtain wall. Sections of the bastions are revetted with stone while an external ditch or dry moat is evident around the external length of the fort with an approximate width of 15m. This outer fort encloses an area of *c.*100m by 120m (Power et al. 2004, 288). The inner complex consists of a rectangular fort with four corner bastions with external dry ditch, two internal towers and a complex of garrison buildings grouped around a courtyard (O'Donnell, 2002). The works were carried out under the supervision of Josias Bodley who had been governor of Duncannon fort from 1604 to 1607. Bodley reports at the time that the walls of this inner defensive complex were 5.5m high and backed with earth, the square towers were to be used for storage while remaining buildings were garrison lodgings. While this work was taking place at Castlepark Bodley was also involved in works at Duncannon, Haulbowline and Limerick castle. At Duncannon the rampart was enlarged, the external ditch widened and a new gatehouse and gun platforms were built (Kerrigan 1995, 60). A new gatehouse was also built at Haulbowline, described as being in a ruinous state prior to 1611, while a square central tower was erected centrally, new garrison quarters were built and the existing fortifications repaired. Work on a fort at Haulbowline had started in the summer of 1602 after the Lord Deputy had requested a magazine be built to service Cork (Mulcahy 1959–60, 127). A southeast bastion was constructed at Limerick castle and the existing gatehouse was repaired.

garrison and dignitaries continued to use an old circular blockhouse on the quay. A blockhouse was built at Castlepark following various proposals put forward in 1605, 1621 and 1626. This was a semi-octagonal fronted battery with double-splayed embrasures designed to accommodate seven guns with 2m thick walls on the ground floor. It was built on the waterfront below Castlepark fort immediately above the high water mark, and accessed from the fort by a covered way. This low-lying location ensured it adopted a highly strategic position for controlling ship movement in and out of the inner harbour area. A number of rooms are located at the rear of the ground floor, one of which served as a domed magazine, with the remainder serving as administrative and accommodation quarters. By July 1636 Castlepark is reported as being in ruins but Charles I designated Kinsale as the base for his Irish fleet off the south coast. Proposals were put forward for the erection of a storehouse, wharf and crane with officer's quarters (Kerrigan 1995, 84). Captain Thomas Kettleby subsequently visits the town in 1637 to advise on the building work and the construction of a dock to the southwest of the fort.

Post-1641
The eruption of violence throughout Ireland in 1641/2 gives rise to a further prolonged period of unrest. Some refortification of existing garrisons takes place including the erection of earthwork defences at Bunratty by the English garrison in 1646. In the final years of the uprisings Prince Rubert sponsored the expansion of defences at Kinsale in 1649 to protect his fleet including the erection of outworks at Castlepark consisting of southerly square redoubts linked to the main fort with entrenchments. Two further gun platforms were built on both sides of the entrance to the harbour and a demi-bastion and two bastioned fortification were added to the southwest of the town walls creating a 'New Line' of defence running down to the water's edge. However, it is not until 1651, following Cromwell's successful campaigns and the later emergence of the Commonwealth, that a further phase of fortification took place. Much of this new work was supported by the parliamentary forces in anticipation of an external rather than an internal threat, in particular a number of coastal forts were erected around the south western Munster coast. During the course of the Anglo-Dutch Wars in 1652–3 forts were established at Valentia Island, Kenmare, Dunboy and Bantry.

Protecting Bantry Bay
Lord Broghil, later earl of Orrery and lord president of Munster, was responsible for the construction of a star-shaped fort one mile north of Bantry at Newtown and a second irregular fort surrounding Dunboy Castle (*Cal. Clarendon State Papers* 1660–1726, vol. V, 544; Bodleian Library). These two forts were built in

1652 to protect against Dutch shipping and to safeguard the important anchorages in the lee of Whiddy Island and in Berehaven. Details on the construction of the star-shaped fort at Newtown are somewhat confused. This area was one of the most south westerly geographical areas affected by the Cromwellian wars. Smith suggests that sometime in the 1650s Henry Ireton, Cromwell's son-in-law, built the star-shaped fort north of Ballygubbin (Smith 1750). However, in May 1663 Orrery wrote to the duke of Ormonde about the possibility of a French invasion and listed a number of garrisons in Ireland. He records 'the small fort at Bantry opposite Whiddy Island built by the writer during the last Dutch War [1652–3] which has a company in it' (*Cal. Clarendon State Papers* 1660–1726, vol. V, 544). On 25 May 1666 Lord Orrery writes from Charleville about the fort at Bantry saying that

> It is a small one, but regular, and consists of four small bastions, the faces of which are but forty-eight feet long, and the planks eighteen; the curtain ninety feet long. All the stoccadoes, which were on the inside on the brick of the graff, and placed there in the nature of a false bray, are rotted away, the guns unmounted, the drawbridge broken, and but one company of sixty men in it, commanded by Captain Manly (*Cal. S. P. Ire.*, 1666–9, 92; Bennett 1869, 389).

It then appears that following the fort's construction in the early 1650s it was not maintained well. Certainly by the end of the Cromwellian period it had fallen into a state of disrepair but was still garrisoned. However, eleven years later the deterioration of the fort had continued and it was now badly in need of repair. In October 1677 an estimate was put forward for the repair of Bantry Fort. The account records that the

> fort is built of lime and stone, consisting of bastions. In it are houses built for two hundred men, but all are out of repair, and some wholly unroofed, walls defective, gates and drawbridge decayed, the dry graff round the fort to be cleared; all which repair will cost £400. In this fort must be mounted, on standing carriages, eight guns, which will cost £56; making a new platform £15; and for repairing the magazine £80 (Bennett 1869, 389).

This repair, or at least part of it, evidently took place as Philip's 1680s vista of Bantry Bay clearly shows the fort as an intact and functioning entity (NLI MS 3137 (42); TCD MS 12092 (24)). In the vista the fort is shown with upstanding walls which appear to be stone built and are surrounded by a trench (fig. 68). A number of gun ports appear at the head of the southeast facing wall while larger

68 Detail of Newtown fort from Philips's vista of Bantry Bay

cannon ports are shown on the north eastern and south eastern bastions. Each bastion is spear-shaped and a series of three steps are shown leading up to the interior of the north western bastion. None is shown mounted with guns. Two buildings are shown in the interior. A smaller building with a single chimney on its eastern gable is situated in the north eastern sector of the fort. It is built against or close to the fort's ramparts and has two windows and door facing inwards to the centre of the fort. A second, larger, building is shown running the full width of the fort at the south west. It is clearly a two-storey building with a single-storey annex to the rear. Three chimneys are shown on a high gabled roof. This division

Cannon length	Feet	Inches
Demi-culverin (large)	7	8
Demi-culverin (large)	8	10
Saker	8	0
Saker (unserviceable)	8	0
Mynion scald	7	0
Mynion scald	6	4
Falcon scald	6	6
Falcon scald	6	3
Round Shot for Culverin:	8	
For demi-culverin:	57	
For saker and mynion:	32	
Standing carriages:	(unserviceable)	

Table 6.2 A 1677 list of armaments in the fort at Newtown (after Bennett 1869)

of buildings can be interpreted in a number of ways. The small building could
have accommodated the officers while the ordinary soldiers, equipment and the
mess were located in the main building. Alternatively the munitions and
equipment could have been stored in the smaller building. The latter is less likely
given that a chimney is shown on this smaller building.

A well was positioned internally at the south eastern end of the fort. This was
open until 1979 when it was capped (Alec O'Donovan, landowner, pers. comm.).
Local tradition also records that the cannon from the fort were dumped into the well
following abandonment. While this appears unlikely, there is a very high magnetic
signature from this feature indicating a high ferrous content. The entrance to the fort
was centrally placed on the north western facing wall. In 1689 the fort was destroyed
by Irish forces but a later report suggested it should be rebuilt (*Cal. S. P. Dom.*,
1694–5, 94). This report went on to suggest that if it was rebuilt it should be
physically located closer to the sea so that it could better protect shipping lying at
anchor. It is clear this rebuilding never took place and the fort fell into disuse.

The fort now consists of a much overgrown earthwork, 200m south of the
small eighteenth-century demesne house at Newtown (fig. 69). Its interior is
roughly square in shape, measuring 38m in length on its north-west/south-east
axis and 40m on its north-east/south-west axis, giving an internal area of 1520m2,
excluding the internal area of the bastions. It is likely that the fort was originally
very regular in plan taking into account that these measurements are approximate
contemporary dimensions which have to take account of soil slippage and
collapse of the banks of the fort. This modern collapse and destruction has then
affected the original symmetry of the structure. Four identical pointed bastions
are placed at each corner and the capped well is centrally placed at the south
eastern side of the fort, 8m in from the inner bank. This central portion of the
fort clearly had an inner earthen-ramparted bank protecting the interior, as
indicated by the surviving nature of the earthworks and by the excavation
evidence on the site. This bank and rampart would have been in excess of 4m
wide originally, accommodating an outer facing earthen slope built to take the
force of cannon fire. This in turn would have been surmounted by a stone and
timber palisade or *stockade*, which protected a raised walkway or parapet termed
a *false bray*. The bank was surrounded by an earth-cut ditch, which follows the
complete circuit of fort averaging 2m in depth and 4m in width. Stone revetment
survives on both the inner and outer faces of the ditch but much of this has been
robbed out. The ditch is rectangular in profile with straight sides and constitutes
the *dry graff* in seventeenth-century literature. It is unclear as to whether there was
an external bank. Traces of possible earthworks which have this appearance are
visible at various places around the fort.

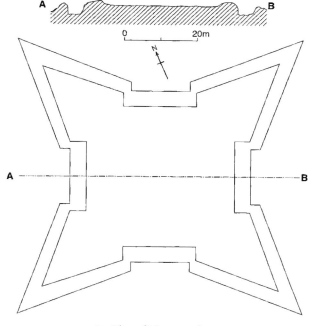

69 Plan of Newtown fort

Newtown Fort excavations

A trial excavation trench measuring 7m by 1m was carried out in the summer of 2000 to try and ascertain the validity of the illustrative depictions of the fort and ground-truth the geophysical survey which had been carried out in the interior (excavation/survey licence no. 00E00849) (fig. 70). Magnetic susceptibility and magnetic gradiometry surveys combined with topographic survey strongly suggested the presence of two large buildings at either side of the fort combined with an internal wall or revetment (Kelly 1999). Subsequent excavations at the southwest of the fort uncovered the collapse of the stone revetment wall for the internal raised walkway and the southwest wall of a large building with an internal cobbled surface. This later feature consisted of the foundation courses of a mortared wall, built using flat sandstone blocks that were faced internally. The wall survived to a height of 0.3m and was 0.6m wide. Interestingly this is a reduction in wall width of 25–30% from the average wall width of structures in the fifteenth and sixteenth century where the church buildings and tower houses invariably had a wider wall width of 0.8m–1m. The building uncovered clearly had a slate roof given the amount of collapsed slate material which overlay the cobbled floor of the building. There are numerous slate quarries in the vicinity

Plan

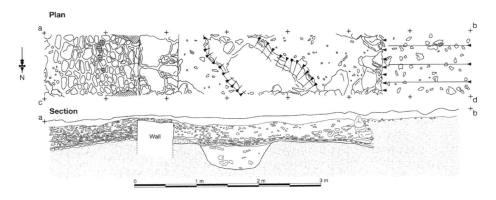

70 Plan and section of excavation trench, Newtown fort

that could have provided this material. A fragment of a roof tile was also recovered from the trench indicating the relatively high status the building originally had and of the level of investment which went into its construction. The roof tile was a green glazed North-Devon ridge tile with a flat-toped crest of a type dating from the 1650s and 1660s onwards (Wren 1997, 151). Three stab marks appear below the crest on either face of the tile. This stabbing helps consolidate the thicker part of the tile during the firing process but may also be a decorative feature (Wren 1997, 151). Few of these tiles have been found on Irish excavation sites which provides an indicator of their possible status.

The excavation also clearly defined the chronology of activity at the site. The first phase of fort development involved the selection of the site for construction, the highest point on a drumlin positioned directly south of Newtown that provided good vistas over the entrances to the Bay and to the anchorage between Whiddy Island and the mainland. The fort was then laid out symmetrically and drainage trenches were dug from the corner bastions to ensure a well-drained site. One of these drains crossed the excavation trench and measured 0.7m in width and 0.4m in depth and was flat-bottomed with straight sides. Drainage was of primary importance to these site-types because of the need to keep the ordnance and munitions dry (Gowen 1979). Ramparts were then built utilizing the natural topography of the drumlin. The inner face of the earthen rampart was vertical and faced with stone consisting of small rough uncut sandstone boulders that are naturally plentiful both in the fields and on the foreshore below the fort. The inner garrison buildings were then erected and an inner cobbled surface laid down. The fort was then occupied (periodically?) for at least 30 years before being abandoned and left to deteriorate. This abandonment is marked by an initial collapse of some roof material which was trodden into the ground surface, indicating that the fort was still in use albeit in a very limited way. At a later period this was followed by a large-scale collapse of the slate roof, especially obvious to the east of the building wall located in the excavation trench where there is a denser layering accumulation of roofing slates. This roof collapse was followed by the removal or robbing out of the garrison building walls and the rampart revetment. Some collapse also took place following robbing with slumping of the rampart occurring as a consequence of this.

Material culture

Interestingly the amount of artefactual material that came from this trench was limited, consisting of two pot sherds, five clay-pipe fragments, one button, one fragment of window glass, the roof tile and eight iron nail fragments. This is in direct contrast to the significantly higher quantity of artefacts recovered from an identical sized trench placed on the periphery of the associated settlement. This difference in artefact quantity, especially in terms of the pottery and clay-pipe evidence, must surely point to the mono-functionality of the fort buildings limited to their military function with little domestic, industrial or leisure activity taking place. The roof tile combined with the fragment of good quality green window glass recovered from the trench are indicative of the high status of the fort building but the two sherds of North Devon gravel free ware and five clay-pipe fragments (two of which are clearly datable to the mid-seventeenth century) are evidence of the limited activity taking place. One flat copper alloy button with a broken loop may be a military button but the artefact was recovered from the topsoil and appears to be nineteenth century in date.

Dunboy fort

In 1666 Orrery also recorded that he built the star-shaped fort at Dunboy but states that it was destroyed by 'usurpers' (*Cal. S. P. Ire.*, 1666–9, 92). The fort itself is an irregular-shaped structure containing six salient angles and a possible entrance breach to the east. It has an internal east-west width of 34m and a north-south length of 33m giving an approximate internal area of 1122m². This is of course a misleading area size given the angular nature of the structure and the presence of the earlier tower house in the centre of the fort. The walls of the fort are 5m wide on average and were revetted by a dry stone wall on the interior and exterior. Excavations revealed the basal 2–3m high sections of the wall and demonstrated that it was constructed by laying down a series of layers of rubble and earth (Gowen 1978, 15). The lower layers largely consisted of large stones and boulders while the upper layers consisted of lighter coloured earthy rubble. Of the six angles on the fort the two eastern examples were clearly designed to function as gun platforms or bastions. A third angle at the northwest may also have served this function. The north eastern platform measures 13m by 10m and consists of a substantial rubble triangular base. The south eastern bastion has an identical structural makeup and has very similar approximate measurements. A set of four 2m-wide flagged steps lead from the interior of the fort into this bastion. The placement of both of these gun platforms to the east is of interest. They were clearly designed and positioned to protect the entrance into Bearehaven through the channel which runs between the mainland and Bere Island. They were not located to fire at attacking terrestrial forces but instead were positioned to attack enemy shipping. This further supports the assertion that the forts in this region were designed to protect against Dutch shipping during the course of the Anglo-Dutch war (1651/2) as opposed to playing a primary role in the Cromwellian conflicts in Ireland. A gun may also have been placed on the north western angle as there appears to be refurbishment of this corner in an attempt to increase its area size. A cannon placed at this angle would have protected the natural anchorage and sheltered inlet which lies below the fort's walls. The remaining three angles are considerably smaller and would have been defended by a stockade with infantry positioned behind it. Interestingly the basal foundations of a circular stone structure were found adjacent to the south western angle. The feature consisted of a circular walled feature built using flat slabs with walls that were 0.3m thick and with a smooth inner face and rough exterior (Gowen 1978, 16). The original excavator interpreted this was the base of a tower but Gowen suggested that it may constitute the remains of a bread oven or more likely be a munitions store. Unfortunately no trace of this feature is now visible but it is likely that Fahy was correct in his tower interpretation. Increasingly small towers of this kind are being excavated on sites of this date and type. They are known as *guerites* in the contemporary literature and were built to accommodate one or two men on sentry or look-out duty (Gowen 1978, 16). Many appear to have a stone foundation with a wooden tower or super structure. There was no foundation ditch on the outside but the nature of the surrounding topography militated against such a construction. Bedrock is very high over much of the site which would have made the excavation of a ditch extremely difficult. The western area of the site is also occupied by a deep north-south running gully that provides natural protection for the western terrestrial approaches to the site.

The site was clearly only occupied for a short period of time given that it was built early in the 1650s but had been destroyed by 1666, and more likely by the end of the 1650s. We are then only looking at eight to ten years maximum occupation. Much of the reason for the greater longevity of the fort at Newtown was its role in protecting the economic interests of a new settlement that had been established on the waterfront directly to its north. Unfortunately, most of the original records from the 1970s excavation of Dunboy are missing and few of the finds are labelled. However, the surviving finds, currently stored at University College Cork, can be used as an indicator of the material culture of the fort's occupants. The only clearly datable finds from the mid to late seventeenth century are pottery sherds and clay pipes. A large portion of the pottery recovered from the site and dated to this period is English and dominated by North Devon wares as demonstrated by the table below.

Pottery name	Quantity	Type	Date
North Devon sgraffito	'large numbers'		17th
North Devon platters	8		17th
North Devon green-glazed			17th
Fine ware	80	inc. pilchard jars	
Gravel-tempered	180		
Slip-trailed (Bristol)	1	dish	mid-late 17th
Black-glazed earthen	4	bases	17th
Southwark manganese	1	cup	17th
Staffordshire combed	1	cup	17th

Table 6.3 Mid to late seventeenth-century pottery types recovered from Dunboy excavations (compiled from Gowen 1978)

This collection is clearly demonstrable of a garrison hierarchy. There are a small number of high-quality table-wares which would have been used by the officers. On the other hand the vast majority of the wares are either functional kitchen or utility wares or storage types used in the fishing industry. The presence of such a high quantity of gravel-tempered wares is especially indicative of this. No imported pottery is readily attributable to this period which in turn points to self dependence and self sustainability among the English forces and points to the provisioning of the garrison through English agents and routes of supply. The absence of Continental wares is also in sharp contrast to the situation in the late medieval period when Dunboy was the focus of a fishing industry dominated by European fleets as evidenced in the historical sources and the pottery evidence from the site. This industry in turn became dominated by English fleets in the seventeenth century. The fact that Newtown was established as a fisheries centre at this time would argue against a downturn in stocks. This is further supported by the presence of pilchard jars within the later seventeenth-century assemblage. The presence of such jars can be taken as an indication of a continuation of fishing activity at the fort with the support or protection of the garrison. It could also be an example of the provisioning of the garrison with fish.

Regional Cromwellian developments

Elsewhere, away from Bantry, Robert Gookin was involved in the construction of a fort at Rosscarbery. In 1654 it had a garrison of 100 horse and foot and some 300 people were settled 'within a musket shot of it' (Kerrigan 1995, 99). The fort was a rectangular enclosure with corner bastions, located just south of the main street in the town. At the blockhouse in Kinsale new guns and equipment were added in 1652 and a tower was built between it and the fort at Castlepark in 1654–6. Both forts at Corkbeg and Haulbowline were still in operation and remained part of the strategic plans of the English. A small fort was built at Tarbert on the southern shores on the Shannon Estuary. This was probably originally an internally square structure with a diameter of *c*.30m with corner bastions and an external 4m wide ditch. While these star-shaped forts were predominantly a feature of the coast a series of citadels were built in a number of urban sites. Both Cork and Waterford were protected by large forts but citadels were built in both Limerick and Clonmel. The Limerick complex was refurbished in the early years of the Commonwealth with the walls of its bastion over 2m thick and an entrance with drawbridge across the external ditch. A further bastion-shaped ravelin constituted a further element to its defences. The Clonmel citadel appears to have been placed internally within the town and incorporated sections of the town wall before being demolished in 1673.

In 1659 the *Calendar of State Papers* (*Commonwealth*) *for Ireland* contains a 'list of Garrisons which were thought fit to be constantly kept if any invasion should be made into Ireland by a foreign enemy' dated 23 April 1659 (*Cal. S. P. Ire.*, 1659, 687). Twenty-two garrisons are mentioned with Limerick City and its three citadels recommended as having a garrison of 200 while Waterford, Kinsale and *Bantry Fort* are all listed as having 100 soldiers. Clonmel, Cork Fort, Valentia and Dingle and Mallow each have 60 (*Cal. S. P. Ire.*, 1659, 687). Following the Restoration a period of calm ensues. A brief crisis during the Dutch War of 1665–7 results in the refortification of Castlepark while a new gun platform was built at Ringcurran Castle, the site of Charles Fort built a decade later. A cable and boom were fed across the harbour, reflective again of the perceived external naval threat that underlay most of the seventeenth-century fortifications. The work at Kinsale appears to be the exception as Orrery reports in 1666 that the forts at Valentia, Bantry, Crookhaven, Sherkin and Kinsale were once again in a poor state of repair while Dunboy had been destroyed. Few developments take place over the following two decades and it is only with the advent of the Williamite wars in the 1680s that the defensive structures enter a new phase of development.

CHAPTER 7

Economy and Industry

Landscape is a complex and multi-layered series of entities. Previous chapters dealt with settlement and communications activity, the most visible surviving physical expressions of past cultural activity, but these are only part of this multi-layered system and are just some of the facets which constitute past cultural activity. Other features include the way people exploited the land and attempted to organize it in order to make a living and derive profit. Indeed, much of past human endeavour during the time period under study was involved in developing new and innovative ways of extracting the maximum surplus from individual resources and finding new ways in which to capitalize fully on productivity. This chapter attempts to address aspects of the surviving evidence for these activities throughout the region under discussion. The major landscape changes that altered the character of the landscape during the 'improvements' of the eighteenth and nineteenth centuries have hidden much of this evidence (Aalen, Whelan and Stout 1997, 91) but detailed analysis of the surviving documentary and carto-graphic sources coupled with targeted field survey can aid in the reconstruction of these activities.

Seventeenth-century enclosure

While the main period of enclosure occurs in the eighteenth century enclosure of fields in the later part of the sixteenth century and throughout the seventeenth century is well documented (Aalen, Whelan and Stout 1997, 136–44; O'Keeffe 2000, 64–66). This corresponds to a general upsurge in the enclosure of common fields, pasture and wasteland in England during the sixteenth century (Rippon 1996, 101; Newman 2001, 106–11). Of course the physical enclosure of sections of landscape into field units was not a new process within Ireland. Enclosure on varying scales has taken place on the island of Ireland since at least Neolithic times, as evidenced by the Céide fields complex. Varying forms of enclosing activity can be seen taking place over the following millennia but it is argued here that it was only in the early part of the seventeenth century that we see large-scale intensification of this activity and large tracts of previously unenclosed land is now taken over as part of this process. Enclosure was undertaken on a number of different premises. At this time agricultural thinking was of the opinion that enclosure would increase productivity and lend itself to the better management of the land and greater yields (Buchanan 1973, 599), although it has been shown that enclosure did not result in improved productivity (Allen 1992, 17). Johnson (1996, 108) argues that enclosure in England began a process of commodification of the landscape and paved the way for the generation of individual wealth through private ownership. This was clearly taking place across the study region and can be perceived on a number of different levels. The development of large-scale enclosures marked a fundamental change in the character of the landscape of Munster. Its parcelling up by individuals and entrepreneurial enterprise marked a fundamental shift away from the open sept lands of the earlier period. Enclosure was stamping new marks of ownership on the landscape and creating a differing set of identities on it. It was also establishing an overt expression of private property. The vast majority of the new planters were English and not only did they bring their lifeways and cultural identity with them but they can also be seen to be bringing their landscape identity with them as well. Of course this is not solely an English process, enclosure was happening in many different places and ways at this time, but in the study area it can be seen in this way in so far as it marks such a critical shift from the past. It also represents a breakdown in the traditional perception of landscape that preceded these developments. The effective closure of many units of landscape is a physical demonstration of a change in socio-economic practice and political structures of power. Whereas tower-houses and other high status residences were the previous manifestation of these expressions, enclosure represented new investment and new arrivals in the area. Not only were they erecting protective structures around their settlements but they were also physically ring-fencing their land investments. This form of private enterprise is then an expression of the beginnings of capitalism, the origins of which can be traced in England from the middle of the sixteenth century onwards (Newman 2001, 5). This can be seen in the direct association of enclosure with the individualism of enterprise and of the highly visible nature of the enclosed private property. The sheer size of the enclosure fences or banks, in excess of 2m in height on Whiddy Island for example, also literally changed the way people could view the landscape. Vistas were now broken and the same expansive examinations of the landscape were simply not possible any more due to the height of the enclosing banks. This enclosure then, probably more than any other factor, represents the most obvious break with the past. It is something that appears to begin in the last years of the sixteenth century and early part of the seventeenth century with the arrival of English planters to the area.

Numerous examples of the enclosing process can be identified in the historical records. Sir William Hull's deposition of 1641 makes a claim for £180 in lieu of the

> Cost of breaking rocks at Lymcon [near Schull, West Cork] and stoninge the land five times all over to make it arable land and so divided it into many fields of 8–10–15–20 acres in a field which before a plough could not work in it also in draining the bogs and making gutters and for ditching and hedging the saued land (Donovan 1993, 35).

This reference clearly implies that this enclosure was a new thing and that Hull was investing in and working land that had previously been neglected or ignored; at least this was the perception that the planters wished to give. Richard Beacon, in his grant of the area around Bantry in 1590 was to pay rent on each acre of 'waste' land enclosed (*Eliz. Fiants* 5536 (6558) 1590–1, 139). He also undertook to enclose 300 acres for horse and deer, in a possible attempt to create a deerpark (*Cal. Patent & Close Rolls, Elizabeth*, 35, February 1594, 266). There is very strong cartographic evidence for this particular example of early enclosure. An early seventeenth-century map of Inner Bantry Bay and Whiddy Island clearly shows the parcelling-up of land (East Yorkshire archives DDCC(2)) (fig. 71). Each unit is assigned a letter of the alphabet but unfortunately the key that this relates to does not survive. It is likely, however, to relate to the ownership or tenantship of each plot. The exciting thing about this map is the fact that many of these boundaries still survive and a number still function as townland boundaries. The surviving seventeenth-century boundaries from the map are illustrated in the accompanying survey map. The existing townland boundaries, taken from the first edition OS 6-inch map are shown as the dotted lines while the seventeenth-century boundaries are shown as solid unbroken lines. It is argued here that the seventeenth-century planters adopted existing townland boundaries in whatever form they appeared and repartitioned them in a distinctive manner. Each townland is named and where an original property unit still survives it is labelled with its original alphabetic letter. The property boundaries highlighted in bold are those that also correspond to a route or roadway. From this particular evidence there does appear to a correlation between routeways, townland boundaries and the seventeenth-century divisions. Certainly the main boundary bordering Kilmore to the north is still the primary east-west running roadway on the Island. These seventeenth-century boundaries are very distinctive and clearly different to

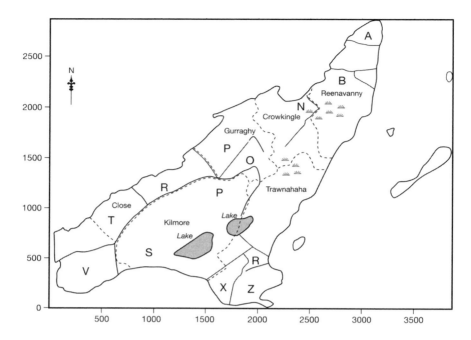

71 Seventeenth-century land divisions on Whiddy Island

what came both before and after them in chronological terms. They are immediately identifiable from their size and are totally unlike the later eighteenth- and nineteenth-century divisions. The Whiddy boundaries average 2.2m in height and *c*.1.2m in width with *c*.12km of the banks surviving across the Island. They were constructed by first creating a substantial earthen bank and then facing it with large stones and boulders at their basal levels, presumably cleared from the surrounding fields. Many of the banks now incorporate large mature trees and are grass covered. This type of structure differs greatly from the low-lying stonewalls constructed as field fences in more recent centuries in the area.

Pastoral and arable

Arable activity is viewed traditionally as being the dominant practice in rural medieval Ireland but this assumption is too much of a generalization and requires a far greater degree of investigation. Regardless, with the arrival of the English planters in the later half of the sixteenth century, pastoral activity greatly increased across Munster. Significant new investment took place in flocks of sheep and herds of cattle by the English. The 1615 visitation records that 'there is very little tillage … they have converted the arable ground into pasture, and graze cattle, garrons, "studds", young cattle out of which the Church hath not any tithe, excepting 2d. for a milch cow' (Dickson 2005, 21). Some indicators of the size of these holdings are contained in the historical sources. Sir Philip Perceval had 5,200 sheep and lambs and 200 cows (Dickson 2005, 21). Grenville's seignory is recorded as having two English bulls, seven English rams, 12 English oxen and four English horses with Irish stock also present (MacCarthy-Morrogh 1986, 130). Herbert has 120 cows, 50 oxen, 200 sheep, 50 pigs and six mares while Norris kept English sheep at Mallow. The increasing significance of sheep is supported by export figures from Youghal and from excavated evidence. Dickson (2005, 18) has illustrated how over 65% of Irish wool exports were passed through the Cork ports of Youghal, Cork and Kinsale in the period 1632–5 dropping to just over 50% by the 1640. This pattern is repeated archaeologically. McCarthy (2005, 148) found that sheep were clearly the dominant and most important animal at Spenser's Kilcolman where they were kept until they were at least three years old to accommodate the wool trade. The 1994 North Gate excavations in Cork recovered a relatively small quantity of bone of which 63% belonged to cattle, 22% sheep and 15% pig (McCarthy 1997, 156). A number of duck bones also recovered. Spenser in the 1590s records that booleying was still in practice amongst the Irish 'to live in herds, driving their cattle continually with them and feeding only on their milk and white meats' (Tierney 2005, 149).

Arable activity continued but our information on its nature and extent is more limited. Currently most information is derived from excavations of securely dated contexts in both urban and rural settings. Excavations of a number of seventeenth-century contexts in Grattan Street produced plant remains including fig, corn, hazelnut, blackberry, apple and elder (McClatchie 2003, 396). Possible rye grains, six-row hulled barley and oat were also present. At Kilcolman cereals dominated the samples recovered with oats, barley and wheat represented (Tierney 2005, 151). Again an inherent bias in the archaeological record needs to be noted here as vegetables do not survive in acidic soils and are normally only found in water-logged deposits.

FISHING

It has been noted elsewhere (Breen 2005) that the seas and seabed off the southern coasts are good fishing grounds, a statement borne out in the historical sources. The fact that these fisheries were seemingly so productive during the fifteenth and sixteenth centuries was not a chance occurrence. Certain fish stocks, like herring, are very susceptible to the slightest change in the oceanographic conditions – a slight rise in water temperature for example will lead to a significant increase in stocks. Recent oceanographic research from Norway is then of direct relevance to this study. Here detailed analyses of benthonic foraminfera, stable isotopes and other sedimentary material obtained from a core extracted from a fjord in western Norway, derived a relative temperature history of the region that spanned the last 5,500 years (Mikalsen, G., Sejrup, H.P. and Aarseth, I. 2001). Four cold periods characterized by 1.5–2°C reductions in bottom-water temperature were identified: 2150 to 1800 BC, 850 to 600 BC, 150 BC to AD 150, AD 500 to 600, and a cooling that may correspond to the 'Little Ice Age' (AD 1625). The authors note there is a good correlation between the cold periods and cold events recorded in other studies. Significantly they identify a warm period from AD 1330 to 1600 that had the highest bottom-water temperatures in Sulafjorden during the last 5,000 years (Mikalsen, G., Sejrup, H.P. and Aarseth, I. 2001, 444). The authors' results clearly establish the reality and importance of the Medieval Warm Period in the North Atlantic region. The rise in water temperatures in the middle of the fourteenth century also appears to signal the start of a burgeoning fishing industry in Ireland. From this period onwards continental fishing fleets begin to arrive off the coast and begin the systematic exploitation of the fishery resource.

The historical evidence would appear to indicate that fishing was largely carried out by visiting fleets with minimal involvement from the local populations (Dickson 2005, 20). Local groups were probably limited to small localized fishing and to the overall control of the operations. An indication of how this actually was carried out comes from an Inquisition that took place in 1609 into the extent of the holdings of the neighbouring O'Driscolls of Baltimore and Roaring Water Bay (O'Donovan 1849, 104; O'Mahoney 2000, 129). This document outlines in great detail how the O'Driscolls operated and gained monetarily from visiting fishing fleets. It is likely that the O'Sullivans were operating a very similar system and this in turn provides an indicator of what physical remains we may expect to find. The O'Driscolls charged each ship four pence sterling to anchor in the sheltered anchorage in Baltimore Sound, while fishing boats were charged an additional nineteen shillings, a barrel of flour and salt, a hogshead of beer and a dish of fish three times a week for use of the fishing grounds and anchorage. Additionally if the crew were to bring the catch ashore for drying on a 'rock' then they were to be charged six pence and eight shillings. In terms of provisioning the fleet O'Driscoll Mór charged eight-pence for every 'beef they [visiting crews] kill … and for every sheep and pig that is killed likewize one penny' (O'Donovan 1849, 104). In addition O'Driscoll was entitled to receive four gallons of every 'butt' of wine landed in the area and all goods imported into the area had firstly to be offered to him at a lower rate. All of these tariffs and other licensing rules were enforced by galleys belonging to the lord and through a weekly court held at Baltimore. This evidence in particular shows that the Gaelic lordships were not economically retarded but instead had comprehensive economic management systems in place. English planters in the early part of the seventeenth century were then taking on, commercializing and developing existing enterprise rather than inventing or creating new enterprises.

Seventeenth-century fisheries

With the arrival of the English planters in the seventeenth century the fishing industry further developed. Significant investment now went in to the development of fishing settlements and facilities associated with these. Dickson (2005, 19–20) suggests that at its height the pilchard industry employed in excess of 2,000 people, a significant percentage of the new English population. It is also remarkable that between 1619 and 1634 37% of the customs receipts of the ports of Kinsale and west Cork were due to the export of pilchards. To what extent this was seasonal employment remains to be seen with these individuals also being involved in other industries outside of the fishing season. The location of these sites and historical information associated with them has been outlined but there is as of yet little supporting archaeological information for the nature of this fishery during the first half of the seventeenth century. Sir William Hull's depositions of 1641 provide an insight into fishing operations at Leacom near Schull in West Cork at this period (Went 1947, 59–60). It details 12 seine boats, 'fish houses', 1200 barrels of salt, thousand of barrels, nets, planks oars, tar and a large variety of other material that was all used in the fishery. Seine boat fishing appears to have been the primary method of catching the extensive pilchard stocks off the coast at this time. Richard Boyle records the purchase of a seine net in 1616 (*Lismore Papers*, 1st ser. I, 13), while Charles Smith, writing in 1750, describes this type of fishing in good detail

> Pilchards are taken either by day or night, but mostly in the day, by means of hewers [look-outs or experienced fishermen] placed on the adjacent high grounds above the bays. The nets are from 100 to 140 fathoms long and from 6 to 9 fathoms deep; the net being shot or dropt into the sea, they surround the fish, having two boats to attend them, one of which is called the seine boat and the other the follower. The pilchard being thus enclosed between the two boats, by drawing both ends of the net or poles together they begin to haul up the net, and bring the bottom and top of it together, this is called tucking the net; then by means of oval baskets … they empty the net of the fish into their boats. The fish are brought out of the large baskets and laid in the fish-house, which they call a palace (Smith 1750, 310).

Numerous depictions of this type of fishing exist, the most relevant in this context being the early seventeenth-century Stafford folio of Baltimore which clearly shows two seine operations underway (wwm str p20/100:8/388/6, Sheffield Archives (published in Breen 2001, 423; Kelleher 1998).

Once brought ashore the fish then had to be processed and preserved. This could be done in three ways – smoking, pressing or pickling. Initially the fish had to be salted and this was normally done by placing the fish in stacked salted layers in a cellar or stone building over a number of days until the excess of salt and blood was soaked from the fish, after which they were washed. The fish could then be smoked on sticks in a drying room but this does not appear to have been common in Ireland. Here, the fish were mostly placed in barrels which, later in the century, were pressed in order to extract the fish oil (Went 1946, 153). It is not clear when pressing was first introduced into Ireland but it seems to have begun in the third quarter of the seventeenth century in Cornwall (Fox 1878, 84). The fish could then be stored or exported immediately in the barrels.

Fish palaces

Fish houses or fish palaces were a common feature of these seventeenth-century fisheries. The actual form of these buildings is unclear as it is usually only the wall with the beam-press niches that survives. It may be that originally these were simple stone- or wooden-built storage structures that became more elaborate later in the century with the development of pressing. It is clear also that in a number of cases they consisted of simple stone walls or utilized the walls of existing buildings. A number of ancillary buildings such as salt stores and coopering yards must also have been associated with the stores to allow for the intensive activity that went on at these processing sites. Smith (1750, 292) recorded that there were 'several fish palaces ... built for saving, preserving and salting Pilchards' in the many creeks around Bantry Bay. In 1798 DeLatocnaye (1798, 168) states that in several parts of Whiddy Island there 'are walls which served for the purpose of extricating oil from pilchards'. Viscount Kenmare records the presence of 'large palaces or receptacles for carrying on a fishery on it' at Donemark, over one kilometre north of Bantry town (Went 1946, 148). Finally, the site of a fish palace is also recorded on the first edition OS map in Laharn townland on the southern shores of Reenadisert inlet. None of the above sites, all situated in the inner Bantry Bay area, now survive. The only surviving fish-palace in the Cork section of Beara is at Ardgroom Inward. Here a seventeenth-century central press-beam wall, 13.5m in length and standing to a height in excess of 3m, contains eight rectangular niches set 1.2m above ground level with eighteen support press-beam niches at ground level. A number of low-lying walls are present on all sides of this

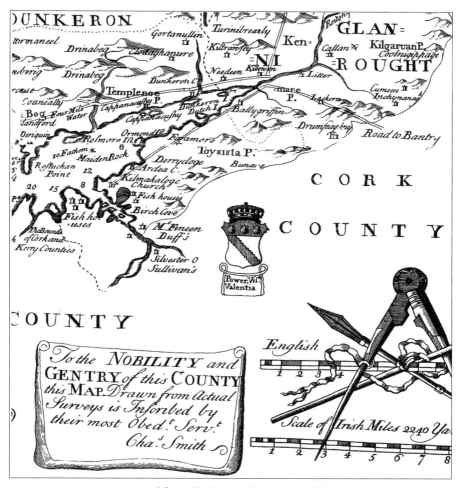

72 Detail from Charles Smith's 1756 map of Kerry

central support. Killmakilloge harbour served as the focus for the pilchard fishery in the Kerry. Smith (1756), on a map accompanying his *History of Kerry*, records fish-houses on both the east and west shores of the harbour (fig. 72). Went (1946, 150) records that William Petty started the fishery here in 1672. No trace of any of these sites now exists but local tradition records that a number of houses and buildings in the area were formerly used for that purpose. Beam presses are visible on the external face of Ballinskelligs castle where Petty was known to also have had a fishery. Foundations lying between the castle and the abbey may represent the remains of the fishery settlement associated with this location.

Fish ponds

A number of fish ponds located at Dunboy and Ardaturish Beg bear further testimony to the fishing industry. Fish ponds were used for storing fish after they were caught and were then taken out when needed. While fish ponds are known to have been extensively associated with medieval ecclesiastical and settlement sites (Aston 1988) their dating is less clear in the study area. At Dunboy a fishpond is clearly marked on the first and second edition OS 6" map (no. 128). The feature is located 400m west of Puxley manor and now consists of a marshy hollow, in excess of 100m in length, fed from Dunboy inlet by a very narrow channel, 3–4m wide. No structural evidence can be found at the site which would help with dating and the landscaped nature of the area immediately surrounding the feature has masked any possible associated earthworks. It is possible that this was an eighteenth-/nineteenth-century estate landscape feature but it may also be associated with earlier fishing activity. The Ardaturish Beg site is a marine site that uses a natural break in the exposed foreshore bedrock that has been artificially enclosed to create a pond. The entrance at its seaward section consists of the foundations of a low wall standing three courses high at either end. It is built of rough and cut sandstone blocks. The blocks are laid flat and joined flush together with mortar with an original sluice entrance at the Southeast end of the wall. A small, red brick extension to the sandstone wall marks the location where a wooden sluice gate was evident over 50 years ago. At the landward end of the pond where the bedrock terminates at the beach a wall was erected consisting of upright overlapping slates, bonded with mortar and running around the landward edge of structure. A slate wall constituted the internal face of the feature while the external face was made up of upright sandstone slabs set on edge and joined overlapping each other and bonded by mortar. A series of slabs were then laid in the gap between the slates and slabs which were unbonded but aided its watertightness. The wall ran above HWM (High Water Mark) across the storm beach and has a maximum thickness of 1.7m. The slate inner face ran for 75% of the SE section of the wall before a number of large sandstone boulders extended the line. The pond would originally have had a depth in excess of 1m. While the red bricks and recent usage of the pond suggest that this feature in its current form is a later eighteenth-/nineteenth-century estate feature, its presence and usage and the long continuity of maritime traditions in the study area is evidence of pond usage and indicative of a tradition that may stretch back into earlier centuries.

INDUSTRY

There is little current archaeological evidence relating to industry in the later medieval period in the study area, although the seventeenth century is better represented. Rynne (1998) has addressed technology and industry in Anglo-Norman Munster concentrating on mills. Barry (1998) has addressed industry for Ireland and has shown that the paucity of data from the study area is a feature of Munster as a whole. The limited information that is available relates to iron working at Bouchier's Castle (Cleary 1983) and mills. Hurley (1997, 45–9) located a high medieval water-powered forge in Cork City while Colin Rynne (1998, 79) has identified a post mill at Youghal, depicted on the *Pacata* illustration of the town, and shown rotating around a central wooden pivot in order to face its sails into the prevailing direction of the wind. One of the most significant monument types which is little represented in the archaeological record across the study area during the later medieval period is the mill. These would have been very important for the processing of cereal grain. Corn-drying kilns are also largely absent but the dual absence of both these site types is indicative of a broader pattern of poor survival throughout Ireland (O'Keeffe 2000, 66–7). One key-hole shaped kiln, post medieval in date, was found in excavations in Waterford City, of which three masonry courses survived (Hurley and Scully 1997, 277). Associated features included a small stone platform and rake-out from kiln. This has been interpreted as a possible corn-drying kiln but may post date the study period given the presence of red brick.

Iron-working

Throughout the medieval period wrought iron was produced in a bloomery (Rynne 2001). This was a process where iron was smelted from its oxides in a furnace often consisting of a lined and covered hollow in the ground. Charcoal is used to initially heat up the furnace and the ore after which bellows were used to increase temperatures to in excess of 1,000°C, with water-powered bellows making this process more efficient in the fifteenth and sixteenth centuries. Internally the oxides were reduced to metallic iron which collect at the base of the furnace and form a bloom amid slag. This bloom could then be removed and beaten into wrought iron. This form of production continued into the seventeenth century in Ireland but was rapidly replaced by the advent of blast furnaces late in the sixteenth century. This new form of furnace was designed to produce molten metal using constant 'blasts' of air and reaching very high temperatures. There were a number of different stages to iron-working at this commercial level. Wood firstly had to be cut down and then burnt for charcoal.

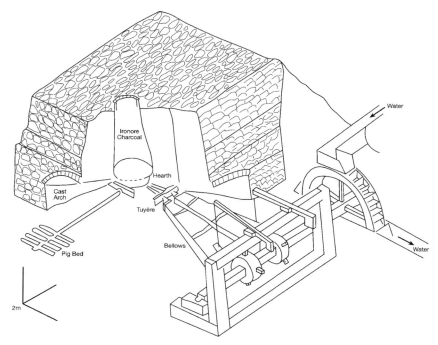

73 Reconstruction of an Iron furnace (after Rynne 2001)

Charcoal-making sites are readily identifiable in the landscape as very low-lying mounds or depressions with dense concentrations of charcoal and burning evident. They show up as circular cleared spaces in contemporary or former areas of woodland (Newman 2001, 116). The charcoal was then placed in a furnace with the iron-ore and fired to very high temperatures to reduce the ores to metallic iron. These blast furnaces were substantial stone-built structures which were square in section with a firebrick-lined interior that tapered downwards to a crucible in which the collection of the molten iron took place (Palmer and Neaverson 1998) (fig. 73). Suitably high temperatures could only be reached by applying continual artificial blasts of air usually generated by water-powered bellows or cylinders driven by a waterwheel. The furnace would normally have 2–3 basal arches, two of which contained tuyéres through which air was blasted while the third arch was used to give access to the molten iron. Furnaces were normally built against a bank or accessed by a bridge so as to allow the iron-ore to be loaded from the top (Jones 1996, 19).

There were a number of topographic and environmental considerations in the siting of these furnaces. They would normally be located in woodland so as to provide a ready supply of charcoal used for fuel. Water was also an important consideration and most furnaces are positioned down-slope of a stream or river so as to allow the operation of a bellows or water-wheel. In an Irish context close or direct access to the sea and landing places was also a necessity to allow for the importation and export of the necessary raw materials and finished products. The continuous operating cycle of the furnaces also required its workers to live close by. Woodland was crucial to this emergent iron-working industry. Certainly by the middle of the seventeenth century English wood resources were under serious threat and iron-workers increasingly turned to Ireland to source wood (Andrews 1956b, 139–41). There is some dispute as to the extent of surviving woodland across the province at this time but it is apparent from both the surviving documentary and cartographic sources that significant tracts or pockets existed. In November 1608 Thomas Wilson, Dudley Norton and Thomas Crooke of Baltimore purchased lands and woods lying around Bantry Bay for development purposes (*Cal. S. P. Ire.*, 1608, 101). Boate (1726), writing in the middle of the seventeenth century, records the survival of large tracts of woodland across Munster – 'There be still sundry great forests remaining in the counties if Kerry, and of Tipperary; and even in the county of Cork, where the greatest destruction thereof hath been made, some great woods are yet remaining, there being also store of scattered woods both in that county, and all the province of Munster over.' Wood was an important commodity for shipbuilding, general construction and increasingly for charcoal production for use in the iron smelting process. Given its value as a commodity we need to question whether there were attempts to ensure the sustainability of the woodland as a resource or whether it was exploited to the point of virtual ecological collapse. Certainly in England numerous examples of the enclosure of woodland for coppicing have been identified (Newman 2001). These enclosures involved protected areas being physically enclosed by low banks and ditches, often topped with a fence. This form of enclosure also took place in order to create areas of leisure activity, such as game hunting, in earlier centuries but it is argued that the later enclosures were far more regular and were well associated historically with various industrial practices. No systematic survey of such enclosing activity has yet to be undertaken in Ireland but is likely to exist. One of the key issues will be discerning between enclosure for leisure or commercial purposes but detailed palaeo-ecological analysis such aid the investigative process.

Andrews (1956a) identifies two primary phases to the development of the iron-working industry. The first originates in the later part of the sixteenth century when a number of the early planters become involved. This expands in the early decades of the seventeenth century but declines dramatically with the outbreak of conflict in 1641. The industry is subsequently redeveloped post-Restoration and emerges as a significant economic entity late in the century. Amongst the earliest attempts to establish an iron-works was in the 1590s when George Goring and Herbert Pelham attempted to set up a venture in east Cork on Raleigh's estates following on from Norrey's works at Mogeely in 1593 (Rynne 2001, 102–3). Subsequently Richard Boyle's estates became the central focus for these activities when furnaces are located across the Blackwater valley. The port of Youghal consequently becomes a principal exporter of iron product during the profitable period of these ventures up to 1631.

Date of establishment	Location	Owner/ developer
1593	Mogeely, Co. Cork	Thomas Norreys
1596	Raleigh's estates, east Cork	Herbert Pelham and George Goring
1608	KIlmackoe, Co. Waterford	Richard Boyle
1612	Dundaniel, Co. Cork	English East India Company
1615	Lismore, Co. Waterford	Richard Boyle
1615	Cappoquin, Co. Waterford	Richard Boyle
1620	Lisfinny, Co. Waterford	Richard Boyle
1625	Araglin, Co. Waterford	Richard Boyle
1668	Clonmeen, Co. Cork	
1670	Kenmare, Co. Kerry	William Petty
1683/4	Dunboy, Co. Cork	

Table 7.1 Iron-working furnaces, Munster (after Rynne 2001)

Rynne (2001) has produced a detailed study of seventeenth-century blast furnaces in Munster and recounts in lucid technical detail their operation. He has also identified a number of surviving sites including Araglin in Waterford, Derrycunihy and Muckross in Kerry and Dunboy and Adrigole in Cork (Rynne 2001, 106). The location and debris associated with the works at Dundaniel is also well known. In the seventeenth century west Cork becomes a significant iron-working centre, an industry largely generated by newly arrived English entre-preneurs (Hourihane 1985, 87). This corresponds to a massive increase in iron-working in England associated with the ordnance industry (Kearney 1953, 156). The extensive woodland in the study area would have been especially attractive to these settlers which provided a plentiful supply of charcoal.

There were three primary seventeenth-century iron-working areas in Beara area – Coomhola, Dunboy and Glanarought. It is no coincidence that these are the places which appear to have the densest woodland cover during this period. The earliest historical reference to large-scale iron-working occurring at these sites is from the 1670s when William Petty established his iron-works at Kenmare and Glanaroughty while an iron-works had been established at Dunboy shortly before 1685 (Andrews 1956a, 218; Barnard 1982). It is somewhat surprising though, that there is limited historical information associated with any of these sites and their workings. A furnace was located in woodland at Dunboy situated on the south-eastern bank of a small inlet. It is a semi-circular structure, *c.*4m high constructed of flat, shale stone set in earth and mortar. There appears to be an earthen floor with stones beneath 1.5–2m above lane level. This is surrounded by a semi-circular stonewall which is open towards the water's edge. The ends of the arms are not faced so it is not clear when or how they were finished. Beneath the floor is a large slab, set at an angle, with a 0.3m hollow beneath. Stone-facing splays out on either side of this hollow which defines the end/edge of the structure, at one point reaching 2m wide. There may have been an outer face to the structure which would have come round to meet the stone facing at the front. The structure is set into a natural earthen bank to facilitate loading from behind and appears to be tapering towards the top to form a possible corbelled roof. This appears to be a blast furnace associated with the later seventeenth-century iron-working industry established at Dunboy, given its typical seventeenth-century construction and form (Rynne 2001, 116). Unfortunately access to the woodland was not possible due to private ownership but this area certainly warrants further study due to its undeveloped nature and potential to preserve further sites.

A second blast furnace was uncovered during the course of excavations at a seventeenth-/eighteenth-century iron-working site at Adrigole (Cotter 2000, 13). Excavations adjacent to a small rectangular stone shed, listed as a furnace on the first edition OS map, exposed a 2.55m-wide mortared stone wall foundation aligned west-north-west/east-south-east in line with the south wall of the ruined structure. This had been subject to intense heat and was associated with a large quantity of vitrified stone and iron slag and burnt stone rubble. A wide silted-up channel was also located which appears to have functioned as the water-channel which drove the bellows. Evidence for iron-working can also be seen at Gortamullin outside Kenmare in the form of dense scatterings of vitrified stone. However, this complex was destroyed during the construction of a modern housing estate in the 1970s.

The Coomhola valley has probably got the best preserved evidence for iron-working in the region. The operations appear to have been concentrated in two townlands in the area, Mill Little and Mill Big, both located at the confluence of the Cooleenlemane River with the larger Coomhola River. A large dry stone dam cuts off the mouth of the smaller tributary. It consists of an inner facing of large boulders facing upstream standing 1m above present ground level and clearly designed to catch and hold the running water in a reservoir-like area directly in front. This could presumably have been used to channel water into a water-wheel structure for the furnaces. Further up the valley there are a large number of probable charcoal burning sites. Could it be that some of the fulacht fiadh referred to in the archaeological record throughout the country are actually charcoal working sites? Charcoal was made by clearing and levelling an area of ground and delimiting it with a circle of stones enclosing a cleared earthen area to prevent the spread of the fire. A central hearth or burning area was then created and wood was stacked in an ordered pile onto this. The mound was then covered with clay and set alit and left to burn for a number of days. It was a highly specialized operation requiring great skill and constant attention to maximize the amount of charcoal you could extract from the pile. The danger was always that the pile would simply burn away or only partially burn. These types of sites manifest themselves in the archaeological record as large circular levelled areas which show intense burning, are located in areas of former woodland and positioned near water. Morphologically they appear very similar to fulacht fiadhs, especially ones that are considered to have been levelled. There are a large number of fulacht fiadh recorded in the region in known areas of former iron-working. There are, for example, ten sites recorded as such in the *Record of monuments and places* in the townland of Rossnashunsoge in the uplands (over 400m OD) above Glengarriff while four fulacht fiadh are recorded in Derroograne townland in Coomhola. Similarly, three fulacht fiadh are recorded in Derrymihin West and ten sites are recorded in the Derreenataggart area, both in the former woodland east of Dunboy. No morphological analysis on charcoal burning sites has been carried out in Ireland to date so any comments made on the sites in terms of their possible later dating can only be arbitrary. A programme of intrusive investigation or sampling of a number of these sites is now required in order to substantiate their actual dating and function.

Pottery production

The period from the late sixteenth century to the seventeenth century is a difficult time for study of pottery in Ireland. Excavated assemblages are dominated by English and European wares but the identification of locally made pottery is extremely difficult. This was, of course, a transitory time with numerous conflicts and disruption to industry but it is unlikely that no production took place throughout Munster. The problem arises with the assignation of a source to the many undecorated earthenwares found on sites. Production of this type of pottery was certainly taking place locally and Claire McCutcheon has identified Youghal as a possible source given its suitable clays and the fact that significant quantities of earthenware and bricks were produced there from late in the seventeenth century (McCutcheon 2003, 199). We should remember also that the artefactual record is also an intrinsically biased one and only presents us with a limited surviving sample of past objects. The soils of rural Munster have a high acidic nature and the consequent preservation of organic material is low. Certain exceptions do of course occur in some 'wet' urban contexts but for the most part there is limited organic survival. Thus, it is likely that ceramics constituted only one part of the tableware of a household. Considerable quantities of wooden items must also have been used including bowls, plates and drinking vessels. Their poor survival rate may account to some extent for the limited quantity of local wares currently identified. Pewter would also have been used but there is no historical mention of production in southern Ireland. The 1590 Castleisland inventory of Sir William Herbert includes a large amount of pewter including platters, dishes, basins, plates, spoons, candlesticks and chamber pots (Chinnery 2004). Similarly the Cork merchant Nicholas Faggan in 1578 had nine pewter trenchers while Thomas Roinane, a second Cork merchant, had 24 pewter dishes recorded in his 1641 inventory

Post-medieval wares are dominated by English and European wares, in particular wares from the southwest of England. North Devon gravel tempered and gravel free wares predominate, with domestic wares including cooking pots, jugs, bowls and dishes the most common forms. In Waterford North Devon wares account for 53% of wares recovered from the later levels (Hurley and Scully 1997, 338). Black wares from north Wales and south Lancashire are also strongly represented. Tin glazed earthenwares are most common for the finer domestic wares including plates, cups and decorated bowls, and were made in Britain for much of the seventeenth century. Many Continental forms are also represented but the English wares in terms of individual pieces are the most numerous. There is some evidence of local production but identification is difficult; McCutcheon has identified a number of sherds of locally made pottery at Kilcolman Castle (McCuthcheon 2005, 147). Potters were certainly present in Cork by 1683 and both Rosanne Meenan and Clare McCutcheon have identified a possible kiln site at Red Abbey in Cork City where substantial quantities of kiln waste from brownwares or glazed red earthenwares have been recovered. The pottery dates to the late seventeenth/early eighteenth century. This form of ware was extremely common across Britain and Ireland throughout the post-medieval period so it should not be surprising that it was being produced locally in Cork. They were largely undecorated and consist of a sandy earthenware, coloured from light orange to brown, with a clear lead glaze (McCutcheon 2003, 233). Fragments of possibly locally produced ridge tiles with low cockscomb crests and incised decoration were also recovered from this site and probably date to the later part of the seventeenth century.

CLAY PIPES

Clay pipes began to appear in Ireland in the 1580s associated with the recent rise in tobacco availability. Production in Ireland began in the middle of the seventeenth century apparently commencing in Cork in the 1650s and in Limerick from *c*.1670. These mostly consisted of pipes with small bowls, thick stems and large bore diameters. A number of distinctive clay pipe types that were made in the study region have been identified. As of yet no seventeenth-century kiln has been identified but the distribution of local pipes shows that pipe manufacture was certainly undertaken after the middle of the century and expanded rapidly in the following centuries. Sheila Lane (1997a and 1997b) recorded 45 pipes from the Skiddy's Castle and Christ Church excavations in Cork City of a type which seems to be from the Cork/ Limerick region. These pipes, dating from the period 1650–90, have a flat heel, a 'slightly bulbous bowl with rouletting at the rim and a mark in relief on the base with a central *fleur de lis* and the letters 'NC' either above or either side' (Lane 1997a, 231). Pipes of this type have been recovered from excavations throughout Cork City, Dunboy castle, Lough Gur, King John's Castle and Charlotte's Quay in Limerick (Lane 1997b). A possible example of this mark was also found at Kilcolman Castle in the construction layer of a later-seventeenth-century cottage (Lane 2005, 147). The Waterford City excavations produced locally made examples as well but here the pipes were also largely imported from England with 17 bowls found dating to 1640–50 and seven from 1660–80 (Hurley and Scully 1997).

FUTHER INDUSTRIAL ENTERPRISE

A variety of other industrial ventures were also undertaken across Munster. As early as 1583/4 Sir Francis Walsinghan sponsored English miners to locate silver and copper miners near Youghal (MacCarthy-Morrogh 1986, 23). Two years later Wallop wrote a report for Walsingham on a alum mine in Kerry and recommends that a mining venture be undertaken there. The subsequent fate of these enterprises is unclear but more successful ventures were undertaken in the southwest. Exploratory silver mining appears to have taken place on Dursey Island while copper mining took place on the Beara Peninsula and on Sheep's Head later in the seventeenth century.

SUMMARY

Agricultural and industrial activities were an important part of both the physical character and socio-economic structure of the landscape throughout the time-period under study. There had been management of the landscape during the high and late medieval periods but it was undertaken on a more intensive and ordered manner in the seventeenth century. Previously the landscape appears to have been largely unenclosed but was still named and divided through the use of townlands and management units consisting of ploughlands and quarters. Demesne land was also in evidence. Much of the agricultural activity of this time was dominated by pastoralism with pockets of arable activity evident throughout the study area. Fishing, however, appears to have been the primary source of income for the lords at this time resulting from an upsurge in fish stocks from the middle of the fifteenth century associated with the rise in sea-temperature. The combination of all of this factors supports the fact that the lordship was an economically viable entity.

The advent of the late sixteenth-century and early seventeenth-century plantations fundamentally changed the character of the landscape and the nature of industrial operations occurring in the study area. There was rapid and pronounced development of enclosure and the commercialization of maritime trade and individual entrepreneurial investment in the fishing industry is evident. In many ways the planters were taking over existing enterprises and this is especially true of the fisheries. Their investment into this and other industries leads to much greater expansion and commercialization. There is also the development of large-scale industrial operations associated with charcoal burning and iron production. All of these efforts radically alter the landscape through division, deforestation, commercial development of the foreshore through the erection of piers and quays, and the establishment of nucleated settlements with large, diverse and often transient populations associated with industrial activity. These developments herald the advent of modernity and early capitalism, marked primarily by the emergence of a mercantile elite.

CHAPTER 8

Conclusion

The period under study was one that saw immense change across southwest
Ireland, marked by fundamental shifts in power structures, new forms of land
management and renewed investment in economy and infrastructure. By the
1560s the first elements of these changes begin to emerge and a number of Gaelic
lords responded in an attempt to maintain their position within society. The
Desmond revolt is traditionally viewed as a conflict between Catholicism and
Protestantism and as an attempt to reassert individual Gaelic power but in reality
was more complex than that. The rising was reflective of increased insecurity
amongst the Gaelic elite and landholders and constituted an attempt to reassert
their influence. The subsequent undertakings laid the foundation for large-scale
plantation not only across Munster but the rest of Ireland. These were originally
highly planned and organized schemes but actual experience on the ground led to
local adaptation (fig. 74). A degree of formality was maintained but both settlements and landholdings developed on more individual grounds. Whatever the
premise for these ventures they were to have a significant effect on political and
social relations across the region. The Gaelic lords became involved in a disparate
set of responses to the new arrivals ranging from militaristic resistance to
economic accommodation. Similarly, the Old English now engaged in a complex
set of socio-political and economic negotiations in an attempt to retain their
positions and holdings. Expansionist English policy intrinsically linked to emergent colonial enterprise was ultimately to lead to the outbreak of almost nationwide hostilities in the 1590s. Conflict was to drag on for nearly nine years and was
marked by uncoordinated activity, misunderstanding and ultimately some
damming examples of poor leadership during the major events of 1601 and 1602.

Following the defeat at Kinsale Gaelic power suffered a significant setback.
Undertakings gave way to large-scale plantation and rapid economic expansion.
This was especially evident in the larger urban centres and was exemplified by the
emergence of Bandon, encouraged largely by the entrepreneurial activity of a
small number of individuals. The early seventeenth century saw the beginnings of

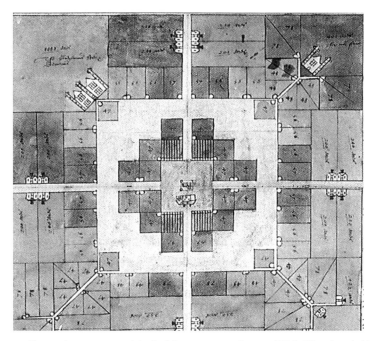

74 Sixteenth-century model of a Munster-type seignory (PRO SP 63/122 (55))

rapid growth in Cork. Between 1602 and 1641 the number of streets and lanes doubled and significant infrastructural work took place at its waterfront (McCarthy 1999, 85). Imports during this period were dominated by commodities including wine, iron, salt and other food stuffs coming from the ports of south-west Britain while exports consisted primarily of rugs, hides, tallow, woolfells and pipestaves. The rural landscape was subject to a similar intensification of activity. Widespread enclosure takes place, new agricultural estates were developed and industrial activity intensified. The 1610s and 1620s were largely peaceful but events both in Europe and in other parts of Ireland gradually led to the re-emergence of Gaelic confidence and the outbreak of rebellion in 1641. Historically, this was a complex event helped by a myriad of personal ambitions, religious division, ethnic tension and power brokering.

The wars of the 1640s and subsequent Cromwellian intervention saw widespread displacement and upheaval. There was a marked intensification of militaristic activity and fortification across the region and a renewal of garrison strength. Town fortifications were strengthened by elaborate earthen ramparts and siege defences were erected. The sustained period of conflict led to an economic downturn and a prolonged period of unrest. The 1650s saw the end of the conflict and a brief period where Ireland becomes part of the parliamentary regime. The subsequent Restoration of Charles II exposes the self-centred nature of the social and political elite across the region as they change sides and negotiate at will to maintain their status and wealth. Could any of these individuals truly have had a moral or ethical belief system grounded in anything else other than self-advancement? Following 1659 the power of Gaelic lords had essentially been broken. Landownership lay with a small number of individuals who came to play a pivotal role in the economic, political and societal development of the region over the following thirty-year period. This predominantly Protestant elite dominated the upper social classes in both urban and rural environments. They influenced the macro-political climate and largely dictated economic direction. Towns again experienced significant expansion as urbanization and population rise combined to facilitate economic growth associated with a rapidly developing north Atlantic world economy.

LIFE IN SEVENTEENTH-CENTURY TOWN

Life in a seventeenth-century town was negotiated through a complex set of hierarchical relationships marked by daily toil and an established set of ritual and leisure activities. Daily life was structured and conformed to an established set of rules and principles created and dictated from the top down. Towns functioned almost as semi-autonomous entities administered by mayor and aldermen. These individuals were elected found within a small circle of the upper echelons of society consisting of the town's leading merchants and gentlemen. They conducted regular meetings in a Tholsel or meetinghouse where they laid down the set of regulations and dictates that governed town activity. Many of these were self-developed by the corporation while others represented centralized sets of legislation enacted from Dublin or the Crown. Each of the important documents that contained legislative or administrative tracts was stored centrally in one or more chests, the keys of which were held by a number of designated individuals. These corporations functioned then in a very similar manner to contemporary town and city corporations. The aldermen maintained control over the central provision of town services and administration. Street cleaning services were maintained as were other services including fire prevention and forms of policing. Scavengers were employed to keep the streets clean operating a number of times a week to clear refuse. Drainage and regulations for waste dispersal were also in place. Each night the town watch would assemble to ensure night-time security within the walls. Access to the towns was closely controlled by a series of gates and walls, not just for security but also to protect economic enterprise and prevent abuses of the custom and tax systems. Gates were locked at night but there are repeated references to illegal entrances into towns as well as private gates or doorways that would have had far less rigid control. Schoolhouses and masters were often centrally supported while wealthier individuals also supported schools and almshouses built to provide housing and care for the town's poor or infirm. Aldermen further controlled town lands and were in charge of associated leases and rent. Building was closely controlled and a number of regulations were in place governing the location, type and form of buildings that could be constructed. Outside of the town significant amounts of common land was used for grazing and crop growing. A number of towns also had bogs where cutting was controlled.

Each of the towns in the study area essentially consisted of a single main street with a number of smaller side streets and laneways running off the main artery. The main street would have been lined by the houses and shop fronts of the town's leading merchants and retailers. In many cases the shop and house were interchangeable entities with the ground floor of the building serving as a display and storage area and the upper floors consisting of domestic space. These were largely timber and stone buildings often two or three storeys high with an attic and a slate roof. Thatch had been used widely but was increasingly falling out of use in the central urban areas due to the risk of fire. Lying off and behind the main street were lesser laneways and concentrations of lower quality houses. Here many of the town's artisans and workers lived in smaller dwellings. There was less of a sense of formal layout and planning in these areas that became increasingly poorer outside of the town walls in the concentrations of workers houses which developed in these areas. Each of the towns had a designated and recognizable central place. This would have been an open space often marked by a cross and it was here that daily, weekly or otherwize regular markets would have taken place. As with most other activity within the town the market was controlled by an established set of rules and regulations. A bell sounded to mark its opening and various stages of its operation. Indeed the sounding of town bells marked out the passage of day from the commencement of business through to the 8 p.m. drum calling of the night watch. A clerk oversaw the market and ensured good practice through weighing and inspection of goods. Tolls were charged to the sellers with preference being given to local traders with outsiders only allowed to commence trading a number of hours later and attracting higher charges.

The markets reflected the wide diversity of activity and occupations that took place within the towns. Many crafts and professions would have been represented including butchers, candle makers, bakers, shoe makers, apothecaries, masons, carpenters, sailors, merchants, weavers, millers, brewers, blacksmiths and tailors. In many cases individuals also served a number of different functions with many households having the capacity to brew their own beer. Numerous inns and hostels also served the towns and played an important social role for both residents and visitors. The town's waterfront, if it had one, was often the busiest area and focus of economic activity. Increasingly port activity becomes structured and formalized as the seventeenth century progressed and extensive facilities were created to accommodate this activity. Associated customs and tolls were a major source of income for the town and government. Numerous facilities were put in place to protect this activity ranging from port forts, protective waterfront structures and quarantine stations. Most towns also had garrisons and the men of the town could be called up to serve the town or Crown's defence during times of crisis. Many households would then have kept weaponry and each town would also have had a storehouse for ordnance, powder etc.

Religious activity was an important element of life. There was a certain degree of religious diversity present with towns having at least two communities represented, Catholic and Protestant. Other forms of worship must also have taken place in meeting houses and been conducted by individuals from other faith groups who moved through the port towns as part of the extensive networks created through seventeenth-century shipping. Sectarianism was not an overt part of urban society but did exist. It was probably more manifest on a macro political level than one experienced in everyday life. People came together for a number of celebrations throughout the year. Bonfires were often lit and the affairs could often become raucous following excess consumption of alcohol and the re-ignition of inter group feuds.

PLANTATION AND COLONIALISM

Later sixteenth-century English activity in Ireland heralds the beginnings of colonial enterprise and larger-scale imperial ambition on behalf of the English Crown. The initial undertakers pave the way for the colonial process and associated structures under the guise of plantation. Parts of Ireland subsequently become colonies immersed within the larger empire, a hugely complex and contested process. What drives a nation or more correctly a set of individuals to undertake colonial activity? What were the justifications and benefits of such enterprise? These events did not take place randomly or without a theoretical or philosophical framework. Many contemporary English commentators were at pains to justify and move the colonial project forward. Ireland then became a trial ground for future colonial activity and form future projects in the Americas and elsewhere. Contemporary discourse justifies this process and became an advocate for state sponsored intervention.

The initial agendas for colonization were justified by agendas of reform (Morrisey 2004a, 91). Justifications for the process included replacing the overly publicized barbarity of the 'native Irish' with the civility of the English. As early as January 1567, the Lord Deputy set out on a visitation of Munster and Connacht. In his official account he describes Munster as follows

> Like as I never was in a more pleasant country in all my life, so never saw I a more waste and desolate land. Such horrible and lamentable spectacles are there to behold – as the burning of villages, the ruin of churches, the wasting of such as have been good towns and castles; yea, the view of the bones and skulls of the dead subjects, who, partly by murder, partly by famine, have died in the fields as, in truth, hardly any Christian with dry eyes could behold'. He goes on to state that the territory of the Earl of Ormond was subject to 'a want of justice and judgment' and labels the Earl of Desmond as 'a man devoid of judgment to govern, and will be to be ruled'.

Three years later Sir Thomas Smith was granted possessions in the Ards, Co. Down in what was to be probably the earliest formal undertaking, albeit a short lived and ill fated enterprise. The broader territory in Ulster was described as laying 'waste, or else was inhabited with a wicked, barbarous, and uncivil people'.

Edmund Spenser (fig. 75) one of the primary advocates of the colonial process (quoted in Canny 2001) writes that there 'was never so great waste in any place, Nor so foul outrage done by living men; For all the cities they shall sack and raze, And the green grass that groweth they shall burn, That even the wild beast shall die in starved den'. Spenser in turn argued for a colonialism firmly supported by military activity in order to suppress dissent and secure newly planted areas with forts and garrisons. In doing so he was following classical models of military-led conquest and social domination. A strong military was also essential to protect the new emergent markets and ensure the sustainability of the

75 The poet Edmund Spenser from a portrait belonging to Pembroke College, Cambridge

economic reforms in the developing global capitalist world. Whole-scale change was required to ensure the success of the process and this entailed replacement of Gaelic traditions with those of the colonizers. Existing legal frameworks and institutions would need to be removed and replaced by structures approved by the new colonial powers.

It would be easy to suggest that the colonial project was only associated with a small group of people. Of course there were individual architects of the process, but in reality each landholder, each individual and artisan also had a role in shaping and developing the emergent colonial model as applied to the region. Each aspect of contemporary society was then used to develop and support this model. Settlement, and more particularly towns, became colonial institutions; for example, the port towns of the southwest coast developed as crucial militaristic and economic entities. They held key strategic positions in the maritime markets and communications networks of Northwest Europe and increasingly with the emergent markets of the Americas. The ports and harbours were also of strategic value in terms of fleet deployment and coastline protection in the ever-volatile political climate of Europe throughout the sixteenth century. It is unsurprising then that the ports also emerge as garrison towns associated with pivotal roles in defence, communications and provisioning. A number of more innovative tools were also used in the colonial process including map making and text (Smyth 2006). In the middle of the sixteenth century a certain sense of geographical order existed but this was one built on tradition and centuries-old understandings of territorial borders and established urban centres. This system was built upon the old urban nuclei surrounded by the virtually autonomous sept lands. There was no single source of centralized control but a significant amount of cultural and economic interchange was undertaken. The development of maps as a tool for quantifying and creating a new sense of place and territory emerges from the 1560s onwards before becoming an integral part of the political process in the 1650s when maps were used for assessing wealth, ordering displacement and solidifying new ownership. Maps were then tools in the creation and moulding of the landscape to suit the order imposed and imagined by the colonial architects and masters.

Text can also be recognized as a colonial mechanism. The actual writing of history and the creation of an administrative bureaucracy are all intrinsic agents of colonialism. We must recognize the inherent agenda of the writers and the subsequent product as those mostly written by an elite for the maintenance of an elite. This recognition warns against these writers as 'purveyors of the truth'. In this study we must then question the racial and cultural stereotypes created by contemporary writers. Similarly we must be cautious of accepting the values and belief frameworks individual writers forward. Texts that survive are not multi-vocal vehicles but rather selective and limiting documents that have to be viewed within the context of their time and creation. They are, of course, valuable as one of the means with which we can interrogate the past but constitute just one of the avenues open to us.

MODERNITY AND CAPITALISM

Many of the events and processes that occur in Munster at this time mark the beginnings of modernity across the region. Key indicators include the development and intensification of industrial activity and an associated rise in production linked to changing consumption patterns. There was a noticeable demand for produce both on a private and public level made possible through the increased availability of capital across a growing population and expansive economy. These processes are evidenced by a huge increase in the range and diversity of artefactual material, a proliferation of affluence across the social spectra and fundamental shifts in various industrial processes, for example the change from bloomery to blast furnace technology. Scale of production is an important component of these changes taking place on varying levels from industrial, through to craft and down to domestic activity. The archaeology of early modernity is then closely identified with the archaeology and emergence of early capitalism. Other key indicators in this linkage with industrial activity include the large-scale loss of woodland as the landscape was cleared for charcoal burning. Widespread enclosure and the reclaiming of waste land reflected shifting patterns and perceptions of land management and ownership. The construction of designed areas within the landscape to facilitate leisure activity, including gardens and parks, were also reflective of this process and of changing displays of affluence and wealth.

These shifts in process are paralleled by significant change within society's hierarchies. The emergence of a more affluent mercantile class is pronounced and overtly expressed through housing, dress and material culture. These classes engage in substantive renegotiations of status within society with new forms of bureaucracy being formed and new mechanisms for power brokering developed. The Gaelic lords who formerly held sway over much of the rural territory due to sept tradition are gradually displaced by a plethora of new leadership structures intrinsically linked to the new economic order and a restructured and divided class profile.

ETHNICITY AND IDENTITY

Extrapolating population sizes, ethnic diversity and constructions of identity across the region is difficult. No accurate census records exist and significant variations exist in the various calculations undertaken by historians on population size. Much of this has consisted of attempting to quantify settler numbers from the 1580s onwards (see MacCarthy Morrogh 1986; O'Flanagan 1993; Canny 2001). From the combination of studies it seems reasonable to suggest that Munster then had a settler population of over 20,000 immediately prior to 1641. The numbers of so-called Gaelic Irish or Old English are more difficult to determine. This is especially true given the significant impact the late sixteenth- and early seventeenth-century upheavals had on rural populations. Any calculation here would be spurious and ill considered. We can, however, with confidence suggest that there must have been considerable fluctuation in the demographic profile of the rural Gaelic Irish and the poorer classes during the later part of the sixteenth century. The numerous famines, periods of shortage and war attested to in the documentary sources must have had an effect on population size. Better estimates can be made for a number of the larger urban areas. Cork had an estimated population of just less than 3,000 in 1602 but this had risen to nearly 8,500 in 1641 (McCarthy 1999, 85). Significantly prior to the outbreak of conflict in 1641 the majority of the city's residents were Catholic. By 1659, however, only 33% of the residents of the walled town were Catholic but 72% of those who lived in the poorer quality houses outside of the walls in the suburbs were of that faith.

A similar pattern emerges when we examine the nature of landholding during this period. Prior to 1641 Catholics owned 65% of land. By 1660 this had fallen to 33% and after 1690 only 8% of landownership was in Catholic hands. Specific figures are also available for Waterford immediately prior to the outbreak of the revolt in 1641. At this time the Old English held 81% of land (121,198 acres), the New English had 15% (22,638 acres), while Gaelic families held the remaining 4% (6372 acres) (Ketch 1992). The New English become far more dominant following the end of the conflict and we see a corresponding rise in their population levels; for example, by 1659 there were 1291 New English in Waterford City. The New English were the undoubted victors of the tumultuous events of the middle of the century and come to command a far greater role in all aspects of society in the second half of the century.

The terminology used in the above paragraphs is interesting and implies an implicit tripartite ethnic division of society at this time. This can be misleading and is possibly too neat and a simplistic way of examining the composition of past society. It may have been a useful division for society's political hierarchy to adopt in order to create political and social allegiances and categorize society according to their needs but was it necessarily a true reflection of social make up? Did the so-called lower classes and poor within society necessarily view themselves as belonging to any of the above categories? Did they have a sense of belonging to any particular nation or were they more interested in the necessities of day-to-day living and survival? Previous rural populations along the western and southern seaboards would have owed allegiance to a variety of sept lords and would probably have grounded their sense of space and place within the traditions of the wider clan like group. As this older traditionalist model broke down these familial based allegiances must have waned. Accordingly we see the suburban populations of the towns increase in size as people left the countryside and the bonds of the sept to place themselves in a far more individual context within the domain of the expanding capitalist system. We can postulate that what we are seeing at this time is the movement away from being a sept labourer to that of a waged labourer. Even this analogy is simplistic and must be placed within a far wider set of processes and interactions taking place across society.

Constructed difference emerges throughout the period. We see differing versions of Englishness dependent on length of time spent in the country competing against, and indeed accommodating, groupings drawn from older insular-based identities; New English are pitted against Old English who are pitted against Gaelic Irish in a seeming never-ending cycle of agreement, disagreement, conflict and collaboration. Yet the island had been subject to so many political and economic arrivals over many centuries that it would truly be hard to find a 'cultural thoroughbred' from any of the labels adopted. There are dichotomies between urban and rural relationships, very apparent class divisions and a disparate array of communication and mercantile interactions in the maritime environment, itself being in a state of continual fluidity and international mixing. The resulting complex series of social negotiations, facilitated by the colonial process and economic intercourse, does not then lend itself to simple black-and-white patterns of ethnicity. No one individual concept of identity can in reality become dominant or all invasive and totally replace pre-existing traditions and cultural norms. Instead theorists like Homi Bhabha suggest that a hybrid or creole culture emerges that adopts, creates and selects new forms of cultural expression and traditions (Gosden 2001, 241). So, we do not see the total abandonment of so-called Gaelicness in Munster at this date: language, musical traditions, dress and other forms of expression survive. This is not to say that what went before was in anyway a pure culture but rather one that had been accumulating and integrating multivariate influences over many centuries. The southwest of Ireland was not an isolated geographically remote entity cut off from external contact for the previous millennia but was instead an area open to extensive external and in many cases internal influences. The notion then that colonialism fundamentally changes the cultural constructs of society is outdated. Instead societies engage in very varied ways to the colonial process involving multi-faceted responses and continual renegotiation. The constraints to these responses lie within imposed or evolving power relations and the agencies of change and development within societies.

GAELIC NEGOTIATION/ACCOMODATION/RESISTANCE

The varied responses to the colonial project in Munster is of interest. Traditional histories tell of a fight for survival between the indigenous Gaelic Irish against the invasionary forces of the English, a fight for religious survival and Gaelic nationhood. Again the reality the situation was far more complex than this. Initial resistance did take place, most notably the Desmond revolt, but this was not fought over national sovereignty or sole religious issues but was rather an attempt by a regional lordship to maintain its power base. It is suggested here that this is the key feature that characterizes Gaelic resistance. There is no real defined sense of a Gaelic nation defending itself in the 1560–80s but instead we see pronounced individualism and regionalism emerging and voicing its sense of insecurity and feelings of threat as a result of the Crown's designs on sept land. The militaristic resistance by the Clandonnell Roe and other groups and individuals across the southwest can be seen in this light. These small groups were operating in an uncoordinated and often ineffective way to disrupt settler life. An increasing commonality of cause emerges in 1590s when religion acts as a cultural bind among the lordships. This was not a nationalist movement but was again a concerted attempt by an established form of lordship to retain its power and influence. There was recognition of cultural commonality but to what extent this transcended into a movement advocating national unity is highly debateable. By the 1640s such feelings can be detected more overtly with an emergent sense of national cohesion but this was across complex cultural entities operating in a disjointed and often conflicting manner.

Many of the Gaelic Irish across the study region did not engage in resistance but instead saught to maintain their influence through varying forms of accommodation. A number of mechanisms were used to facilitate this negotiation including marriage, building styles, dress and language. The O'Briens of Inchiquin survived through religious adoption, political accommodation and strategic marriage alliances. Sections of the O'Sullivan Beare sept also engaged in marriage alliances with the settlers and more effectively use the tool of land mortgage to integrate themselves into the new economic order. Indeed such mortgaging activity and the leasing of lands became a key financial tool for a number of lordships in maintaining economic survival. Other forms of negotiation also take place. English was now widely spoken by the Gaelic lords and there are documented cases where rivals were derided for speaking in the native tongue. One of the most obvious forms of accommodation was the widespread adoption of material cultural and architectural fashion. The abandonment by the new O'Sullivan Beare of his tower house at Carriganass for a mansion house at Reenadisert is reflective of this change as is the MacCarthy mansion house at Kanturk. This was a house that adopted a number of building trends from England but also exhibits two entrances. The main doorway is an elaborate structure built in an English style but a second arched doorway is of a typical sixteenth-century Gaelic type. These two features reflect the duality of existence and the extent individuals went to in order to appeal to different communities or audiences.

FRAMEWORK FOR FUTURE RESEARCH

If nothing else this work has illustrated how much further work is required in this region. A cursory glance through the previous chapters will reveal the limited extent of archaeological investigation undertaken to date. Sustained and integrated programmes of research are now required to develop this subject area further. Existing research has only begun to touch on the historical resource that exists across the province. A number of key themes require formulation with subsequent research frameworks established and properly funded. In the urban areas recognition needs to be given to the important changes which took place in terms of town morphology and building styles at this time. Greater effort needs to take place during the course of urban investigations to elucidate evidence of these changes. In particular targeted programmes of investigation could be sponsored at the important towns of Youghal and Bandon. The precinct of St Mary's in the former town stands out as a spectacular monument complex that requires far greater attention. In all of Munster's urban areas greater attention also needs to be paid to the historic fabric of each building. It is likely that there is a far greater level of survival of seventeenth-century features in these buildings than previously thought. Archaeologists then need to engage with conservation architects in targeted investigative programmes of research to examine the evolution of these buildings. Similarly buildings and settlement morphology in the rural environment require greater attention. Traces of these settlements will be subtle and existing archaeological practice may not be as finely tuned to their presence. The physical fabric of the Church during this period is also little understood yet its buildings and practice were undergoing profound change. Construction and publication of digital artefactual databases would be of great use while greater analysis of the ecofactual resource from this period is also a priority.

Finally, more theoretical engagement with the multitude of sources is required. There is an opportunity here for archaeologists to immerse themselves in examining the social processes and contexts of this formative period in Ireland's history. Many of the political and social interactions of that time resonate in contemporary society. Examinations of the underlying processes and outcomes can then be used to inform our approaches to contemporary society and the issues we currently face in relation to Ireland's role in an increasingly globalized world. Other subjects must also recognize the contribution archaeology can make to develop our understandings of this period. Archaeology is not a hand maiden to any other subject area but yet cannot alone singularly reconstruct past society in the late sixteenth-seventeenth century. Greater discourse between the various branches of the social and historical sciences needs then to take place in an attempt to create a more engaged, discursive and holistic view of this important period in the development of society on this island.

Late sixteenth-/seventeenth-century findings: excavations in southwest Ireland, 1975–2002

Appendix: A provisional list of significant excavations which have took place in the southwest region which produced evidence of late sixteenth- and seventeenth-century material. This should not be viewed as an exhaustive list and has been drawn largely from the annual excavations bulletin now published by Wordwell and edited by Isobel Bennett. The first column details the county where the excavation took place. The second column lists the site name, relevant grid reference and site type. Column three lists the site's excavation bulletin number, its relevant SMR number(s), the excavation code and the name of the principal excavator(s). Finally, the fourth column lists the primary material recovered from the excavation which is relevant to this current study.

County	Excavation name and type	Excavation no. and excavator	Description
Cork City	South Main Street – W670716 Urban	1975:10 Dermot Twohig	17th-century stone houses and almshouses; unfinished well-shaft adjacent to one of the 17th-century houses contained a large quantity of slates, ridge tiles, pottery, clay pipes and wine bottles. A number of stone-built refuse pits in which was found a good range of 17th- and 18th-century pottery.
Cork City	81–83 Grand Parade W671715 City Wall	1992:022 Joanna Wren	City Wall surviving to a maximum height of 1.35m. Above this the wall had been rebuilt probably sometime in the late 17th or early 18th century. This later wall was built of well-coursed limestone ashlar. All of the late 16th and early 17th century maps show a mural rower on this stretch of the city wall and the perpendicular wall may have formed part of such a tower. Parts of the city wall particularly in its later life, may have functioned as quay wall and

→

County	Excavation name and type	Excavation no. and excavator	Description
(contd)			this wall may have been a boat tie-up or a dock. Finds: 17th-century harp tuning peg from unstratified material.
Cork City	Grand Parade/ Washington Street 16781 07123 Urban post medieval	2002:277 SMR 74:122, 74:34 (01,02) 02E0034 Hilary Kelleher	No structures predating 18th century found on Grand Parade. Sections of town wall – roughly dressed limestone blocks with some sandstone, 1.5 to 2m wide, basal batter – found on Washington Street. Wall demolished after 1690. Clear rebuilding evidence in upper section of wall in one trench – late 16th/ early 17th-century rebuild.
Cork City	Kyrl's Quay/ North Main Street W671721 Urban	1992:023 Maurice Hurley	Section of original 6m high city wall located, now serves as defence and waterfront wall in 17th century.
Cork City	Red Abbey Yards, W675714 Urban	1992:024 Cathy Sheehan	Augustinian Priory, 17th-century cobbled surface located and an east-west wall, randomly-coursed, roughly-dressed limestone with slight batter, may be northern limit of abbey complex. Slob land to north and habitable areas to south. Slob land infilled in late 17th century.
Cork City	17 Grattan Street, Cork City W675717 Urban	1997:036 97E0387 Maurice Hurley	Section of medieval town wall found to have collapsed outwards in mid- 17th century due to being built on unstable ground. Wall rebuilt using original as a foundation. Finds: pottery.
Cork City	Philips Lane/ Grattan Street, Cork City 16698 07205 Urban	1997:038 97E205 Mary O'Donnell	15m stretch of town wall uncovered, shows rebuilding in 17th century. 17th century gateway through this wall from Philips Lane onto modern Grattan Street. Possible 17th-century stone building, measuring 6.8m N/S and 7.8m E/W built on earlier medieval house using sections of the earlier building.

County	Excavation name and type	Excavation no. and excavator	Description
Cork City	Grattan Street, Cork City 16727 07202 City Wall	1998:068 98E0105 Tony Cummins	Section of 17th century rebuilding of city wall uncovered. Wall survived to a height of 1.2–1.3m. Masonry roughly hewn limestone, size rage (0.1m x 0.1m to 0.4 m x 0.4m) with some sandstone and slate inclusions. Bonded with lime mortar.
Cork City	South Main Street /Hanover Place/ Liberty Street/ Cross Street, Cork City W670720 Urban	2000:0132 RMP74:03401, 74:122 Maurice Hurley, John Trehy, Vincent Price	Structural features found in Hanover Place trench with quantities of post-medieval pottery, oyster shells and animal bone 1.4 m below present ground surface. Section of inner (east) wall face of city wall, built of random courses of red and green sandstone located at western end of Liberty Street, 0.8m below present ground surface. Multi-phased stone walls, possibly associated with later 16th-century Droop's mill, located. Wall F43 built of slabs of red sandstone and limestone. Mortar-bonded limestone and sandstone 1.1m wide wall built on timber piles set into estuarine clays found in Cross Street.
Cork City	Cornmarket Street W670720 Urban Post medieval	2001:154 00E0124 ext. SMR 74–122 Maurice Hurley	East Marsh, adjacent to channel at Cornmarket Street, reclaimed late in the 17th century. Quay walls and 'The Walkabout' constructed. Sections of these quay walls uncovered including 6.95m length of the 'Potatoe Quay Wall'. Wall was *c*.0.4m wide, to a height of 1–1.45m and survived to 0.95m below the modern road surface, orientated north–south and constructed of lime-mortared green and red sandstone and limestone. Further south a 2.25m north-west/south-east length of quay wall was uncovered and was 1.4m in width and stood to a maximum height of 1.9m. This wall was of eight courses and was composed of limestone and red sandstone blocks. The bottom two courses had an ope (0.6m x 0.5m) which probably functioned as a drain – excavator suggests that this was early 18th-century in date. Third section

→

County	Excavation name and type	Excavation no. and excavator	Description
(contd)			of quay wall uncovered at the east side of the street. Section measuring 4.6m north–south length was located and was *c.*0.5m wide and stood to a height of 1.75 m. It consisted of nine to ten courses of limestone and green and red sandstone blocks bonded with lime mortar. Probably a remnant of Newenham's (Newman's) Quay, which stretched from the Cornmarket to the North Channel of the River Lee. When quays became obsolete the channel was culverted in the late 17th/early 18th century. Section of a rough limestone and sandstone wall orientated north–south and exposed for a length of 7m with an average width of 0.5m and stood to a height of 1.1m. It comprised four to five regular courses of limestone bonded by lime mortar lying over an earlier poorly preserved section of wall, clay bonded with only five courses of sandstone. Excavator suggests this may be the inner face of 'The Walkabout'.
Cork City	Urban 16716 7177 Post medieval	2002:270 01E0984 ext. SMR 74:34 (01, 02), 74:122 Hilary Kelleher	Excavations revealed components of suburb development on reclaimed river channels and marshes in late 17th century (South Mall, Oliver Plunkett Street, Grand Parade and Parnell Place). Culverts demonstrated the covering or infilling of river channels at end of 17th century. Many stone-lined and capped drains also found. Extensive post medieval artefactual assemblage uncovered.
Cork Co.	Glanworth – R757041 Castle	1980–84:0057 Conleth Manning	Tower house occupied into 18th century. Further south against the west wall remains of a large bread oven, in use in the early 17th century were found.

County	Excavation name and type	Excavation no. and excavator	Description
Cork Co.	Bridgetown Abbey Medieval priory	1998:060 98E0377 SMR 34:02702 Eamonn Cotter	Post dissolution domestic stone-built building uncovered with cobbled surface on west side of refectory, walls rendered internally. Small rectangular chamber also uncovered to the west of the church with a chimney below ground surface. Iron slag also suggests iron working on site. Features are likely to be late 16th/ early 17th century in date. May be associated with granting of site to farmer.
Cork Co.	Barryscourt Castle, Carrigtwohill 1822 0725 Late medieval castle	1998:061 96E0238 Dave Pollock	Kitchen extended in 16th century but damaged probably in 1581. Rebuilt shortly afterwards with an enclosing mortared bawn wall and buildings range to west. This included a timber hall built on unmortared stone footing. Garden beds and trees now set out. Possibly early in 17th century this enclosed area of bawn raised and revetted with mortared wall (garden feature/artillery placement).
Cork Co.	Kilcolman Castle R58113 Medieval castle, post-med. Fortification and plantation residence	1994:029 94E108 Eric Klingelhofer 1995:030 94E108	Purchased by Edmund Spenser in 1587–1617, attacked 1598. Building with possible measurements of 3mx10m uncovered with internal cobble floor, clay-bonded walls, 2m wide internal fireplace, possible hipped roof with timber framing walls – possibly the 'convenient English house' erected by 1622 to replace the burned 'fair stone house' of Spenser. Earlier hall also possibly present. Finds: Elizabethan window glass and lead window fittings, pewter spoon – late 16th and north Devon gravel-tempered pottery.
		1996:051 94E108	Uncovered 'parlour' underlying timber-framed house of previous season. Wooden floored, window with iron mullion, 0.3m-high surviving plaster wall face (clay-bonded), undecorated. Structure was probably 10mx6.5m between tower house and probably hall site – destroyed c.1600. Finds: clay pipes of first quarter of 17th century, base of Rhenish stoneware drinking pot.

County	Excavation name and type	Excavation no. and excavator	Description
(contd)			Uncovered rebuilt hearth for parlour, destroyed in fire of c.1615 (Spenser's son Sylvanus now leaves for English-style house elsewhere). Late 17th-century cottage built on site with cobbled farmyard. Finds: butchered animal bones, domestic artefacts, early 17th-century clay pipe Well-worn bone (or ivory) lute turning-peg.
Cork Co.	Kill-Saint-Anne-South, Castlelyons 8412 9262 Adjacent to fortified house	1997:042 96E308 Eamonn Cotter	Adjacent to Ballymore Castle, possible midden associated with house located. Finds: Oyster shells, significant quantities of animal bone and small mammal bones.
Cork Co.	Dunasead Castle, Baltimore 10468 02649 'Fortified house'	1998:056 SMR 150:03602 98E0186 Eamonn Cotter	Possible '17th-century fortified house', rectangular measuring 18.5m N/S and 5.82 E/W internally. Two storeys high, with attic and high gables. Enclosed by bawn wall 28m N/S and 14m E/W. Floor foundation layer found directly overlying bedrock consisting of shale hard-core overlain by compacted mortar and small shale fragments. Foundations of garderobe tower on east wall, stone-lined well (0.7m diameter – predated house construction) and exterior paved and cobbled areas also located. Stone-lined drain uncovered in bawn. Finds: late medieval pottery (in fill of well also), two fragments of ceramic ridge tile (similar to North Devon tiles), some metal (possible railing around well).
Cork Co.	Baltimore 10468 02649 Fortified House	2002:225 SMR 150:36(02) 98E0186 ext. Eamonn Cotter	Interior of site excavated. Two hearths, one standing on a probable grate, uncovered which appear to predate site. Contained within rectangular structure. Excavator suggests this was a two roomed structure dating to 17th century, orientated north/south with northern room measuring 4.3m x 3.6m N/S. Hearths in each room in walls.

County	Excavation name and type	Excavation no. and excavator	Description
Cork Co.	Charles Fort, Forthill, Kinsale W652495 Star-shaped fort	1998:080 SMR 125:7 98E0536 Margaret McCarthy	Trench opened opposite to main entrance and located traces of recent military activity. Previous monitoring in 1979 had located a substantial wall close to citadel and section of ditch cut into bedrock.
Cork Co.	Jame's Fort, Old-Fort, Kinsale 16463 04963 Star-shaped fort	1998:082 SMR 112:36 98E0279 Mary O'Donnell	South Bastion – Excavations of inner fortification showed inner works made up of rampart, enclosed by outer facing wall of bastion. Possible setting for flagpole found ontop of bastion. Evidence of burning on rampart slope. Finds: post medieval pottery, lead musket shot, animal bones, clay pipes, glass and slate roof tiles. Entrance – causeway running across moat to bastion gateway with flagstone surface and low stepped wall. Moat – moat cut was 3.6m wide and 1.2–1.4m deep. Steep sided with flat to rounded base. Moat filled by building collapse under mortar layer under a silt layer. One cutting (1A) showed evidence of burning, possibly associated with that on south bastion. Finds: post-medieval pottery, clay pipes, lead musket shot, bottle glass, animal bone. North Bastion – roughly flagged surface found in interior.
Cork Co.	Gully townland, Bandon 14890 05515 Urban	2000:0115 SMR 110:19/01 00E0857 Maurice Hurley	Richard Cox, in the 1680s describes the town as 'built within the memory of man and walled about with a handsome and strong wall of lime and stone, and fortified by eleven flankers and three of the stateliest gatehouses or castles in any town in Europe' (quoted in O'Flanagan 1988, 4). Bennett (1869, 67) described the town walls of Bandon as under construction in 1621 but noted a reference of 1616 describing a house as 'built with out the walls, by the west gate'. He described the walls as being 'mainly composed of a thick, black slate. There [sic] were ➤

	County name and type	Excavation and excavator	Excavation no.	Description
(contd)				generally about nine feet thick, and varied in height from thirty feet to fifty. There were six bastions – one at each corner of the walls, one in the river, and one midway on the south wall.' Section of wall located 2.47m wide and standing to 1.7–1.9m in height. Wall face rendered with hard lime mortar below ground level. Outer western face also likely to have been rendered.
Cork Co.	Casement Road, Bandon W487545 Town wall	1998:057 98E05003		Testing adjacent to outer face of town wall uncovered no trace of archaeological material.
Cork Co.	MacSweeny Quay, Bandon 14900 05497 Urban	1999:076 99E0158 Eamonn Cotter		An area within Bandon that was probably An area within Bandon that was probably gardens in the 17th century. Excavations uncovered a silt-loam layer 0.6m overlying the natural gravels.
Cork Co.	Gully, Bandon Town wall	2001:122 00E0857 Sheila Lane		Base of the town wall located at a depth of 1.9m below present ground level. Approximately 0.6m of the wall foundation was identified and the wall was found to measure 1.5m in width.
Cork Co.	College Grounds, Emmet Place, Youghal X101782 Urban	1995:039 95E076 SMR67:29/06 Catyrn Power		College, grounds and gardens of 15th-century College of Youghal, acquired by Richard Boyle who added towers and walling. Possible late 17th/early 18th century building located north of 17th-century wall. Underlying medieval ditch found, possibly representing earlier defensive fortification in 13th century.
Cork Co.	Chapel Lane, Youghal X104782 Urban	1994:034 94E165 Rose Cleary		Three 17th-/18th-century buildings recorded.

	County name and type	Excavation and excavator	Excavation no.	Description
Cork Co.	2–3 South Main Street, Youghal Urban	1998:090 98E0163 Jacinta Kiely		No archaeological stratigraphy was recorded.
Cork Co.	Ashe Street, Youghal 21064 07783 Post medieval	2001:240 SMR 67:29(01) 01E0876 Maurice Hurley		A number of 17th-century ceramic sherds and clay pipe stems in an area that has past few centuries. Finds appear to have been introduced with garden soil/manure.
Cork Co.	Hill Cottage, Gaol Steps, Youghal 210475 777225 Town Wall	2002:371 02E0424 SMR 67:29 (01, 02) Daniel Noonan		Area largely used as gardens in post medieval period. Excavations revealed late 17th/early 18th-century earthenware ceramics
Cork Co.	Black Rock, Bantry House 09869 04814 Later medieval settlement	2001:123 01E0648 SMR 118:75 Colin Breen		Currently a greenfield site, known as the West Lawn, directly to the west of Bantry House, a large 18th-century estate house. This site appears to have been abandoned in the middle of the 17th century, There are clear earthworks in the field, Extensive archaeological deposits were found, including a mid-17th-century house represented by the survival of its western gable foundations, which in turn overlay a more substantial and better-built rectangular structure, interpreted as a timber-built English administrative building. A palisade trench, dug late in the 16th or early in the 17th century, presumably to provide a stockade around the early plantation settlement, immediately pre-dated this building. Sixteenth-century cultivation ridges were uncovered which, interestingly, cut the foundations of a 15th-16th-century Gaelic domestic structure.
Cork Co.	Kilcoe 10192 03282 Tower-house	2001:184 01E0310 SMR 140:32 Eamonn Cotter		Late-medieval bawn features uncovered.

County	Excavation name and type	Excavation no. and excavator	Description
Cork Co.	Ballinvinny South 173953 079681 Post medieval Settlement	2001:210 01E0111 Eamonn Cotter	Excavation of medieval moated site. Two houses found internally associated with Saintogne ware. Both houses measured 10mx5m with one orientated E/W and the second N/S. This second wooden house had stone chimney foundation in NE . corner. Three 17th-century domestic houses found overlying medieval moated site. House walls identified by shallow foundation trenches which may have held wooden sill-beams. One house measured *c.*11m by 5m, containing one large room at each end, and a small central room. A hearth was placed in the east gable wall and the entrance appears to have been in the centre of the south wall. In the external area a shallow U-shaped channel with a metalled surface ran along the east wall and downslope, along the north wall of the house. Excavator suggests that this was to carry water dripping from the roof. A hoard of 68 coins wrapped in cloth was found in this house, identified as James II 'gun money', dated 1689–90. To the immediate south-west of these houses a pair of parallel ditches ran southwards. A late medieval boundary consisting of a pair of parallel ditches was found to the south-west of the settlement.
Cork Co.	Ballinvinny South 173953 079681 Post-medieval smithy	201:111 01E0633 Eamonn Cotter	Part of a wider settlement complex dating from the late or post-medieval period, including domestic structures 80m to the north and a post-medieval roadway. The area has been identified as a smithy floor identified as area of burnt clay and charcoal with layer of metal fragments/ smithying 'scales', tiny metal fragments struck off by the smith's hammer as iron shaped and moulded. Smithy fire located to north while anvil was to south. Stake holes for metal supports for smithy fire and bellows structure found, as well as possible anvil pit. Metalled surface of fine

→

County	Excavation name and type	Excavation no. and excavator	Description
(contd)			pebbles found to north-west and identified as possible pathway Artefactual evidence suggests smithy complex dated from the late 17th into the 18th century.
Cork Co.	'Rathbarry Castle', Castlefreke W340352 Adjoining tower house	1993:019 SMR 143:7402 93E0072 Richard Crumlish	A 15th-century tower house besieged for eight months in 1642. In the 18th century, the landowner, Lord Carberry, converted site to farmyard when new residence built at Castlefreke. Test trenches produced fills of dumped material including post medieval ceramics and walls from later farm buildings. Possible traces of section of original curtain wall also found.
Cork Co.	Rathbarry Church, Castlefreke 13258 03524	2002:257 SMR 143:76(03) 02E0209 Eamonn Cotter	Western end of church 17th or 18th century in date. Tower at this end of church extensively excavated and examined.
Cork Co.	Carriganass 104802 05659 Tower-house and bawn	2002:248 SMR106:1 02E0834 Colin Breen	Excavations in the bawn area uncovered the foundations of the tower house and bawn wall. 17th-century artefactual assemblage recovered under extensive 18th-century farm yard development.
Cork Co.	Carrigohane Castle W1614807168 Tower house and fortified house	2002:255 SMR 73:49(01) 02E1375 Florence Hurley	15th-century castle in ruins by late 16th century. Fortified house built adjacent to it. 17th-century projecting tower removed in 1990s.
Cork Co.	Castledonovan 11134 04955 Tower house	2002:256 SMR119:17(02) 02E1569 Annette Quinn	Drainage channels uncovered in caphouse at NW corner at top of tower house. Fill of channels included animal bone, a lead musket shot, roof slates and a 17th-century ridge tile.

County	Excavation name and type	Excavation no. and excavator	Description
		KERRY	
Kerry	*'St Brendan's Cathedral', Ardfert Medieval cathedral Q786214	1990:066 SMR 20:46 Fionnbar Moore	Extensive evidence of late medieval burials. South transept extended into a pre-existing cemetery in the 17th century. Three post-medieval statues, roof slates and post-medieval ridge tile fragments also recovered.
Kerry	St Brendan's Cathedral, Ardfert Medieval cathedral Q786214	2000:0407 RMP 20:46 E000493 Fionnbar Moore	Probable late medieval/17th-century doorway level found at north east doorway.
Kerry	Ballinskelligs Castle, Ballinskelligs Tower house V434654	1988:27 John Sheehan	Small rectangular tower house. Two poorly preserved post medieval external buildings found on either side of the castle doorway. Eastern structure, probably of timber construction, measured 4m x 3m with cobbled Evidence for the second building survived only as a small area of a stone wall 1.5m by 0.55m. Irregular trench found to south west with fill of soil and post-medieval pottery. Small section of northeast interior and intramural chamber of tower house excavated. Original floor of the castle was formed by a series of large stone flags set in a mortar base with finds consisting mainly of iron nails, post-medieval pottery and early wine bottles. Cutting beneath garderobe ope-chute uncovered a shallow, broad pit, 2.7m in maximum width and 0.4m in maximum depth, containing a highly organic deposit including quantities of post-medieval pottery, bones and shells. Collapse layer with post-medieval pottery overlay this feature. Post medieval pottery dominated assemblage from excavation with gravel tempered ware most common with stoneware, combed slipware, sgraffito, Westerwald, brownware, mottled ware and beauvais also present.

County	Excavation name and type	Excavation no. and excavator	Description
Kerry	'Ballinskelligs Castle', Ballinskelligs Tower house V 434654	1991:064 John Sheehan	Large portion of internal ground-floor original paved floor uncovered on a bedding layer of silty clay loam. No earlier floor level was evident. Finds from the interior largely consisted of post-medieval pottery, iron nails and fragments of corroded iron. Majority of artefacts recovered consisted of post-medieval pottery sherds, with gravel-tempered wares predominating. Other finds included a number of early buttons, early wine bottle fragments and a bronze book-mount.
Kerry	Dingle Monitoring in medieval town Q447013	1994:122 SMR 43:224 93E192 Richard Crumlish	In Holy Ground organic layer with charcoal inclusions found containing a large quantity of oyster and periwinkle shells, and a small number of animal bone fragments. Ten sherds of 17th-century pottery found within this context. Undisturbed context also located in Main St consisting of sandy deposit with a large quantity of stones, some shell and animal bone fragments and three sherds of post-medieval pottery Two shell middens (both found within the undisturbed context in Main St, and a culvert of post-medieval date (located in Green St) were also uncovered.
Kerry	Bray Head (Valentia Island) Early medieval farm and village V344737	1997:231 97E278 Alan Hayden	Extensive early medieval and later evidence found of agricultural activity. In the later medieval period a street of houses was built on top of the medieval fields and continued to be occupied until the 16th or 17th century at this site.
Kerry	Bray Head (Valentia Island) Early medieval/ post-medieval farm and settlement 343000 736000	2001:549 01E0814 Alan Hayden	House VII was was a very poorly preserved rectangular stone building. No floor levels survived within it. Excavator suggests it is likely to be of late medieval date but no datable finds were recovered from it. House I was excavated at Site 2. A well built rectangular house, 4.6m x 7.6m

→

County	Excavation name and type	Excavation no. and excavator	Description
(contd)			was erected against the high lynchette at the downhill end of one of the larger medieval fields of the farm. It is associated with a number of small fields, which are subdivisions of older and larger fields. Two-phased structure – original drystone and sod walls were replaced by totally drystone walls and interior refloored in the later 17th century. Several hearths, drains and post-holes were uncovered in its interior, as were extensive deposits of ash. The house was built inside a small enclosure defined by a narrow ditch and a bank. Sections were opened across these features. Two raised cultivation beds, delimited by stone walls, were also uncovered south of the house within the enclosure.
Kerry	Castleconway, Killorglin Tower-house 7774 9640	1998:278 SMR 56:25 98E0319 Lar Dunne	Multi phased tower house rebuilt in 17th century.
Kerry	Tailor's Row, Castlegregory 062140 013350	2002:773 SMR27:8 (adjacent) 02E1858 Niamh O'Callaghan	Near castle site, possibly built by Gregory Hoare, a tenant-in-chief of Desmonds, in 16th century. A number of architectural fragments survive including two inscribed arched sections, gun-loop and a dripstone. Garden soil found at lowest levels of trial trenches but no artefactual or structural material found.

WATERFORD

Waterford	St Augustine Street ('Friary Street'), Dungarvan Urban District Town ditch and well X226930	1989:095 X226930 Catryn Power	At Junction of Friary Street and Emmet Street ditch uncovered with 17th-19th-century layers consisting of dumped glass, ceramics and animal and fish bone. Town wall was in use into the 17th century and excavator suggests that this ditch may have been moat associated with wall.

County	Excavation name and type	Excavation no. and excavator	Description
Waterford	'Dungarvan Castle', Dungarvan Medieval castle X262930	1995:265 95E080 Dave Pollock	East end of shell keep redeveloped to accommodate artillery. D-shaped tower slighted in 16th or 17th century.
Waterford	Dungarvan Castle 2262 0927	1997:571 95E0080 Dave Pollock	South side of hall fallen in 17th/ 18th century. Platform of rocks and clay, interpreted as possible artillery platform, found behind 15th/16th-century D-shaped tower. Tower and wall mined at end of 17th century when barracks built and wall reconstructed.
Waterford	Dungarvan Castle Medieval and post-medieval castle 2262 0927	1998:635 95E0080 Dave Pollock	Ditch between the keep and the curtain wall was largely infilled by the 16th century; in the 16th or 17th century the depression directly outside the main entrance to the keep was further infilled with fill revetted with a clay-bonded wall. Battered base of the keep was blanketed with a layer of rubble and clay, for protection against artillery attack and supporting internal rampart. Traces of buildings were found in the disturbed ground inside the north curtain wall. A door in the curtain was inserted or rebuilt, probably in the 1640s, and provided with a flanking tower. Curtain wall was mined from the inside and exploded at the end of the 17th century.
Waterford	Dungarvan Castle Medieval and post-medieval castle 2262 0927	1999:847 95E0080 Dave Pollock	Passage between the D-towers had been lowered in the late medieval period and resurfaced with beach gravel. Later fire in the passage associated with considerable destruction pre-dating the slighting at the end of the 17th century.
Waterford	Carberry's Lane, Dungarvan 2262 0930 99E0115	1999:844 SMR 31:4 99E0115 Dave Pollock	Section of 17th-century development of town wall examined with construction consisting of drystone foundations with mortar occasionally poured in. Linear clay pit found floored with beach cobbles and used as laneway to beach.

County	Excavation name and type	Excavation no. and excavator	Description
Waterford	Davitt's Quay/ Old Market House, Dungarvan 2263 0930	1999:846 SMR 31:4 99E0666	Quay constructed possible late in 17th/early 18th century. Old Market House appears to be of a similar date. 17th-century ground surface present over beach gravels.
Waterford	Castle Street, Dungarvan 2263 0929	2002:1784 SMR 31:40 02E0120 Dave Pollock	Series of mettaled surfaces, clay floors and infilled clay pits all dating to late medieval and early 17th century uncovered.
Waterford	Shandon, Dungarvan Post medieval 2589 9440	2002:1791 SMR 31:41 020809 Daniel Noonan	Possible late 17th-century house. Excavations largely uncovered 18th-and 19th-century farm activity.
Waterford	Castle Avenue, Lismore Urban 20465 09843	2001:1244 SMR 21:29 01E0289	Extensive 17th-century garden landscaping consisting of platforms and ditches uncovered.
Waterford	Duncannon Bar, Waterford Harbour Shipwreck 272590 106200	2001:1259 01E0363 Niall Brady 2002:1821	Timbers, iron cannon balls and a piece of copper sheathing recovered from dredging works. Wreck site identified consisting of a timber ship with six iron cannon, four lead pots in area 40m x 20m.
Waterford City	21 George's Street, Waterford Urban medieval 26044 11204	2001:1251 RMP 9:5 01E0775 Anne Marie Lennon	Excavations adjacent to town wall uncovered post medieval structures and pottery assemblages.
Waterford City	Grady's Yard, John Street, Waterford Urban medieval 26074 11198	2001:1252 SMR 9:5(18) 01E0323, 01E0987 Dave Pollock	John's bridge built in late medieval period along with wall from the Bastion to St John's Gate.
Waterford City	Lady Lane, Waterford Urban medieval defences	2001:1254 00E0276 Jonna Wren	Throughout late medieval and early 17th-century external fosse was gradually infilled and land becomes 'marginal'. Area now landscaped in early part of 17th-century and used as a pathway and ➤

County	Excavation name and type	Excavation no. and excavator	Description
(contd)			probably a garden. Are covered with boulder clay and demarcated by a stone kerb. Drains also cut. Features gone out of use by end of century when demolition debris covers site, possibly associated with demolition of gate-tower *c.*1698.
Waterford	Knockhouse Upper/ Woodstown Post medieval 255611 112036 – 256008 112486	2002: 1799 02E0274 Deirdre Murphy	Spread of archaeological material including North Devon gravel-tempered ware.

Abbreviations

JWAHS	*Journal of the Waterford Archaeological and Historical Society*
OS	Ordnance Survey
PRO	Public Record Office (London)
RIA	Royal Irish Academy (Dublin)
TCD	Trinity College Dublin

PRINTED SOURCES

The Book of Rights	J. O'Donovan (Dublin, 1847).
Cal. Carew MSS	*Calendar of the Carew manuscripts preserved in the archiepiscopal library at Lambeth.* J.S. Brewer and W. Bullen (eds), 6 vols (London, 1867–73).
Cal. S. P. Ire.	*Calendar of State Papers relating to Ireland*, 24 vols (London, 1860–1911).
Cal. Pat. Rolls Ire.	*Calendar of patent and close rolls of chancery in Ireland, Henry VIII to 18th Elizabeth*, ed. J. Morrin (Dublin, 1861).
Cal. Pat. Rolls Ire., Jas I	*Irish patent rolls of James I: facsimile of the Irish record commissioners' calendar prepared prior to 1830*, with foreword by M.C. Griffith (I.M.C., Dublin 1966).
Cal. Stat. Rolls	*Statute Rolls of the Parliament of Ireland, Reign of Henry VI.* H. Berry (ed.), (1910, London).
Civil Survey	*The Civil Survey 1654–6, Miscellanea.* R.C. Simington (ed.), vol. 10. (I.M.C., 1961, Dublin).
The Cloyne Pipe Roll	P. MacCotter, and K.W. Nicholls (eds), (1996, Cork).
Fiants	*The Irish Fiants of the Tudor sovereigns*, 3 vols (Dublin, 1994).

HCA   *A Calendar of Material relating to Ireland from the High Court of Admiralty Examinations, 1536–1641.* J.C. Appleby (ed.), (I.M.C., Dublin, 1992).

MIA   *Miscellaneous Irish Annals (A.D. 1114–1437),* ed. S.Ó. hInnse (Dublin Institute for Advanced Studies, 1947).

NHI   *A New History of Ireland* (Oxford 1976).

Ormond Deeds   *Calendar of Ormond Deeds,* ed. E. Curtis, 6 vols. (Dublin, 1932–43).

Pacata Hibernia   or *A History of the Wars in Ireland.* S. O'Grady (London, 1896).

Rep. Fran. Man.   *Report on Franciscan Manuscripts* (Historical Manuscripts Commission, Dublin, 1906).

Bibliography

Aalen, F.H.A., 'Origin of enclosures in eastern Ireland', in N. Stephens and R.E. Glasscock (eds), *Irish geographical studies in honour of E. Estyn Evans* (Belfast, 1970), pp 209–23.

— , K. Whelan and M. Stout, *Atlas of the Irish rural landscape* (Cork, 1997).

Allen, R.C., *Enclosure and the yeoman* (Oxford, 1992).

Andrews, J.H., 'Notes on the historical geography of the Irish iron industry', *Irish Geography* 3 (1956a), 139–49.

— , 'A note on the later history of the Irish charcoal industry', *Journal of the Royal Society of Antiquaries of Ireland* 86 (1956b), 217–19.

— , 'Robert Lythe's Petitions 1571', *Analecta Hibernica* 24 (1967), 232–42.

— , *Plantation acres; an historical study of the Irish land surveyors and his maps* (Ulster Historical Foundation, 1985).

— , *Shapes of Ireland, maps and their makers, 1564–1839* (Dublin, 1997).

Appely, J.C. (ed.), *A calendar of material relating to Ireland from the High Court of Admiralty examinations, 1536–1641* (Dublin, 1992).

Appelby, J.C. and M. Dowd, 'The Irish Admiralty: its organisation and development', *Irish Historical Studies* 95 (1985), 299–326.

Appiah, A., 'Out of Africa; topologies of nationalism', *Yale Journal of Criticism* 12 (1988), 23–6.

Arendt, H., *The origins of totalitarianism* (London, 1951).

Aston, M., *Interpreting the landscape–landscape, archaeology and local history* (London, 1985).

Barnard, T.C., 'Sir William Petty as Kerry Ironmaster', *Proceedings of the Royal Irish Academy* 82C (1982), 1–32.

— , *Irish Protestant ascents and descents, 1641–1770* (Dublin, 2004).

Barrett, J.C., 'Chronologies of landscape', in P. Ucko and R. Layton (eds), *The archaeology and anthropology of landscape* (London, 1999), pp 21–30.

Barrington, T.J., 'Sir William Petty, 1633–1689', in *Tuosist 6000* (Dublin, 1999), pp 124–7.

Barry, T.B., *The archaeology of medieval Ireland* (London and New York, 1987).

— , 'Late Medieval Ireland: the debate on social and economic transformation, 1350–1550', in B.J. Graham, and L.J. Proudfoot (eds), *An historical geography of Ireland* (London, 1993), pp 99–122.

— , 'Rural settlement in Ireland in the Middle Ages: an overview', *Ruralia* 1 (1996), 134–41.

— , 'Socio-economic aspects of Irish medieval settlements', *Ruralia* 2 (1998), 78–86.

— , *A history of settlement in Ireland* (London, 2000).

— , 'Excavations at Piperstown Deserted Medieval Village, Co. Louth 1987', *Proceedings of the Royal Irish Academy* 100C (2000), 113–35.

— , 'The chronology and development of medieval rural settlement in Munster', *Journal of the Cork Historical and Archaeological Society* 105 (2000) 191–98.

— , 'An introduction to dispersed and nucleated medieval rural settlement in Ireland', *Ruralia* 3 (2000), 6–11.

— , 'Ireland', in P.J. Crabtree (ed.), *Medieval archaeology, an encyclopedia* (London, 2001), pp 176–9.

Bender, B. (ed.), *Landscape, politics and perspective* (Oxford, 1993).

Bennet, G., *The history of Bandon* (Cork, 1869).

Boate, N., *A Natural history of Ireland* (Dublin, 1726).

Bolster, E., *A History of the diocese of Cork from the earliest times to the Reformation* (Shannon, 1972).

— , *A history of the diocese of Cork from the Reformation to the penal era* (Cork, 1982).

Boroughs, J.J. *The Plymouth Colony Archive project: a new insight into the early settlement of Plymouth Plantation* (BA, University of Virginia, 1997).

Brady, W.M., Clerical and parochial records of Cork, Cloyne and Ross. 3 vols (privately published, 1863).

Breen, C. *Integrated marine investigations on the historic shipwreck 'La Surveillante'*, Centre for Maritime Archaeology Monograph Series No. 1, (Coleraine, 2001).

— , 'The Gaelic maritime lordship of O'Sullivan Beare', *Journal of the Cork Historical and Archaeological Society* 106 (2001), 21–36.

— , 'The maritime cultural landscape in medieval Gaelic Ireland', in P.J. Duffy, D. Edwards and E. FitzPatrick (eds), *Gaelic Ireland c.1250–c.1650: land, lordship and settlement* (Dublin, 2001), pp 418–37.

— , 'Blackrock', in I. Bennett, (ed.), *Excavations 2001* (Bray, 2003), p. 31.

— , *The gaelic lordship of the O'Sullivan Beare* (Dublin, 2005).

Breen, C. and W. Forsythe, *Boats and shipwrecks of Ireland, an archaeology* (Stroud, 2004).

Buchanan, R.H., 'Field systems of Ireland', in A.R.H. Baker, and R.A. Butlin, *Studies of field systems in the British Isle* (Cambridge, 1973), pp 580–618.

Butler, W.F.T., *Confiscation in Irish history* (Dublin and London, 1917).

— , *Gleanings from Irish history* (London, 1925).

Byrne, C.F., 'Philip O'Sullivan Bear', *Journal of the Cork Historical and Archaeological Society* 2 (1896), 392–522.

Byrne, M.J., *Ireland under Elizabeth, being a portion of the history of Catholic Ireland by Don Philip O'Sullivan Bear* (Dublin, 1903).

Cairns, C.T., 'The tower-houses of County Tipperary' (PhD, Trinity College Dublin, 1984).

— , *Irish tower-houses, a Co. Tipperary case study* (Athlone, 1987).

Caldwell, D. et al., 'Post-medieval settlement in Islay – some recent research', in J.A. Atkinson, I. Banks and G. MacGregor (eds), *Townships to farmsteads: rural settlement studies in Scotland, England and Wales*. British Archaeological Reports, British Series 293 (Oxford, 2000), pp 58–69.

Canny, N., 'The 1641 Depositions as a source for the writing of social and economic history: County Cork as a case study', in P. O'Flanagan and C. Buttimer (eds), *Cork: history and society* (Dublin, 1993), pp. 249–308.

— , *Making Ireland British, 1580–1650* (Oxford, 2001).

Carroll, M.J., *A bay of destiny* (Bantry, 1996).

Caulfield, R., *Council Book of the Corporation of Cork* (Surrey, 1876).

— , *Council Book of the Corporation of Youghal* (Surrey, 1878).

Chinnery, V., 'Barryscourt Refurnished; the reinstatement of a late sixteenth-century Irish domestic interior', in J. Ludlow and N. Jameson, *Medieval Ireland; the Barryscourt Lectures, I–X* (Kinsale, 2004), pp 177–224.

Cleary, R.M., 'Excavations at Lough Gur, Co. Limerick, Part II', *Journal of the Cork Historical and Archaeological Society* 87 (1982), 77–106.

— , 'Excavations at Lough Gur, Co. Limerick, Part III', *Journal of the Cork Historical and Archaeological Society* 88 (1983), 51–80.

— , 'Excavations at Chapel Lane, Youghal', *Journal of the Cork Historical and Archaeological Society* 102 (1997),

Cleary, R.M. and M.F. Hurley (eds), *Excavations in Cork City, 1984–2000* (Cork, 2003).

Conry, M. and P. Ryan, 'Soils', in *An Foras Taluntais Report* (Dublin, 1965).

Cooney, G., T. Condit and E. Byrne, 'The archaeological landscape', in N. Buttimer, C. Rynne, and H. Guerin (eds), *The heritage of Ireland* (Cork, 2000), pp 18–28.

Corish, P.J., 'The Cromwellian conquest, 1649–53', in T.M. Moody, F.X. Martin and F.J. Byrne (eds), *A New History of Ireland*, III: *Early Modern Ireland 1534–1691* (Oxford, 1976), pp 317–35.

— , 'The Cromwellian regime, 1650–60', in T.M. Moody, F.X. Martin and F.J. Byrne (eds), *A New History of Ireland* III: *Early Modern Ireland, 1534–1691* (Oxford, 1976), pp 353–86.

Cosgrove, D., *Social formation and symbolic landscape* (London, 1984).

Cosgrove, A. (ed.), *A New History of Ireland*, II: *Medieval Ireland, 1169–1534* (2nd edition) (Oxford, 1993).

Cotter, E., 'Adrigole post-medieval ironworks', in I. Bennett (ed.), *Excavations 1999, summary accounts of archaeological excavations in Ireland* (Bray, 2000), 13.

— , 'Architectural change and the parish church in post-Refomation Cork', in E. FitzPatrick, and R. Gillespie (eds), *The Parish in medieval and early modern Ireland* (Dublin, 2006), pp 266–77.

Cowman, D., 'Two Kerry lead-silver mines: Kenmare and Castlemaine', *Journal of the Kerry Historical and Archaeological Society* 8 (1993), 65–75.

Cox, R., 'Regnum Corcagiense: or a description of the Kingdom of Cork', *Journal of the Cork Historical and Archaeological Society* 8 (1902), 65–75.

Creighton, O., *Castles and landscape* (London and New York, 2002).

Crowley, J.S., RJ.N. Devoy, D. Linehan and P. O'Flanagan, *Atlas of Cork City* (Cork, 2005).

Cuppage, J., *Archaeological survey of the Dingle Peninsula* (Dublin, 1986).

Curtin, P.D., *The rise and fall of the Plantation complex: essays in Atlantic history* (Cambridge, 1990).

Dalglish, C., *Rural society and the Age of Reason: an archaeology of the emergence of modern life in the southern Scottish Highlands* (New York, 2003).

Deetz, P.S. and J. Deetz, *The Plymouth Colony Archive Project: vernacular house forms in seventeenth century Plymouth Colony* (Virginia, 1998).

Delle, J.A., 'A good and easy speculation: spatial conflict, collusion and resistance in late sixteenth-century Munster, Ireland', *International Journal of Historical Archaeology* 3:1 (1999), 11–25.

De Latocnaye, Mon., *Rambles through Ireland by a French emigrant* (Cork, 1798).

Dickson, D., *Old World colony, Cork and south Munster, 1630–1830* (Cork, 2005).

Dixon, P., 'Nuclear and dispersed medieval rural settlement in southern Scotland', *Ruralia* 3 (2000), 252–72.

Donnelly, C.J., 'The tower-houses of Co. Limerick' (PhD, Queen's University of Belfast, 1994).

— , 'The I.H.S monogram as a symbol of Catholic resistance in seventeenth-century Ireland', *International Journal of Historical Archaeology* 9:1 (2005), 37–53.

Donnelly, C.J. and N. Brannon, 'Trowelling through history, historical archaeology and the study of early modern Ireland', *History Ireland* 6:3 (1998), 22–5.

Donnelly, C.J. and A.J. Horning, 'Post-medieval and industrial archaeology in Ireland', *Antiquity* 76 (2002), 557–61.

Donovan, M.R., 'Notes on Sir William Hull and Leacom', *Mizen Journal* 1 (1993), 30–8.

Donovan, B.C. and D. Edwards, *British Sources for Irish history, 1485–1641: a guide to manuscripts in local, regional and specialized repositories in England, Scotland and Wales* (Dublin, 1997).

Dúchas, *Recorded monuments, County Kerry* (Dublin, 1997).

Dúchas, *Recorded monuments, County Cork, Volume 2 O.S. sheets 79-end* (Dublin, 1998).

Duffy, P.J., 'The territorial organisation of Gaelic landownership and its transformation in Co. Monaghan, 1591–1640', *Irish Geography* 14 (1981), 1–26.

— , D. Edwards and E. FitzPatrick (eds), *Gaelic Ireland c.1250–c.1650: land, lordship and settlement* (Dublin, 2001).

— , 'Social and spatial order in the MacMahon Lordship of Airghialla in the late sixteenth century', in P.J. Duffy, D. Edwards and E. FitzPatrick (eds), *Gaelic Ireland, c.1250–c.1650* (Dublin, 2001), pp 115–37.

Dunlop, W., 'A catalogue of maps in the Public Records Office', *English Historical Review* 10 (1905), map no. 33.

Durrell, P., *Discover Dursey* (Cork, 1996).

Durrell, P. and F. Kelly, *A tour of Beara* (Cork, 2000).

Edwards, D., 'Legacy of defeat: the reduction of Gaelic Ireland after Kinsale', in H. Morgan (ed.) *The battle of Kinsale* (Bray, 2004), pp 279–99.

Ellis, S.G., *Tudor Ireland: crown, community and the conflict of cultures, 1470–1603* (Harlow, 1985).

Foras Taluntais, *West Cork Resource Survey* (Dublin, 1965).

Fenlon, J., *Ormond Castle* (Dublin, 1996).

Field, W.G., *The handbook for Youghal* (Youghal, 1896).

FitzPatrick, B., *Seventeenth-century Ireland: the War of Religions* (Dublin, 1988).

FitzPatrick, E. and C. O'Brien, *The medieval churches of County Offaly* (Dublin, 1998).

Flangan, L., *Ireland's Armada legacy* (London, 1989).

Flavin, S., 'The development of Anglo-Irish trade in the sixteenth century' (MA Bristol University, 2004).

Foster, R.F., *Modern Ireland, 1600–1972* (London, 1988).

Fox, H., 'Observations in further illustration of the history and statistics in the Pilchard Fishery', *Report of the Royal Cornwall Polytechnic Society* 1 (Cornwall, 1878).

Gahan, A., C. McCutcheon, and D.C. Twohig, 'Medieval pottery', in R.M. Cleary, M.F. Hurley and E. Shee Twohig (eds), *Skiddy's Castle and Christ Church Cork: Excavations, 1974–77 by D.C. Twohig* (Cork, 1997), pp 130–58.

Giddens, A., *Capitalism and modern social theory: an analysis of the writings of Marx, Durkheim and Max Weber* (Cambridge, 1971).

Gosden, C., 'Postcolonial archaeology: issues of culture, identity and knowledge', in I. Hodder (ed.), *Archaeological theory today* (Cambridge, 2001), pp 241–61.

Gowen, M., 'Dunboy Castle, Co. Cork', *Journal of the Cork Historical and Archaeological Society* 83 (1978), 1–49.

— , 'Irish artillery fortifications, 1550–1700' (unpublished MA thesis, University College Cork, 1979).

Graham, B.J. and L.J. Proudfoot (eds), *An historical geography of Ireland* (London, 1993).

Gras, N.S.B., *The Early English Customs System* (Cambridge MA., 1918).

Grenville, J., *Medieval housing* (Leicester, 1997).

Gwynn, A. and Hadcock, N.D., *Medieval religious houses: Ireland* (London, 1970).

Hadfield, A. and W. Maley (eds), *Edmund Spenser, a view of the state of Ireland* (Oxford, 1997).

Harrington, J.P., *The English traveller in Ireland: accounts of Ireland and the Irish through five centuries* (Dublin, 1991).

Harris, A.L., 'The funerary monuments of Richard Boyle, earl of Cork', *Church Mons.* 13 (1998), 70–86.

— , 'The Tynete monument, Kilcreadan, Co. Cork: a reappraisal', *Journal of the Cork Historical and Archaeological Society* 104 (1999), 137–44.

— , 'The Fitzgerald monument at Cloyne Cathedral, Co. Cork; a memorial to father and son', *Journal of the Cork Historical and Archaeological Society* 107 (2002), 171–6.

Hayden, A., 'Bray Head, Valentia Island', in I. Bennett (ed.), *Excavations 1994 – summary accounts of archaeological excavations in Ireland* (Bray, 1995), p. 43.

— , 'Bray Head (Valentia Island), early medieval farm to late medieval village', in I. Bennett (ed.), *Excavations 1997 – summary accounts of archaeological excavations in Ireland* (Bray, 1998), p. 82.

— , 'Bray Head (Valentia Island), Early medieval farmhouses', in I. Bennett (ed.), *Excavations 1998 – summary accounts of archaeological excavations in Ireland* (Bray 1999), p. 89.

— , 'Bray Head (Valentia Island), early medieval buildings', in I. Bennett (ed.), *Excavations 2000 – summary accounts of archaeological excavations in Ireland* (Bray, 2001), p. 423.

Hayes-McCoy, G.A., *Ulster and other Irish maps, c.1600* (Dublin, 1964).

— , 'Conciliation, coercion, and the Protestant Reformation, 1547–71', in T.M. Moody, F.X. Martin and F.J. Byrne (eds), *A New History of Ireland*, III; *Early Modern Ireland, 1534–1691* (Oxford, 1976), pp 69–93.

— , 'The completion of the Tudor conquest and the advance of the counter-reformation, 1571–16–3', in T.M. Moody, F.X. Martin and F.J. Byrne (eds), *A New History of Ireland*, III; *Early Modern Ireland, 1534–1691* (Oxford, 1976), pp 94–141.

Hayman, Revd, S. 'The ecclesiastical antiquities of Youghal', *Proceedings and Transactions and Kilkenny and the southeast of Ireland Archaeological Society* 3 (1854–5), 96–119

— , *Memories of Youghal, ecclesiastical and civil* (Youghal, 1879).

Hickson, M.A., *Selections from old Kerry records* (London, 1874).

Hodder, I. et al., *Interpreting archaeology: finding meaning in the past* (London, 1995).

Hodder, I., *Archaeological theory today* (Cambridge, 2001).

Hogg, I., *The history of fortification* (London, 1970).

Horning, A.J., 'Dwelling houses in the old Irish barbarous manner: archaeological evidence for Gaelic architecture in an Ulster plantation village', in P.J. Duffy, D. Edwards and E. FitzPatrick (eds), *Gaelic Ireland c.1250–c.1650* (Dublin, 2001), pp 375–98.

Hourihan, J.K., 'Town growth in West Cork: Bantry, 1600–1960', *Journal of the Cork Historical and Archaeological Society* 96 (1985), 83–97.

Hurley, M.F., *Excavations at the North Gate, Cork, 1994* (Cork, 1997).

— , 'Medieval Cork', in J.S. Crowley, RJ.N. Devoy, D. Linehan and P. O'Flanagan, *Atlas of Cork City* (Cork, 2005), pp 64–73.

Hurley, M.F. and O.M.B. Scully, *Late Viking Age and Medieval Waterford; excavations, 1986–1992* (Waterford 1997).

Jager, H., 'Landuse in medieval Ireland: a review of the documentary evidence', *Irish Economic and Social History* 10 (1983), 57–65.

Jarvis, R.C., 'The appointment of ports', *Economic History Review* II (1959), 455–66.

Jefferies, H.A., *Cork: historical perspectives* (Dublin, 2004).

Jennings, B., 'Sint-truiden: Irish Franciscan documents', *Archivium Hibernicum* 24 (1961), 148–98.

— , 'Sint-truiden: Irish Franciscan documents', *Archivium Hibernicum* 25 (1962), 1–74.

Johnson, G., *The laneways of medieval Cork* (Cork, 2002).

Johnson, M.H., *An archaeology of capitalism* (Oxford, 1996).

Jones, W., *Dictionary of industrial archaeology* (Gloucester, 1996).

Jones, E.T,. 'The Bristol shipping industry in the sixteenth century' (PhD, Edinburgh University, 1998).

Jones, F.M., 'The plan of the Golden Fort at Smerwick, 1580', *Irish Sword* 2 (1954–6), 40–2.

Jope, E.M. et al., *An archaeological survey of County Down* (Belfast, 1966).

Kearney, H.F., 'Richard Boyle, ironmaster; a footnote to Irish economic history', *Journal of the Royal Society of Antiquaries of Ireland* 83 (1953), 156–62.

Kelleher, C., 'The maritime archaeological landscape of Baltimore, Co. Cork ' (MA thesis, University College Cork, 1998).

Kelly, D.E., 'The application of archaeogeophysical techniques at the site of Newtown, Bantry, Co. Cork and at the star shaped fort at Newtown' (MSc. thesis, Applied Geophysics Unit, National University of Ireland, Galway, 1999).

Kenyon, J.R. and K. O'Conor (eds), *The medieval castle in Ireland and Wales* (Dublin, 2003).

Kerrigan, P., *Castles and fortifications in Ireland, 1485–1945* (Cork, 1995).

Ketch, C., 'Landownership in County Waterford c.1640: the evidence from the Civil Survey', in W. Nolan and T.P. Power (eds), *Waterford history and society* (Dublin, 1992), pp 177–98.

Kew, G., *The Irish sections of Fynes Moryson's Unpublished Itinerary* (Dublin, 1998).

King, H.A., *The castle in England and Wales* (London and Sydney, 1988).

Klingelhofer, E., 'The Renaissance fortifications at Dunboy Castle, 1602: a report on the 1989 Excavations', *Journal of the Cork Historical and Archaeological Society* 97 (1992), 85–96.

— , 'Elizabethan Settlements: Mogeely Castle, Curraglass and Carrigeen, Co. Cork (Part 1)', *Journal of the Cork Historical and Archaeological Society* 104 (1999a), 97–110.

— , 'Proto-colonial archaeology: the case of Elizabethan Ireland', in P.P.A. Funari, M. Hall and S. Jones (eds), *Historical archaeology: back from the edge* (London, 1999b), 165–79.

— , 'Elizabethan settlements: Mogeely Castle, Curraglass and Carrigeen, Co. Cork (part II)', *Journal of the Cork Historical and Archaeological Society* 105 (2000), 155–74.

— , 'The architecture of empire: Elizabethan country houses in Ireland', in S. Lawerence (ed.), *Archaeologies of the British* (London, 2003), pp 102–18.

— , 'Edmund Spenser at Kilcolman Castle: the archaeological evidence', *Post-Medieval Archaeology* 39:1 (2005), 133–54.

Lane, S., 'Clay Pipes', in M.F. Hurley, *Excavations at the North Gate, Cork, 1994* (Cork 1997a), pp 102–5.

— , 'Clay Pipes' in R.M. Cleary, M.F. Hurley, and E. Shee Twohig, *Skiddy's Castle and Christ Church, Cork, Excavations, 1974–77 by D.C. Twohig*, 224–238 (Cork 1997b), pp 224–38.

— , 'Clay Pipes' in E. Klingelhofer, 'Edmund Spenser at Kilcolman Castle: the archaeological evidence', *Post-Medieval Archaeology* 39:1 (2005), 147.

Leask, H.G., *Irish castles and castellated houses* (Dundalk, 1941).

— , *Irish churches and monastic buildings*, vol. 2 (Dundalk, 1955–60).

— , *Irish churches and monastic buildings*, vol. 3 (Dundalk 1955–60).

Leister, I., *Peasant openfield farming and its territorial organisation in Co. Tipperary* (Marburg/Lahn, 1976).

Lennon, C., *Richard Stanihurst the Dubliner* (Dublin, 1981).

— , *Sixteenth century Ireland, the incomplete conquest* (Dublin, 1994).

Lesser, A., 'Social fields and the evolution of society', *Southwestern Journal of Anthropology* 17 (1961), 40–8.

Lewis, S., *A topographical dictionary of Ireland* (London, 1837).

Loeber, R., *The geography and practice of English colonisation in Ireland from 1534–1609*. Group for the Study of Irish Historical Settlement (Dublin, 1991).

— , 'An architectural history of Gaelic castles and settlements, 1370–1600', in P.J. Duffy, D. Edwards and E. FitzPatrick (eds), *Gaelic Ireland c.1250–c.1650* (Dublin, 2001), pp 271–315.

— , and G. Parker, 'The Military Revolution in seventeenth-century Ireland' in J.H. Ohlmeyer (ed.), *Ireland from independence to occupation, 1641–1660* (Cambridge, 1995), pp 66–88.

Lynch, A., 'Excavations of the medieval town defences at Charlotte's Quay Limerick', *Proceedings of the Royal Irish Academy* 84C (1984), 281–331.

Ludlow, J. and N. Jameson, *Medieval Ireland; the Barryscourt Lectures*, I–X (Kinsale, 2004).

Lunham, T.A., 'Bishop Dive Downes visitation of his diocese, 1699–1702', *Journal of the Cork Historical and Archaeological Society* 15 (1909), 19, 78, 126, 163.

Lydon, J., *The making of Ireland; from ancient times to the present* (London and New York, 1998).

Lyne, G.J., 'The Mac Finín Duibh O'Sullivans of Tuosist and Bearehaven', *Journal of the Kerry Archaeological and Historical Society* 9 (1976), 32–67.

— , 'Land tenure in Kenmare and Tuosist, 1696–1716', *Journal of the Kerry Archaeological and Historical Society* 10 (1977), 19–54.

Luccketti, N.M., W.M. Kelso, and B.A. Straube, *Jamestown rediscovery, field report 1994* (Virginia, 1994).

Luccketti, N. and B. Straube, *1997 Interim Report on the APVA Excavations at Jamestown, Virginia* (Virginia, 1998).

Macalister, R.A.S., *The archaeology of Ireland* (Dublin, 1928).

MacCarthy Mór, *Historical essays on the Kingdom of Munster* (Missouri, 1994).

MacCarthy-Morrogh, M., 'The English presence in early seventeenth-century Munster', in C. Brady and R. Gillespie (eds), *Natives and newcomers: the making of the Irish Colonial Society, 1543–1641* (Dublin, 1986).

— , *The Munster plantation: English migration to Southern Ireland, 1583–1641* (Oxford, 1986).

McCarthy M., 'Faunal remains', in M.F. Hurley, *Excavations at the North Gate, Cork, 1994* (Cork, 1997), pp 154–8.

— , 'Faunal remains', in E. Klingelhofer, 'Edmund Spenser at Kilcolman Castle: the archaeological evidence', *Post-Medieval Archaeology* 39:1 (2005), 133–54.

— , 'Turning a world upside down: the metamorphosis of property, settlement and society in the city of Cork during the 1640s and 1650s', *Irish Geography* 33 (2000), 37–55.

— , 'Geographical change in an early modern town: urban growth, economy and cultural politics in Cork, 1600–1641', *Journal of the Cork Historical and Archaeological Society* 106 (2001), 53–78.

— , 'Historical geographies of a colonized world: the renegotiation of New English colonialism in early modern urban Ireland, *c*.1600–1610,' *Irish Geography* 36 (2003), 59–76.

— , 'The evolution of Cork's built environment', in J.S. Crowley, RJ.N. Devoy, D. Linehan and P. O'Flanagan, *Atlas of Cork City* (Cork, 2005), pp 119–26.

McClatchie M., 'The plant remains' in R.M. Cleary, and M.F. Hurley (eds), *Excavations in Cork City, 1984–2000* (Cork, 2003), pp 391–414.

MacCurtain, M., *Tudor and Stuart Ireland* (Dublin, 1972).

McCutcheon, C., 'Cork-type pottery: a medieval urban enterprise' (MA, University College Cork, 1995).

— , 'Pottery and roof tiles', in M.F. Hurley, *Excavations at the North Gate, Cork, 1994* (Cork, 1997), pp 75–101.

— , 'Pottery' in R.M. Cleary, and M. Hurley, *Excavations on Cork City 1984–2000* (Cork, 2003), p. 199.

— , 'Pottery', in E. Klingelhofer, 'Edmund Spenser at Kilcolman Castle: the archaeological evidence', *Post-Medieval Archaeology* 39:1 (2005), pp 133–54

McErlean, T., 'The Irish townland system of landscape organisation', in T. Reeves-Smyth and F. Hammond (eds), *Landscape archaeology of Ireland* (Oxford, 1983), pp 315–39.

McErlean, T., R. McConkey, and W. Forsythe, *Strangford Lough, an archaeological survey of the maritime cultural landscape* (Belfast, 2002).

MacLysaght, E. (ed.), *Calendar of Orrery papers* (Dublin, 1941).

McNeill, T.E., *Castles in Ireland, feudal power in a Gaelic world* (London and New York, 1997).

Maher, D., *Kilcrea Friary, Franciscan heritage in County Cork* (Cork, 1999).

Mallio, S. and B. Straube, *1999 interim report on the APVA excavations at Jamestown, Virginia* (Richmond, Virginia, 2000).

Mallory, J.P. and T.E. McNeill, *The archaeology of Ulster* (Belfast, 1991).

Martin, C. and G. Parker, *The Spanish Armada* (London, 1988).

Marx, K., *Pre-capitalist economic formations* (London, 1964 ed.).

Maxwell, C. (ed.), *Irish history from contemporary sources* (London, 1923).

Mikalsen, G., H.P. Sejrup and I. Aarseth, 'Late-Holocene changes in ocean circulation and climate: foraminiferal and isotopic evidence from Sulafjord, western Norway', *The Holocene* 11 (2001), 437–46.

Moody, T.M., F.X. Martin and F.J. Byrne (eds), *A New History of Ireland* III; *Early Modern Ireland, 1534–1691* (Oxford, 1976).

Moore, M., *Archaeology survey of County Waterford* (Dublin, 1999).

Moorman, J., *A history of the Franciscan Order* (Oxford, 1968).

Morales, O.R., 'Spanish army attitudes to the Irish at Kinsale', in H. Morgan (ed.), *The battle of Kinsale* (Bray, 2004), pp 91–100.

Morgan, H. (ed.), *The battle of Kinsale* (Bray, 2004).

Morrisey, J., 'Contours of colonialism: Gaelic Ireland and the early colonial subject', *Irish Geography* 37:1 (2004a), 88–102.

— , 'Geography militant: resistance and the essentialisation of identity in colonial Ireland', *Irish Geography* 37:2 (2004b), 166–76.

Mulcahy, M., 'Elizabeth Fort, Cork', *Irish Sword* 4 (1959–60), 127–34.

Murtagh, B., 'The Kilkenny Castle archaeological project, 1990–1993: interim report', *Old Kilkenny Review* 46 (1993), 78–94.

— , 'Waterford's Watergate', *Archaeology Ireland* 15:2 (2001), 28–33.

Newman, R., *The historical archaeology of Britain c.1540–1900* (Gloucester, 2001).

Nicholls, K.W., *Gaelic and Gaelicisied Ireland in the Middle Ages* (Dublin, 1972).

— , 'Gaelic society and economy in the High Middle Ages', in A. Cosgrove (ed.), *A New History of Ireland*, II. *Medieval Ireland, 1169–1534* (Oxford, 1987), pp 397–438.

— , 'The development of lordship in County Cork 1300–1600', in P. O'Flanagan and C. Buttimer (eds), *Cork: history and society* (Dublin, 1993), pp 157–212.

— , 'The Anglo-Normans and beyond', in J.S. Crowley, R.J.N. Devoy, D. Linehan and P. O'Flanagan, *Atlas of Cork City* (Cork, 2005), pp 104–11.

— , 'Sixteenth- and early seventeenth-century Cork', in J.S. Crowley, R.J.N. Devoy, D. Linehan and P. O'Flanagan, *Atlas of Cork City* (Cork, 2005), pp 112–18.

Noel-Hume, I., *Williamsburg cabinetmakers: the archaeological evidence* (Williamsburg, 1971).

Nolan, W. and A. Simms, *Irish towns: a guide to sources* (Dublin, 1998).

O'Brien, A.F., 'The royal boroughs, the seaport towns and royal revenue in Medieval Ireland', *Journal of the Royal Society of Antiquaries Ireland* 118 (1988), 13–26.

— , 'Politics, economy and society: the development of Cork and the Irish south-coast region c.1170–c.1583', in P. O'Flanagan and N. Buttimer (eds), *Cork: history and society* (Dublin, 1993), pp 83–156.

O'Brien, D.M., *Beara, a journey through history* (Castletownbere, 1991).

Ó Caoimh, T, 'Mocheallóc Mac Uibhleáin of the Corco Dhuibhne', in *Tuosist 6000* (Dublin, 1999), pp 79–84.

O'Carroll, M.J., *A bay of Destiny* (Bantry, 1996).

O'Conor, K.D., *The archaeology of medieval rural settlement in Ireland*. Discovery Programme Monographs 3 (Dublin, 1998).

— , 'The morphology of Gaelic lordly sites in North Connacht', in P.J. Duffy, D. Edwards and E. FitzPatrick (eds), *Gaelic Ireland c.1250–c.1650* (Dublin, 2001), pp 329–45.

— , 'Housing in Later Medieval Gaelic Ireland', *Ruralia* 4 (2002), 197–206.

— , 'Medieval rural settlement in Munster', in J. Ludlow and N. Jameson (eds), *Medieval Ireland; The Barryscourt Lectures I–X* (Kinsale, 2004), pp 225–56.

Ó Corráin, D., 'Corcu Loígde: land and families', in P. O'Flanagan and C.G. Buttimer (eds), *Cork: history and society* (Dublin, 1993), pp 63–82.

O'Donnell, M.G., 'Excavations at James Fort, Kinsale, 1974–98', *Journal of the Cork Historical and Archaeological Society* 107 (2002), 1–70.

O'Donovan, J., *Miscellany of the Celtic society* (Dublin, 1849).

— , *The antiquities of the county of Kerry* (Cork, 1983).

O'Flanagan, P., *Bandon* (Dublin, 1988).

— , and C.G. Buttimer (eds), *Cork: history and society* (Dublin, 1993).

O'Keeffe, P., 'A map of Beare and Bantry, Co. Cork', *Journal of the Cork Historical and Archaeological Society* 63 (1958), 26–31.

O'Keeffe, T., *Barryscourt Castle and the Irish tower-house* (Kinsale, 1997).

— , *Medieval Ireland, an archaeology* (Stroud, 2000).

O'Kelly, M.J., 'Three promontory forts in Co. Cork', *Proceedings of the Royal Irish Academy* 55C (1952–3), 25–59.

O'Mahony, E., 'The O'Driscolls and their revenues from fishing – the 1609 inquisition', *Mizen Journal* 8 (2000), 128–30.

Ó Murchadha, D., *Family names of County Cork* (Dun Laoghaire, 1985).

— , 'Gill Abbey and the "Rental of Cong", *Journal of the Cork Historical and Archaeological Society* 249 (1985), 31–45.

— , 'The castle of Dún Mic Oghmainn and the overlordship of Carbery', *Journal of the Cork Historical and Archaeological Society* 252 (1988), 73–83.

O'Neil, B.H. St J., 'Notes on the fortifications of Kinsale Harbour', *Journal of the Cork Historical and Archaeological Society* 45 (1940), 110–16.

O'Neill, T. *Merchants and mariners in medieval Ireland* (Dublin, 1987).

Ó Ríordáin, S.P. and J. Hunt, 'Medieval dwellings at Caherguillamore, County Limerick', *Journal of the Royal Society of Antiquaries of Ireland* 72 (1942), 37–63.

Ó Ríordáin, S., *Antiquities of the Irish countryside* (5th ed.), revised by R. De Valera (London, 1979).

O'Sullivan, A., and J. Sheehan, *The Iveragh Peninsula, an archaeological survey of South Kerry* (Cork, 1996).

O'Sullivan, A., *Farmers, foragers and fishermen on the Shannon Estuary*. Discovery Programme Monograph 7 (Dublin, 2001).

O'Sullivan, T., *Bere Island, a short history* (Cork, 1996).

Ohlmeyer, J.H., *Ireland from independence to occupation, 1641–1660* (Cambridge, 1995).

Orser, C.J., *A historical archaeology of the modern world* (New York, 1996).

Oswald, A., *Clay pipes for the archaeologist*. British Archaeological Reports 14 (Oxford, 1975).

— , 'On the life of clay pipe moulds', in P. Davey (ed.), *The archaeology of the clay tobacco pipe: IX More pipes from the Midlands and Southern England*. British Archaeological Reports, International Series 146(I) (Oxford, 1985), pp 5–22.

Otway-Ruthven, A.J., 'The organisation of Anglo-Irish agriculture in the middle ages', *Journal of the Royal Society of Antiquaries of Ireland* 81 (1951), 1–13.

— , *A history of medieval Ireland* (New York, 1980).

Palmer, M. and P. Neaverson, *Industrial archaeology, principles and practice* (London, 1998).

Pender, S., *A census of Ireland, c.1659* (Dublin, 1939).

Philips, T., *Londonderry and the London companies* (Belfast, 1928).

Power, D. et al., *Archaeological inventory of County Cork. Volume 1: West Cork* (Dublin, 1992).

Power, D. et al., *Archaeological inventory of County Cork. Volume 2: East and South Cork* (Dublin, 1994).

Prendergast, J.P., *The Cromwellian settlement of Ireland* (London, 1865).

Prendergast, F.J., 'Ancient history of the kingdom of Kerry by Friar O'Sullivan', *Journal of the Cork Historical and Archaeological Society* 4 (1898), 115–19.

Renwick, W.L. (ed.), *A view of the present state of Ireland, by Edmund Spenser* (Oxford, 1970).

Reeves-Smyth, T. and F. Hammond (eds), *Landscape archaeology in Ireland*. British Archaeological reports, British Series 116 (Oxford, 1983).

— , 'Irish gardens and gardening before Cromwell', in J. Ludlow and N. Jameson, *Medieval Ireland; the Barryscourt Lectures, I–X* (Kinsale, 2004), pp 97–144.

Rippon, S., *Gwent Levels: the evolution of a wetland landscape*, Council for British Archaeology Research Report 105 (Oxford, 1996).

Roberts, B.K., *Landscapes of settlement: prehistory to the present* (London, 1996).

Robinson, P., *The plantation of Ulster* (Belfast, 1984).

Rynne, C., *Technological change in Anglo-Norman Munster* (Kinsale, 1998).

— , *Industrial archaeological survey of Cork City and its environs* (Cork, 1999).

— , 'Towards an archaeology of the post-medieval Irish Iron industry: the blast furnace in South Munster', *Journal of the Cork Historical and Archaeological Society* 106 (2001), 101–20.

— , 'An Archaeological Survey of Elizabeth Fort, a seventeenth-century artillery fortification in Cork City', *Journal of the Cork Historical and Archaeological Society* 109 (2004), 199–216.

Samuel, M., 'Coppinger's Court: a document in stone', *Journal of the Cork Historical and Archaeological Society* 248 (1984), 59–76.

— , 'A tentative chronology for tower-houses in West Cork', *Journal of the Cork Historical and Archaeological Society* 103 (1998), 105–24.

Sauer, C., 'The morphology of landscape', *University of California Publications in Geography* 22 (1925), 19–53.

Shanks, M. and C. Tilley, *Social theory and archaeology* (Oxford, 1993).

Sharpe, R., 'Churches and communities in early medieval Ireland: towards a pastoral model', in J. Blair and R. Sharpe (eds), *Pastoral care before the parish* (Leicester, 1992), pp 81–109.

Sheehan, J., 'Ballinskelligs Castle', in I. Bennet (ed.), *Excavations 1992: summary accounts of archaeological excavations in Ireland* (Bray, 1993).

Shiels, D., 'Fort and field: the potential for battlefield archaeology in Kinsale', in H. Morgan (ed.), *The battle of Kinsale* (Bray, 2004), pp 337–50.

Sherlock, R., 'The later medieval fireplaces of County Cork', *Journal of the Cork Historical and Archaeological Society* 105 (2000), 207–30.

Simington, R.C. and J. MacLellan, 'Oireachtas library list of outlaws', *Analecta Hibernia* 23 (1966), 317–68.

Simms, K., *From kings to warlords* (Suffolk, 1987).

— , 'Native sources for Gaelic settlement; the house poems', in P.J. Duffy, D. Edwards and E. FitzPatrick (eds), *Gaelic Ireland c.1250–c.1650* (Dublin, 2001), pp 246–70.

Smith, C., *The ancient and present state of the county and city of Waterford* (Dublin, 1745).

— , *The ancient and present state of the county and city of Cork* (Dublin, 1750).

— , *The ancient and present sstate of the county of Kerry* (Dublin, 1756; 1969 reprint).

Smyth, W.J., 'Social, economic and landscape transformations in County Cork from the mid-eighteenth to the mid-nineteenth century', in P.F. Flanagan and N. Buttimer (eds), *Cork: history and society* (Dublin, 1993), pp 655–98.

— , 'Ireland a colony: settlement implications of the revolution in military, administrative, urban and ecclesiastical structures, *c.1550–c.1730*', in T. Barry (ed.), *A history of settlement in Ireland* (London, 2000), pp 158–86.

— , *Map-making, landscapes and memory; a geography of colonial and early modern Ireland, c.1530–1750* (Cork 2006).

Southward, A.J. and G.T. Boalch, 'The effect of changing climate on marine life; past events and future predictions', in S. Fisher (ed.), *Man and the maritime environment.* Exeter Maritime Studies, No. 9 (Exeter, 1994), pp 101–43.

Stephens, N. and R.E. Glasscock (eds), *Irish geographical studies in honour of E. Estyn Evans* (Belfast, 1970).

Stokes, W., 'Acallamh na Senórach', in W. Stokes and E. Windisch (eds), *Irische Texte,* series 41 (Leipzig, 1900).

Straube, B. and N. Luccketti, *Jamestown rediscovery 1995 interim report* (Jamestown, 1996).

Sweetman, P.D., 'Archaeological excavations at Trim Castle, Co. Meath, 1971–4', *Proceedings of the Royal Irish Academy* 78C (1978), 127–98.

— , 'Archaeological excavations at Adare Castle, Co. Limerick', *Journal of the Cork Historical and Archaeological Society* 85 (1980), 1–6.

— , *The medieval castles of Ireland* (Cork, 1999).

— , *The origin and development of the tower-house.* The Barryscourt Lectures 8 (Kinsale, 2000).

Tabraham, C., 'The Scottish medieval tower-house as lordly residences in the light of recent excavation', *Proceedings of the Society of Antiquaries of Scotland* 118 (1988), 267–76.

— , *Scottish castles and fortifications* (Edinburgh, 2000).

Tarlow, S. and S. West (eds), *The familiar past* (London, 1999).

Taylor, W.W., *A study of archaeology.* American Anthropological Association, Memoir 69 (Washington, 1948).

Thomas, A., *The walled towns of Ireland,* 2 vols (Dublin, 1992).

Thomas, J., 'Archaeologies of place and landscape', in I. Hodder (ed.), *Archaeological theory today* (Cambridge, 2001), pp 165–86.

Tierney, J., 'Plant remains' in E. Klingelhofer, 'Edmund Spenser at Kilcolman Castle: the archaeological evidence', *Post-Medieval Archaeology* 39:1 (2005), 133–54.

Tierney, M., 'Theory and politics in early medieval Irish archaeology', in M.A. Monk and J. Sheehan (eds), *Early Medieval Munster, archaeology, history and society* (Cork, 1998), pp 190–9.

Tietzch-Tyler, D., *The geology of the Allihies mines, Desert Rivers, Slate Mountains and Copper Ore.* Geological Survey of Ireland (Dublin, 1997).

Tilley, C., *A phenomenology of landscape, places, paths and mountains* (Oxford, 1994).

Toal, C., *North Kerry archaeological survey* (Dingle, 1995).

Townshend, D., *The life and times of the Great Earl of Cork* (London, 1904).

Tuosist History and Newsletter Committee, *Tuosist 6000, Turas Staire go Tuath Ó Siosta* (Dublin, 1999).

Wagner, P. and M. Mikesell, *Readings in cultural geography* (Chicago, 1962).

Walsh, C., 'Bray Head, Valentia Island, early medieval hut site', in I. Bennett (ed.), *Excavations 1994 – summary accounts of archaeological excavations in Ireland* (Bray, 1995), p. 81.

Walton, J.C., 'Household effects of a Waterford Merchant Family in 1640', *Journal of the Cork Historical and Archaeological Society* 237 (1978), 99–106.

Watt, J., *The church in medieval Ireland* (Dublin, 1972).

Went, A.J., 'The Irish pilchard industry', *Proceedings of the Royal Irish Academy* 51B (1946), 81–120.

— , 'William Hull's losses in 1641', *Journal of the Cork Historical and Archaeological Society* 52 (1947), 58–60.

Wheeler, S., 'Four armies in Ireland' in J.H. Ohlmeyer, *Ireland from independence to occupation, 1641–1660* (Cambridge, 1995), pp 43–65.

Wiggins, K., *Anatomy of a siege: King John's Castle, Limerick, 1642* (Wordwell/Boydell, 2000).

Williams, P. and C. Chrisman, *Colonial discourse and post-colonial theory: an introduction* (London, 1994).

Woodward, D., 'Irish trade and customs statistics, 1614–1641', *Irish Economic and Social History* 26 (1999), 54–80.

Wren, J., 'Roof Tiles', in C. Walsh, *Archaeological excavations at Patrick, Nicholas and Winetavern Streets, Dublin* (Dingle, 1997), pp 149–52.

— , 'Roofing tiles and slates' in A. Halpin, *The port of medieval Dublin; archaeological excavations at the Civic Offices, Winetavern Street, Dublin 1993* (Dublin, 2000), pp 139–42.

Index